NAVIGATING THE PLANETARY

Navigating the Planetary

Hildegund Amanshauser
and Kimberly Bradley (eds.)

for the Salzburg International
Summer Academy of Fine Arts

Rahel Aima
Hildegund Amanshauser
Kader Attia
Stephanie Bailey
Sammy Baloji
Kimberly Bradley
Sabine Breitwieser
Tania Bruguera
Roger M. Buergel
Clémentine Deliss
Rosalyn D'Mello
Charles Esche
Olamiju Fajemisin
Marina Fokidis
Alexander Koch
Christian Kravagna
Bonaventure Ndikung
Peter Osborne
Fernando Resende
Mohammad Salemy
Shuddhabrata Sengupta
Nina Siegal
Chloe Stead
Sanjukta Sunderason
Kate Sutton
Simone Wille

Verlag für moderne Kunst

Planetary Academy
and *Navigating the Planetary*

Hildegund Amanshauser, Kimberly Bradley

This volume was created as a guidebook for those looking for new points of departure into the literal, figurative, and metaphorical planetary approaches to the contemporary visual art field. But it is also intended for those who don't know where to begin.

Through essays, case studies, and interviews situated in the past, present, and looking into the future, *Navigating the Planetary* explores people, institutions, and thoughts that are dissolving East/West and Global North/South binaries or rendering them irrelevant.

It attempts to reimagine the "planetary" beyond abstract "global" concerns and present different ways to theorize, remap, and find new perspectives. How have artists, curators, and institutions addressed transcultural issues, and how could they in the future? Which methods do such individuals use to root themselves in various regions of the world and make themselves understood to others? In its scope, this book also asks—why navigate the planetary at all? Do global or planetary networks offer solutions to cultural problems, and how are these networks best established and maintained? *Navigating the Planetary* endeavors to answer these pertinent questions, as well as offer selected historical references and thoughts on the planetary art world's potentials.

HOW IT BEGAN

In 2015, the Salzburg International Summer Academy of Fine Arts officially launched the long-term project Global Academy (now Planetary Academy),[1] a research and networking project on the planetary art world and its theory and history, focusing on learning and teaching art. Two conferences (in 2016 and 2018) and numerous lectures in the intervening years provided forums for encounters and discussions, and thus shaped the project. The 2016 conference *Global Academy?* addressed alternative academies in the Global South (these included RAW Material Company in Dakar; ruangrupa in Jakarta; SOMA in Mexico City; the Dhaka Art Summit in Dhaka; and Spring Sessions in Amman); the summer 2018 conference was devoted to various models of transcultural exchange of ideas on contemporary art and the systems in which it circulates.

Each conference created a space for open, honest, and sometimes even contentious exchange, sharing and discussing ideas and concepts on the subjects with experts who are shaping the planetary art world. The organizers recognized that there was and is enormous demand for this kind of forum. These encounters ultimately gave rise to the joint idea (we conceptualized, curated, and moderated the 2018 conference together) of producing this book as the next step in the Summer Academy's Planetary Academy project.

WHY, WHO, WHAT, WHEN?

The *why* was clear; we then moved on to the *who*. Which artists, thinkers, curators, and writers could contribute

1 In 2018, after the Salzburg Summer Academy's conference on transcultural models of artistic exchange, the project title was changed from *Global Academy* to *Planetary Academy*. The keynote lecture *In Pursuit of the Planetary,* appears here in a reworked version, *Planetary Pursuits*, pp. 15–30.

their expertise to this book? And, perhaps even more importantly, what audience(s) is this book intended for? The contributors' work on the following pages was the result of research, many queries, and diving into our respective networks (Hildegund Amanshauser has more than forty years' experience in the art world in Austria and further afield; Kimberly Bradley is a writer, critic, and editor whose networks stretch into fields beyond art), which overlapped in some places and diverged in others. Half of the contributors had already participated in the Planetary Academy in some form. We wanted to present a broad array of entry points into planetary artistic thinking and activity, accessible yet still illuminating.

What we wanted to express took some time to determine: a rather sweeping and by no means complete look at transcultural art history, but also current transcultural issues and even forecasts. Thus evolved the structure, which splits the book into temporal categories (past, present, and future) and "typologies" of essays, interviews, and case studies. As the essays trickled (then flooded) in, topical threads began to emerge, sometimes appearing in texts whose primary themes weren't necessarily analogous. Several writers and interviewees parse the meanings of words like "global" and "planetary" as well as the French *mondialité*, whose meaning diverges from the English but is very close to how we use "planetary." There were of course musings on the Global South or the challenges of decolonization or Dis-Othering institutions ranging from museums to general societies. Other notions became more abstract leitmotifs. For example, how can geographically and linguistically divergent artistic cultures in an interconnected age such as now properly understand each other when communication is funneled through the art world's lingua franca, English? Why do alternative knowledges so far fail to gain traction in a still linearly defined Western hegemony—or do they? And interestingly, some contributions also exhibit a softer yearning, perhaps; the desire for a planetary connection that transcends the economic connotations of the word "globalism" to include wisdom, holistic thinking, mutual respect, new ways of looking at and moving through the spatial and temporal. Preserving local knowledges yet intertwining them, learning from and connecting to each other, and being gentler on our Earth seems to be this book's unexpected subtext. The book, in the end, has become a kind of epistemological/emotional constellation.

As optimistic as it is, creating a book like this is a political endeavor. There were moments in which we—a team of Europeans and North Americans—were acutely aware of the contradictions inherent in producing an Austrian-funded book on planetary art with planetary contributors; the power structures we highlight exist in this very act. Geopolitics, in fact, affected many of the contributors: several writers faced difficulties in their research due to Kashmiri uprisings, for example, then protests in Hong Kong, ongoing Brexit overwhelm, and the outbreak and spread of the coronavirus. Some contributions were written on the road from several countries. Time and space became elastic, which is perhaps one of the markers of our planetary condition.

Some contributions were lost along the way, due to the aforementioned reasons. Nancy Adajania intended to edit the lecture she gave at Dhaka Art Summit in 2018 called *Between the High-Altitude View and The Detail: A Study of Two Decades of American Painting*, which referred to an exhibition organized by The Museum of Modern Art New York and was presented in Delhi in 1967. Adajania spoke about the effects of this show on the Indian art scene, bringing in a new perspective on the center-periphery question. Kimberly Bradley interviewed Irena Popiashvili on the history and current situation of contemporary art in Tbilisi, Georgia, but time constraints precluded approving the text, so we are sadly missing a contribution addressing the positions of Eastern Europe and the Caucasus. And we unfortunately lost track of curator Catherine David during the initial and highly uncertain phase of the coronavirus crisis in Europe. Her interview with Hildegund Amanshauser primarily addressed Documenta X in 1997 as the first major exhibition having globalization in focus as well as her curatorial methodologies and how they might differ from mainstream "planetary" curating.

When this book was just an idea, we couldn't imagine that it would come together at a time in which our planet and its manmade systems are undergoing a paradigm shift whose outcome is still unclear. As we write this, the coronavirus is calling not only world health but also late capitalism and our various political systems into question: borders are closing, states of emergency called, politicizing running rampant. Yet at the same time we've never been more planetary: Chinese medical professionals are sending equipment and doctors to other countries, Italian and Russian patients are being treated in Germany, and international experts are working on solutions, in the best cases transcending national interests. Again, our relationships to time and space—themes that appear in several of the outstanding writings in the following pages—are changing faster and far more irreversibly than what we would have expected.

We talk about returning to normal, but what will that normal be, and will the journey represent a return, or a charting of new territory? Will this book still be a guidebook when it appears, or will it be a historic document of an irresponsible period in human history?

HOW TO USE THIS BOOK

There are three types of texts: essays, interviews with protagonists, and case studies with examples of best practice. There is also a glossary to which many authors contributed. Glossary terms appear in gray on first mention in an article throughout the book as cross-references. Our experience and the different contributions in this book show that many terms used in postcolonial discourse are employed in different senses, so several entries are listed for some terms. Exploring the definitions of these terms is an important basis for meaningful dialogue. This dialogue, central to the *Planetary Academy* project of the Salzburg International Summer Academy of Fine Arts, provides the volume's framework.

On the front cover is *The Blue Marble,* the first and only photograph taken of the whole earth by a human, captured in 1972 from Apollo 17, the final mission in NASA's manned Project Apollo. "The photograph was called *The Blue Marble* for its vivid detail and color," explains Stephanie Bailey in her introductory essay (pp. 31–55) and it changed how humans viewed their own planet. We use it here in its original version, which was not oriented to the North, turned yet another ninety degrees. Likewise, we attempted to collect writings that shift the perspectives on the planetary art field in a multitude of ways. There are different layers to navigating this book, which need not be read in sequence (just as there are different ways to get from any point A to point B, and all points in between); the table of contents appears on the front inside flap to make finding contributions a bit easier.

THANKS

We would like to thank Christian Hoffelner, who has not only created a splendid graphic design, but has also been a valuable and patient collaborator throughout this publication's production and implementation. He also introduced us to the Verlag für moderne Kunst. Our thanks to Jennifer Bressler for her comprehensive and sometimes complicated picture-editing, which presents a narrative level of its own. Many thanks to Chloe Stead for her meticulous copy-editing and proofreading, and to John Barker for his proficient compilation of the index. Warmest thanks to the Verlag für moderne Kunst, Vienna, particularly to managing director Silvia Jaklitsch and our project manager Gabrielle Cram, who gave us wonderfully straightforward and efficient advice. We thank the Summer Academy team of Karin Buchauer, Simone Rudolph, and Gabriele Winter for their constant support. Hildegund Amanshauser would like to thank Sabine B. Vogel, who had the idea for and cocurated the Global Art conference at the Salzburg Summer Academy in 2011, which gave us the self-confidence to go further into this direction. Finally, we thank the grant-awarding bodies, our financial backers, especially regional councilor Heinrich Schellhorn and Deputy Mayor Bernhard Auinger, Olga Okunev of the Austrian Federal Chancellery (arts and culture division), and all other members of the working committee, Eva Veichtlbauer (head of dept. 2, Culture, Education and Society, Province of Salzburg) and Ingrid Tröger-Gordon (head of dept. Culture, Education and Science, Town of Salzburg), whose support has been essential for the production of this book.

Special thanks to the contributing authors, interviewees, and everyone involved in creating the following pages. Without them, the book you are holding would not exist. They have shown commitment far beyond normal measure.

INTRODUCTORY ESSAYS

INTRODUCTORY ESSAYS

Planetary Pursuits

Shuddhabrata Sengupta, Raqs Media Collective

I live in a part of New Delhi—which is both a very new and a very old city—close to a ridge of reddish quartzite rocks that are part of the oldest extant mountain range on earth; the Aravalli Range. The Aravallis are close to 3.2 billion years old. So old that they have been worn down to a stubble of rock, like a rash on the face of the earth. Once they were mighty mountains; now they are mainly gravel, rock, pebble, and hard, rough, thorn-laden ground. Walking on these stones, which I have done, on hot, dry midsummer afternoons, foggy winter mornings, and humid monsoon nights throughout my life, I have a sense of walking on a young, still-changing planet, and being astride an ancient world. It takes me back to a time, a Pre-Cambrian deep time, when the ground that I stand upon today was much closer to Antarctica than it was to the not-yet-risen Himalayas. Perhaps some places offer a greater sense of planetary time than others. I like to think that the city in which I was born, made, and live, is one of those.

What does it mean to be planetary? I'd like to find out by invoking, first, a statement by Gayatri Chakravorty Spivak, which I think we can use as a key with which to open many doors. "I propose the planet to overwrite the globe."[1] But in doing so I immediately want to think of what globes and planets can do to our sense of location, our bearings, in space and time. The word "planet" comes from a Greek expression that suggests a wandering celestial body. Our earth is very much that wanderer. She spins

1 Gayatri Chakravorty Spivak, *Death of a Discipline* (New York, 2003), ebook, no page number.

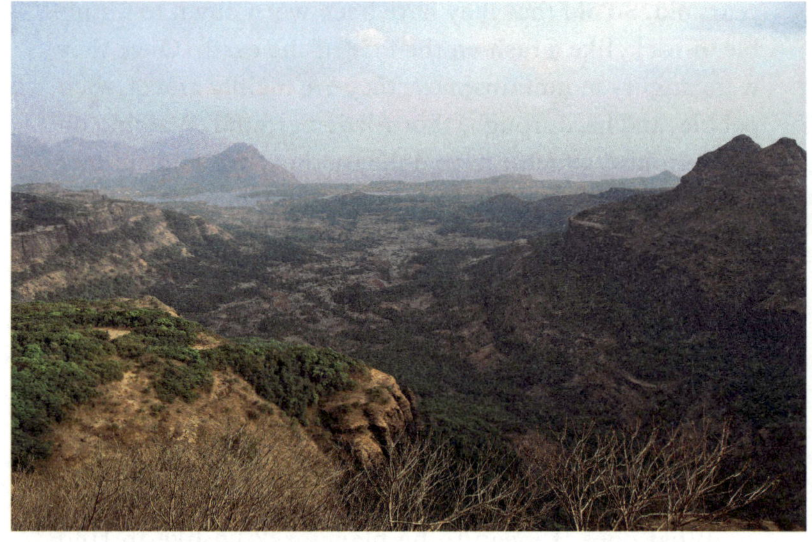

The Aravalli Range at Maharashta, India

about her axis at the rate of 460 meters per second, which is roughly a thousand miles per hour. Her orbit around the sun implies a speed close to thirty kilometers per second, or 67,000 miles per hour. The solar system itself whirls around the center of the Milky Way at around 490,000 miles per hour. This means that depending on which question we are asking—about rotation, orbit, or celestial waywardness—our home, this planet, is anything but still. We are whirling. I have always derived some comfort from this fact when I think about the meaning of the name we give to our practice as artists: Raqs. The word Raqs can mean *whirling* in several languages, but especially in Arabic, and one of our own, Urdu. I enjoy the sense of being synonymous with the restlessness of our planet.

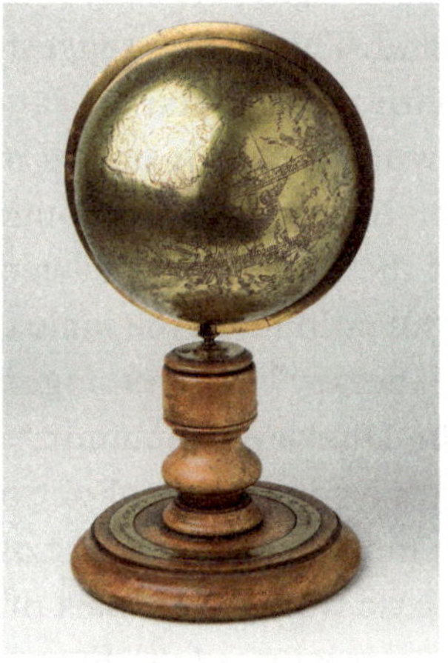

Celestial sphere in brass and silver made for Itiqad Khan, brother-in-law of Mughal Emperor Jahangir, 1623

The other thing about being a coinhabitant of a planet is that we all share a roughly spherical topology. There's a simple law of physics—the principle of isostatic adjustment—which has to do with the fact that all the mass of a body greater than a certain minimum size is uniformly attracted, gravitationally, to a point at its center. This shapes bodies in space of a certain mass into spheres. And it is true of all spheres, that every point on their surface can claim centrality. No point on a sphere is more central than any other point. Being planetary thus means giving up the illusion that any place is more "central" than any other place.

My fascination with spheres, and the globe, reaches back into childhood where I saw a boy my age, the character Apu, in the second part of Satyajit Ray's *The Apu Trilogy*[2] being handed a globe and books on invention, exploration, and discovery by his village school's headmaster. As he grows older, the boy Apu becomes a young man, travels to Calcutta for higher studies, and carries the world, the globe in his hand. This always suggested the possibility of an intimacy with the planetary, a familiarity with the world and with worldliness. It makes me think of what Marx means when he says, "The becoming-philosophical of the world is at the same time the becoming-worldly of philosophy; its realization is at the same time its loss."[3]

The word "planetary" or *Grihojagotik*, came back to me recently at the Dhaka Art Summit,[4] (see pp. 227–42), where it featured as part of a title of one of the exhibitions. It led me to think more about the place of the planetary in the history of artistic work in our part of the world. From globes in Mughal miniatures (the Emperor Jahangir was

2 Ray's *Apu Trilogy* is a 1955 series of feature films focusing on the life a young boy who faces existential struggle; it's widely known as Indian cinema's exemplary *Bildungsroman*.
3 Karl Marx, *Writings of the Young Marx on Philosophy and Society* (Indianapolis, 1997), p. 62.
4 *Planetary Planning*, exhibition curated by Devika Singh, Dhaka Art Summit (2018).

particularly fond of them) to astrolabes and astronomical instruments designed with a sense of planetary movements in mind in medieval Delhi, Jaipur, and Punjab, and images of the avatars of Vishnu playing with the globe as if it were a ball—we have always had different ways of playing with and deploying the planetary idea in South Asian cultures.

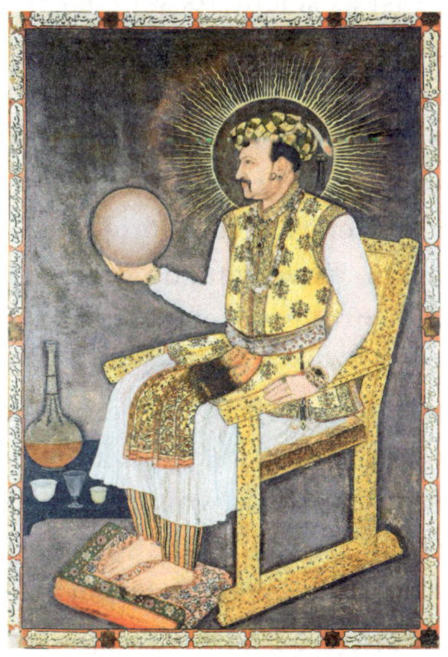

Nadir al-Zaman (a.k.a. Abu'l Hasan), portrait of Emperor Jahangir and sphere, 1617

The idea of the world as a game, as *lila*, has fascinating resonances. The modern Greek philosopher Kostas Axelos reprises Heraclitus's idea of the "world game" when he says, "The world deploys itself as a game. That means that it refuses any sense, any rule that is exterior to itself. The play of the world itself is different from all the particular games that are played in the world."[5]

5 Stuart Elden, "*Mondialisation* without the world," interview by Kostas Alexos, PDF, https://progressivegeographies.files.wordpress.com/2010/05/interview-with-kostas-axelos.pdf (accessed November 24, 2019).

From Axelos, it becomes possible to move to Édouard Glissant, and his sense of worldliness, or, *mondialité*. For Glissant, *mondialité* denotes a meditation of the relational properties of a spherical topology:

> I believe that Relation is the moment when we realize that there is a definite quantity of all the differences in the world. Just as scientists say that the universe consists of a finite quantity of atoms, and that it doesn't change—well, I say that Relation is made up of all the differences in the world and that we shouldn't forget a single one of them, even the smallest. If you forget the tiniest difference in the world, well, Relation is no longer Relation. Now, what do we do when we believe this? We call into question, in a formal manner, the idea of the universal. The universal is sublimation, an abstraction that enables us to forget small differences; we drift upon the universal and forget these small differences, and Relation is wonderful because it doesn't allow us to do that. There is no such thing as a Relation made up of big differences. Relation is total; otherwise it's not Relation. So that's why I prefer the notion of Relation to the notion of the universal ...[6]

Both Glissant and Axelos present an expanded view of worldliness. I view worldliness as something critical to the question of how we overcome the exhaustion of the contemporary. If we are to be serious about what it means to be inhabitants of a wandering star—an errant planet with an eccentric orbit—the paths we must follow are those that

6 Édouard Glissant and Manthia Diawara, "Conversation with Édouard Glissant aboard the Queen Mary II," in *Afro-modern: journeys through the Black Atlantic*, exh. cat. Tate (London, 2010), pp. 58–63.

take us back to the sense of what it means to be planetary. To be contemporary with the prehistoric and with the forms of life which are yet to come. That's the temporal dimension that I think contemporary art has the opportunity at this point in time to actually embrace. Again, it's about being abreast of the minutest fluctuations of our own time, and at the same time understanding the rhythms that take a few million years to resolve themselves.

Let us return to the Aravalli Range. The reason why the Aravalli Hills are so special for me is because they are evidence in their own way of the fact that India, Australia, Africa, Latin America, and Antarctica were once one continent. The man who thought this up was an Austrian geologist, Eduard Suess, who also worked on the mountainous terrain of Salzburg. His theory was based on his observation of the distribution of a fossil plant, *Glossopteris,* that turns up across vast distances in the Southern Hemisphere in a time consistent geological stratum. Unusual and distinctive, *Glossopteris* characterizes an unusual sequence of non-marine sedimentary rocks found through much of the Global South. Subsequent studies of the fossils and the character of the sediments have shown the existence of similar rock formations in South Africa, South America, Antarctica, Australia, India, Madagascar, and other areas, all of which contain common flora and fauna. It is now possible to correlate the succession of freshwater sedimentary strata, beginning in the late Paleozoic and continuing well into the Mesozoic, in these widely separated areas. The *Glossopteridae* arose in the Southern Hemisphere around the beginning of the Permian Period (298.9 million years ago), but became extinct during the end-Permian mass extinction.

By looking at the fossil record, Suess deduced that at some point in the remote past, the now distant continental masses of India, Australia, Africa, and Antarctica were one supercontinent that he called "Gondwanaland." The name "Gondwana" was suggested in 1872 by Henry Medlicott of the Geological Survey of India for a sequence of nonmarine sedimentary rocks. He took the name from the ancient kingdom of the Gonds, one of the principal aboriginal tribes believed to have inhabited a large part of central India in which the most complete sequence of these rocks is found.

And that is why, when I take a short walk from my home on to the red gravel of the Aravalli Ridge in Delhi, I know that under my feet I have found the reason for a planetary sensibility. Let us mark this moment, here, by marking the way this location allows us to address the question of what we call the planetary, which is fluid because it takes the career of the sphere we live on in time, not as a frozen ball suspended in space, but as a fluid wandering star—moving through and in time.

Along with this greater planetary consciousness, there is of course also greater anxiety. Those who captain the ship of contemporary art have expressed concern that perhaps this assumption of the global planetary is premature. I've heard this even from progressive colleagues who say we neglected what was under our eyes, and therefore also neglected the rise of xenophobic nationalism and so on. I don't think the answer is a return to parochial sensibilities. I don't think that's even a way of addressing local realities. This is the delusion intellectuals have when they do not connect with people on the street. If they connected with people on the street, they would understand that ordinary citizens the world over have a fairly good idea about a new cosmopolitanism—a democratic, or I would even say, a proletarian cosmopolitanism. It is only in the noise of political debate and discussion in the *feuilletons* and television studios that anxiety about localisms exists.

So it's necessary for us to have a balanced view of the world. I come from a country in which we are ruled by a form of political power that is exactly like Donald Trump. So do you in Japan. In Turkey, Russia, the United States, India, Japan, we are all ruled by these big men who think they speak to local anxieties. But I think this is the last hurrah of nationalism. It will fall because it produces itself in reaction to the immense tectonic movements taking place within populations all across the world.

The ground beneath our feet is fluid; the earth is a labyrinth of connected and resonant fault lines. Nothing stands still. Nothing ever has. Over one hundred earthquakes are recorded each week across the world. Many remain undetected because their magnitudes are very small, or because there are vast stretches of land and sea where there are no sensors. These earthquakes and microtremors, including those unregistered on the Richter scale, are the signs of geological life, of mobile magma, of evidence of an animate planet.

The world of humans too is active, with cascading microtremors, daily seismic shifts, and the occasional upheaval. Occurrences, varied in tone and intensity, manifest themselves in an increasing frequency of deoccupying workplaces of managements, work riots, work stoppages, slowdowns, tool-downs, "wildcat" acts of wage workers' self-activity, and continuous insubordination—sometimes angry, sometimes joyous, occasionally both—in educational institutions, natural habitats, housing estates, prisons, battlefields, and cities. Power's vision is weakened by its entropic excesses. The rising, falling, sliding, colliding, and overlapping waves of the messianic, the hedonistic, the mystic, the altruistic, the communistic, and the heretical forces of our times, with their countercurrents, constitute a seismic terrain, a discontinuous, broken, abrupt transcript of the daily life of our world.

Perhaps we could speak of a seismic shift displacing capitalism toward a reconfiguration of human life along uncharted lines. The question now is the ability to sense the magnitude of these tremors, with their spin, their charm, their direction, and their intensity. The networked intelligence of a global workplace is quietly turning into a platform for the daily insurgencies that mirror or transcend the fluctuations of the market life of commodities. The crucial question is: can it lead to new, concrete proposals for the material futures of our host planet and its guest life forms? Can the emerging self-consciousness of the networked intelligence of seven billion inhabitants of this planet lead to hitherto unimagined possibilities for reinventing what it means to be a social species?

The work of art, and the imagination, is an antidote to the poison of every inevitability. A work of art challenges the notion that things have to be a certain way. Because every work of art contains within it a myriad of other possibilities in relation to what already exists. Nothing has to be the way it is. Nothing is just the way it is. Everything has a secret wish to be something else. This includes the world at large. The lives of the seven billion-odd people who make up the world intersects somewhere in the republic of the imagination to create a desire for another world. Art is the process of finding that desire, and of making drafts of the future walk into the present on the basis of reading that desire.

For instance, a certain claim was made when the First International[7] produced itself. Unlike the case of Documenta X (1997) or Documenta 11 (2002), the participants were all men, all European, from a tiny fraction of the globe. You could say they were unrepresentative of humanity—which is true, and will always be so, because no matter what collection of people you gather, they will always be unrepresentative of the enormous complexity and diversity of the human condition. But just think for a moment about the ambition they had and the scale of their desire to embrace a global condition.

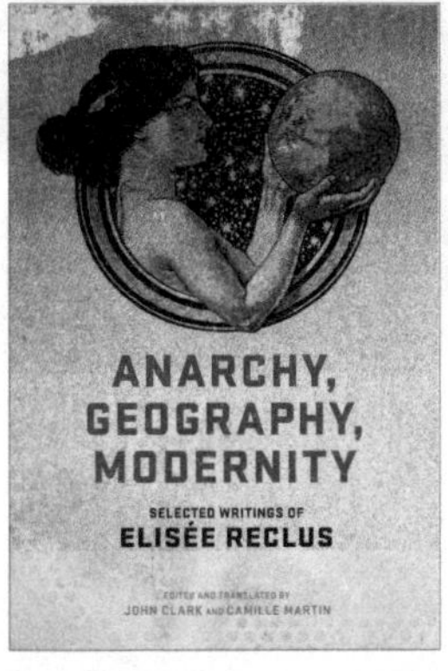

Anarchy, Geography, Modernity:
Selected Writings of Elisée Reclus

That is what is important. For instance, a great thinker who came out of the Paris Commune, the geographer Élisée Reclus, actually thought of urban planning on a planetary scale. And such ambition does not always have to lead to some sort of totalitarian master narrative. We can also think of it as a moment of expansion and

7 The First International is another name for the International Workingmen's Association, an organization founded in London in 1864. It connected left-wing groups based on class and labor struggles.

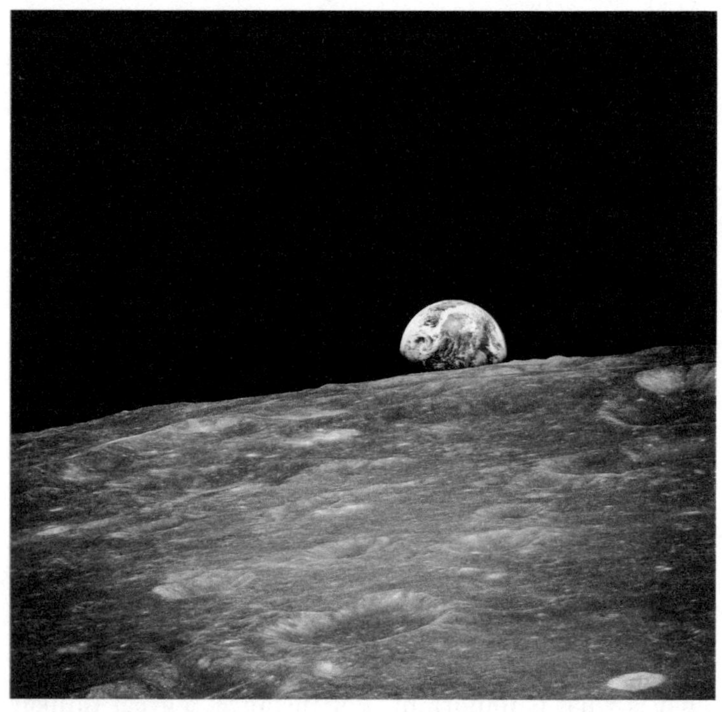

Earthrise, Apollo 8, 1968

imaginative largesse or generosity. Another famous Reclusian image, the one reproduced on the cover of *Anarchy, Geography, Modernity*, a collection of Reclus's essays,[8] contains no such ambiguity. In this image, we see Nature herself contemplating or watching over the earth, which this time is clearly held in her hands. The contemplating and holding seem to be inseparable parts of one process. The image evokes aspects of the contemporary ethics of care, an important dimension of ecofeminism, in which "holding" is a key concept.

The planetary haunts us. It haunts us in the *Earthrise* photographs from the early years of space exploration. It haunts us in Hannah Arendt's meditation on the exploration of outer space, marked by the launch of the Sputnik satellite in 1957:

In 1957, an earth-born object made by man was launched into the universe, where for some weeks it circled the earth according to the same laws of gravitation that swing and keep in motion the celestial bodies—the sun, the moon, and the stars.

To be sure, the man-made satellite was no moon or star, no heavenly body which could follow its circling path for a time span that to us mortals, bound by earthly time, lasts from eternity to eternity. Yet, for a time it managed to stay in the skies; it dwelt and moved in the proximity of the heavenly bodies as though it had been admitted tentatively to their sublime company.[...] The earth is the very quintessence of the human condition, and earthly nature, for all we know, may be unique in the universe in providing human beings with a habitat in which they can move and breathe without effort and without artifice.

8   Published by PM Press in 2013.

The human artifice of the world separates human existence from all mere animal environment, but life itself is outside this artificial world, and through life man remains related to all other living organisms. For some time now, a great many scientific endeavors have been directed toward making life also 'artificial,' toward cutting the last tie through which even man belongs among the children of nature. It is the same desire to escape from imprisonment to the earth that is manifest in the attempt to create life in the test tube, in the desire to mix 'frozen germplasm from people of demonstrated ability under the microscope to produce superior human beings' and 'to alter [their] size, shape and function'; and the wish to escape the human condition, I suspect, also underlies the hope to extend man's life-span far beyond the hundred-year limit.[9]

To be planetary is to understand the limits of being earth-bound, of being finite, of being mortal. This means that we understand our own fragility, and care for our brittleness. It means that claims to power, and to sovereignty, are just that, claims; entitled bits of legal fiction hurled around by those who don't have to care for much. The Earth has no naturally sovereign countries. Sovereignty is only an invention of powerfully armed, ambitious men that slice the globe into sections to be administered.

I return to what Gayatri Chakravorty Spivak meant when she proposed the planet to overwrite the globe:

To be human is to be intended toward the other. We provide for ourselves transcendental figurations of what we think is the origin of this animating gift:

9 Hannah Arendt, *The Human Condition* (Chicago, 1958), prologue.

mother, nation, god, nature. These are names of alterity, some more radical than others. Planet-thought opens up to embrace an inexhaustible taxonomy of such names, including but not identical with the whole range of human universals: aboriginal animism as well as the spectral white mythology of postrational science. If we imagine ourselves as planetary subjects rather than global agents, planetary creatures rather than global entities, alterity remains underived from us; it is not our dialectical negation, it contains us as much as it flings us away. And thus to think of it is already to transgress, for, in spite of our forays into what we metaphorize, differently, as outer and inner space, what is above and beyond our own reach is not continuous with us as it is not, indeed, specifically discontinuous. We must persistently educate ourselves into this peculiar mindset.[10]

The place that art makes in the world does not have to be a palace, a prison, or a promenade. It can be a culvert, a conduit, or a detour off the highway. Off the highway where speed reigns, where the grand procession marches on the spot, very fast, forever, not really going anywhere. It can be that vestibule, that shortcut, or secret passage, that turn in the labyrinth that gets us from here, wherever "here" is, to "there"—that tantalizing lighthouse on the horizon.

The place that art makes in the world is a departure lounge for a time traveling expedition. It can take us to the future as easily as it can take us to the past, or sideways

10 Gayatri Chakravorty Spivak, *Death of a Discipline*, quoted in Susan Abraham, "The Pterodactyl in the Margins: Transcententalizing Postcolonial Theology," in Stephen D. Moore, Mayra Rivera, eds., *Planetary Loves: Spivak, Postcoloniality and Theology* (New York, 2011), p. 79.

into other worlds, concurrently; here, now, inside or outside, but unknown to our own. The place that art makes in
the world is found by ascent to an altitude in which close
companions can become welcome strangers, where strangers can become familiar. It is a mountain peak on the range
called uncertainty. The place that art makes in the world is
the natural habitat of the third man. That strange, delight-
ful companion, the one you find when you hallucinate on
a long, hard climb. Not you, not me, but someone else who
makes it unnecessary to ask whether it is you, or me.

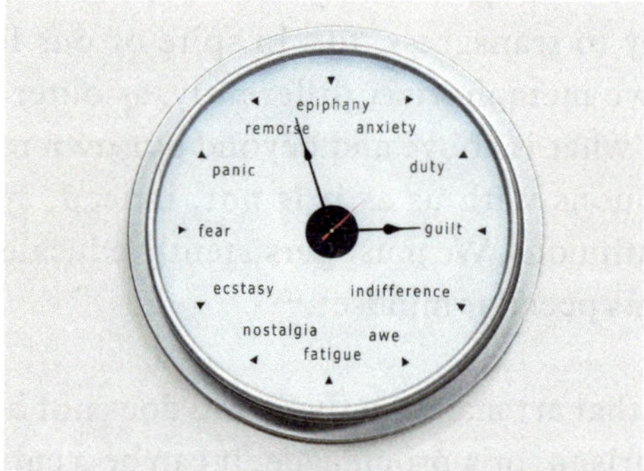

Raqs Media Collective, *Escapement* (detail), 2009

The place that art makes in the world has the taste of
solitude and the texture of solidarity. It has the porosity
of intimacy and lives and breathes like a crowd. The place
that art makes in the world is not a destination, not a
way-station, not a terminus, not a junction, not a spot
on a timetable. No trams, trains, airplanes, or motorboats
can get you there. You walk to get there, not on your feet,
but on the limbs of your questions and desires. It is not far.
It is not close at hand.

This text is based on a lecture given at the conference Global
Academy II, Examples of Transcultural Exchange, Salzburg Summer
Academy of Fine Arts 2018, see: https://youtu.be/cP5bjBhCar4,
(accessed March 2, 2020).

For and Against Definition: Or, How to Dismantle Maps

Stephanie Bailey

The chaos-monde is only disorder if one assumes there to be an order whose full force poetics is not prepared to reveal (poetics is not a science). The ambition of poetics, rather, is to safeguard the energy of this order. Édouard Glissant [1]

In 1977, Charles and Ray Eames released the final version of *Powers of Ten*. The short film famously starts with a bird's-eye view of a man and woman picnicking on a lakefront, zooms out into deep space, returns to that same picnic scene, and then enters the man's body to explore its molecular composition. We pass through skin and flesh to reach a white blood cell, then a DNA molecule, before arriving at a carbon nucleus—"the domain of universal modules," we are told, since protons and neutrons exist in every nucleus, "electrons in every atom," and "atoms bonded into every molecule out to the farthest galaxy." Finally, "a single proton fills our scene, we reach the edge of present understanding."

Powers of Ten is a visual depiction of a planetary perspective: a total view of the material world bound by a vast and intricate spatial relation, from the earth's place among the celestial bodies making up an ever-expanding universe, to the inner space of an earthling. Scholar Derek Woods

1 Édouard Glissant, *Poetics of Relation*, trans. Betsy Wing (Ann Arbor, 1997), p. 94.

describes the film as "an aesthetic event comparable to the first image of the earth from space"[2]—a representation of "all known scales of the universe in one continuous zoom."[3]

There have been many firsts when it comes to images of earth from space. The first official shot is a black-and-white corner of the globe taken some sixty-five miles above the surface of New Mexico in 1946 by a 35mm camera riding a Nazi-designed V-2 rocket launched from White Sands Missile Range, dubbed in one NASA factsheet as "the birthplace of America's Missile and Space Activity."[4] In August 1966, the first photo of earth taken from the moon's orbit was transmitted from NASA's Lunar Orbiter I satellite,[5] and was followed in December by the first full-disk image

2 Derek Woods, "Epistemic Things in Charles and Ray Eames's Powers of Ten," in *Scale in Literature and Culture,* Michael Tavel Clarke, David Wittenberg, eds. (London, 2017), p. 62.

3 Ibid.

4 Tony Reichhardt, "First Photo from Space," in *Air & Space Magazine*, October 24, 2006, https://www.smithsonianmag.com/smart-news/70-years-ago-today-nazi-rockets-and-american-scientists-took-first-photo-earth-space-180960890/ (accessed February 1, 2020); Megan Garber, "The First Image of Earth Taken From Space (It's Not What You Think)," in *The Atlantic,* August 6, 2012, https://www.theatlantic.com/technology/archive/2012/08/the-first-image-of-earth-taken-from-space-its-not-what-you-think/260755/ (accessed February 1, 2020); Jason Daley, "American Scientists Took the First Photo of Earth From Space Using Nazi Rockets," in *The Smithsonian Magazine*, October 24, 2016, https://www.smithsonianmag.com/smart-news/70-years-ago-today-nazi-rockets-and-american-scientists-took-first-photo-earth-space-180960890 (accessed February 1, 2020); "White Sands Missile Range Factsheet," Public Affairs Office White Sands Missile Range, viewable on Nasa.gov, https://www.nasa.gov/pdf/449089main_White_Sands_Missile_Range_Fact_Sheet.pdf (accessed February 7, 2020).

5 Ben P. Stein, "45 Years Ago: How the 1st Photo of Earth From the Moon Happened," in *Space Magazine*, August 23, 2011, https://www.space.com/12707-earth-photo-moon-nasa-lunar-orbiter-1-anniversary.html (accessed February 1, 2020).

Stephanie Bailey

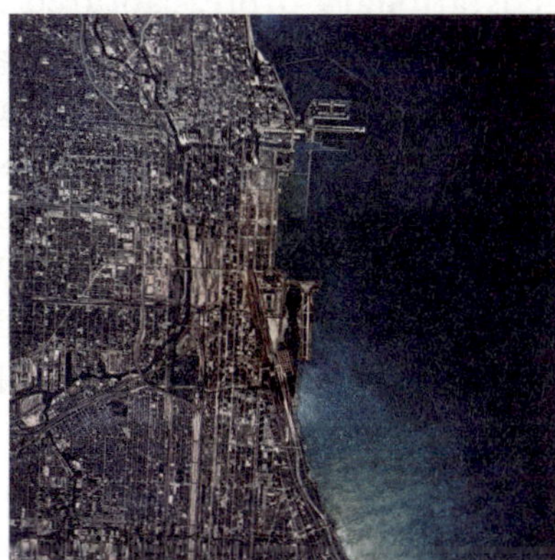

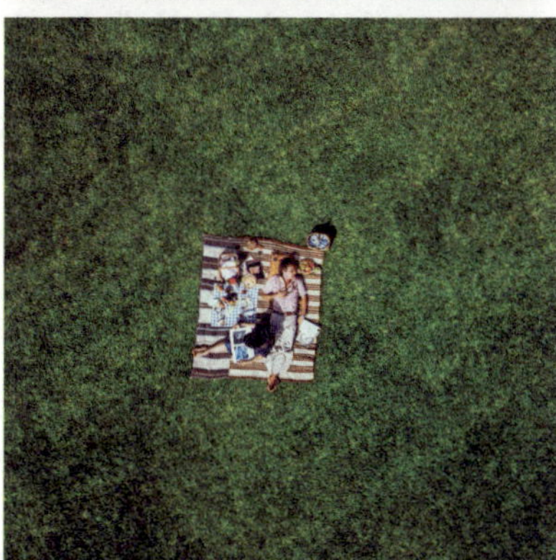

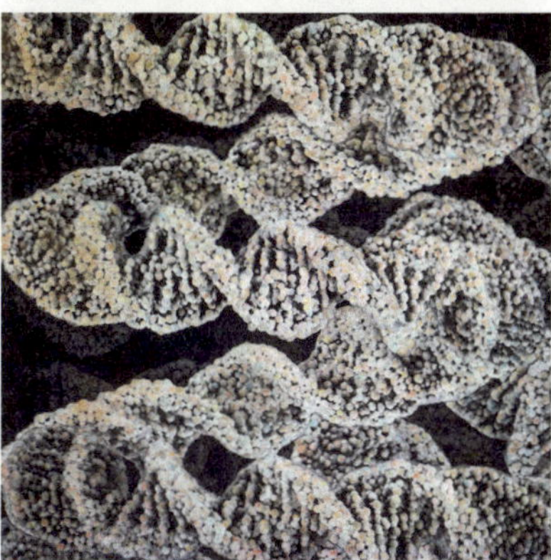

Charles and Ray Eames, film stills from *Powers of Ten*, 1977

recorded in geostationary orbit, captured in black and white via a spin-scan cloud-cover camera aboard the ATS-1 satellite.[6] In 1967, a multicolor spin-scan camera on the ATS-3 satellite captured the first full-color image of earth from space.[7] That composite appeared on the cover of the first *Whole Earth Catalog* in 1968, a publication for an emergent global community that "eschewed institutions in favor of individual empowerment," which Steve Jobs called the Google of the sixties.[8]

Whole Earth Catalog was founded by environmentalist Stewart Brand, who campaigned for NASA to release an image of planet earth in the belief that it "would be a unifying force in the management of global ecological challenges."[9] The first edition opened with a review of four books by Buckminster Fuller, whose insights the *Catalog* credited with its initiation. (Fuller's 1969 publication *Operating Manual for Spaceship Earth*, based on a 1967 lecture, proposed a unified system of planetary governance.) A review of *Cosmic View: The Universe in 40 Jumps* by Dutch schoolmaster Kees Boeke followed.

6 "The 50th Anniversary of ATS-I," National Oceanic and Atmospheric Administration, U.S. Department of Commerce, Satellite and Information Service, December 16, 2016, https://www.nesdis.noaa.gov/content/50th-anniversary-ats-1 (accessed January 24, 2020).

7 Ibid.

8 Anna Wiener, "The Complicated Legacy of Stewart Brand's 'Whole Earth Catalog,'" in *The New Yorker*, November 16, 2018, https://www.newyorker.com/news/letter-from-silicon-valley/ the-complicated-legacy-of-stewart-brands-whole-earth-catalog (accessed November 13, 2019); Carole Cadwalladr, "Stewart Brand's Whole Earth Catalog, the book that changed the world," in *The Guardian*, May 5, 2013, https://www.theguardian.com/ books/2013/may/05/stewart-brand-whole-earth-catalog (accessed February 1, 2020).

9 "Access to Tools: Publications from the Whole Earth Catalog, 1968–1974," MoMA.org, https://www.moma.org/interactives/ exhibitions/2011/AccesstoTools (accessed November 1, 2019).

Described as "a graphic journey through the universe, to the edge of infinity in one direction and to the nucleus of the atom in the other,"[10] it starts with a girl sitting on a chair and moves to outer space, where galaxies are reduced to dots, before returning to earth and entering a sodium atom's nucleus. The book is essentially the scenography for *Powers of Ten*. It was published in 1957, the year the Soviets launched Sputnik—the Space Race's opening shot.

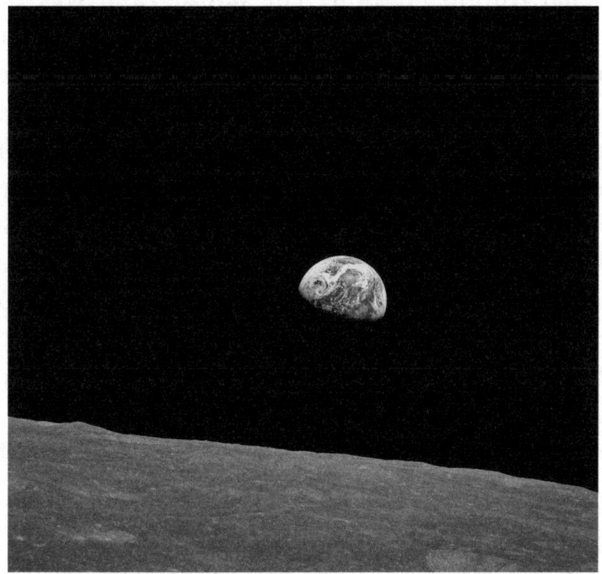

Earthrise, Apollo 8, 1968

Whole Earth Catalog made full use of the imagery coming from NASA's Apollo moon missions.[11] The Spring 1969 edition featured the first color image of the earth taken by a human on its cover—a shot of the half-illuminated planet peering out from beyond the surface of the moon taken in December 1968 from Apollo 8, the first manned orbital

10 Kees Boeke, *Cosmic View: The Universe in 40 Jumps* (New York, 1957), p. 2.
11 Anna Wiener (see note 8).

mission to the moon. Known as *Earthrise,* environmental-ist Michael McCarthy calls the image "one of the most profound events in the history of human culture."[12] This was the first time the world saw itself from a distance, after all, and the impact "is credited with spurring pro-environmental legislation and the inception of Earth Day."[13]

Then came the first and only photograph taken of the whole earth by a human, captured in 1972 from Apollo 17, the final Apollo mission. The photograph was called *The Blue Marble* for its vivid detail and color—"iconic," writes biochemist Gregory A. Petsko, "because it perfectly represented the human condition of living on an island in the universe."[14] Suddenly, Petsko continues, the planet "seemed *whole* in a way that no map could illustrate. Regional conflict and petty differences could be dismissed as trivial compared with environmental dangers that threatened all of humanity."[15] This description aligns with a common feeling that astronauts described after earth-gazing from space: an acute awareness of earth's interconnectedness as a living whole—a phenomenon that space philosopher Frank White called the Overview Effect.

12 Michael McCarthy, "Earthrise: the image that changed our view of the planet," *The Independent,* June 12, 2012, https://www.independent.co.uk/environment/nature/earthrise-the-image-that-changed-our-view-of-the-planet-7837041.html (accessed November 13, 2019).

13 Haley Weiss, "We Only Had One Photograph of the Entire Earth—until Three Years Ago," in *Artsy,* May 18, 2018, https://www.artsy.net/article/artsy-editorial-one-photograph-entire-earth-three-years-ago (accessed November 13, 2019).

14 Gregory A. Petsko, "The blue marble," in *Genome Biology,* 2011; 12, No. 112. Published online on PubMed Central® at U.S. National Institutes of Health's National Library of Medicine, April 18, 2011, https://www.ncbi.nlm.nih.gov/pmc/articles/PMC3218853 (accessed November 13, 2019).

15 Susan Buck-Morss, "Seeing Global," published on the author's website, http://susanbuckmorss.info/text/seeing-global (accessed November 13, 2019).

That firsthand experience was mirrored by those who witnessed the images on land: a collective mirror stage in which people were able to view the world as a singular object—not just as a world or an earth, but as a planet, and beyond that, a collective "I."

Susan Buck-Morss cites philosopher Hans Blumenberg's description of *Earthrise* as the initiation of a rapid and almost silent "transformation in human consciousness," which occurred more through the "cosmic reflection" created in "the stream of transmitted pictures" of earth than the first moonwalk itself.[16] So began what historian Benjamin Lazier terms the Earthrise Era, in which a global vocabulary—from the use of the term "globalization" to phrases like "global economy"—emerged.[17] Earth's image would become "the most prominent symbol of the contemporary global age; vicariously duplicated at the everyday level," writes scholar Neil Turnbull, and "culturally reinscribed as a representation of corporate global prowess and/or ecological concern."[18] Taking into account how one Apollo 17 astronaut, who later became a climate change denier, saw the scientific consensus surrounding the ecological crisis as "an excuse to implement a planetary management regime," this reinscription aligns with the dominant term that defined this new era.[19] Namely, globalization and its derivatives, which, to quote professor Christian Moraru, critics "summed up as *totalization*"—a byword or ideology for a "frictionless," "complete and completed,

16 Ibid.

17 Ibid.

18 Neil Turnbull, "The Ontological Consequences of Copernicus: Global Being in the Planetary World," in *Theory, Culture & Society* 23, no. 1 (January 2006), p. 133.

19 Benjamin Bratton, "Excerpt: 'The Terraforming,'" in *Strelka Mag*, September 18, 2019, https://strelkamag.com/en/article/excerpt-bratton-the-terraforming (accessed November 10, 2019).

perfect world ... whose "smooth surface allow[s] the unimpeded flow of capital, information[,] and language."[20]

Returning to *Powers of Ten*, this materialist view articulated an expanded frame that absorbed everything between the cosmic global and particulate local into its borders—emblematic of an era driven toward the realization of "one world" that *Earthrise* and *Blue Marble* heralded. This projected vision was outlined in a 1997 essay published in *Wired* magazine, which put a smiling blue marble on its cover. Titled "The Long Boom: A History of the Future, 1980–2020," Peter Schwartz and Peter Leyden present a "plausible" scenario for the future, where new technology in the "developed countries of the West" has increased economic growth, and "an unprecedented alignment" has taken place between "an ascendant Asia, a revitalized America, and a reintegrated greater Europe— including a recovered Russia"—creating "an economic juggernaut that pulls along most other regions of the planet."[21] For Schwartz and Leyden, "fundamental technological change and a new ethos of openness" would create "the beginnings of a global civilization."[22]

From the vantage point of 2020, this scenario has not aged well. For one, it is China, not the United States, that is leading the race to develop and build 5G wireless networks described as "the heartbeat of the future," in a competition that has been likened to the Space Race, a battle that unfolded as part of the Cold War.[23] This reality

20 Christian Moraru, *Reading for the Planet: Toward a Geomethodology* (Ann Arbor, 2015), p. 29.
21 Peter Schwartz and Peter Leyden, "The Long Boom: A History of the Future, 1980–2020," in *Wired*, July 1, 1997, https://www.wired.com/1997/07/longboom (accessed November 13, 2019).
22 Ibid.
23 Stu Woo, "In the Race to Dominate 5G, China Sprints Ahead," in *The Wall Street Journal*, September 7, 2019, https://www.wsj.com/articles/in-the-race-to-dominate-5g-china-has-an-edge-11567828888 (accessed February 1, 2020); Kevin Stankiewicz,

underscores the bias not only in Schwartz and Leyden's article, but also in the concept of a global planet communicated through the Apollo-era pictures of earth from space. These images, along with the 1969 moon landing, were engineered during the Space Race. In this frame, they were not only "a triumph of modernity as the technological dream of human progress," to quote Buck-Morss, but "the apogee of American power"—a victory of war.[24] This fact alone arguably problematizes any conception of the planetary as a departure from—or subversion of—the conceptual framework of globalization as a technological project of centralized development, since the images of earth as a planet that became emblematic of the global era were taken in the context of a polarized and tech-driven geopolitical conflict for world supremacy. Even *Powers of Ten*, a planetary view, was financed by IBM, whose complicit business with the Third Reich somewhat mirrors the Nazi technology—and former Nazi engineer—behind NASA's Apollo missions.[25]

"Cramer compares China's lead in next generation 5G wireless to how Russia beat America to space," in *CNBC*, December 17, 2019, https://www.cnbc.com/2019/12/17/jim-cramer-china-lead-in-5gsimilar-to-how-russia-beat-us-to-space.html (accessed February 1, 2020).

24 Buck-Morss (see note 15).

25 On IBM: Jack Beatty, "Hitler's Willing Business Partners," in *The Atlantic,* April 2001, https://www.theatlantic.com/magazine/archive/2001/04/hitlers-willing-business-partners/303146/ (accessed February 5, 2020). The same man who designed the V2 rockets, former Nazi rocket engineer Werner von Braun, developed the Saturn V rocket that carried US astronauts to the moon; Alejandro de la Garza, "How Historians Are Reckoning With the Former Nazi Who Launched America's Space Program," July 18, 2019, in *Time,* https://time.com/5627637/nasa-nazi-von-braun (accessed February 5, 2020); Amy Shira Teitel, "Wernher von Braun: History's most controversial figure?" in *Al Jazeera,* May 3, 2013, https://www.aljazeera.com/indepth/opinion/2013/05/2013521386874374.html (accessed February 5, 2020).

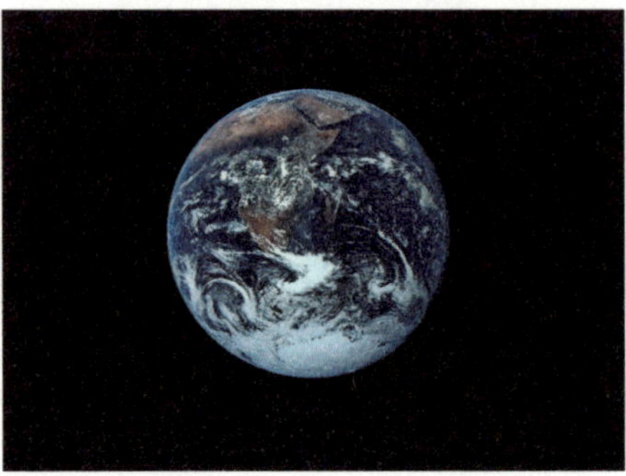

Blue Marble, Apollo 17, 1972

As perception-altering and world-uniting as *Earthrise* and *Blue Marble* were, they were technologies of power. *Blue Marble,* for example, originally showed the South Pole at the top, but the publicly distributed image was intentionally reversed to "maintain mapping conventions and primitive hierarchies"[26]—a fact that supports scholar Jennifer Gabrys's observation that a "total view of the planet suggests complete interconnectedness, but also forms of imperial control."[27] These were not so much world images, then, as they were flags in the ground: myths upon which the planet was claimed.

To quote Édouard Glissant, "… thinking about One is not thinking about All"—"Either the other is assimilated, or else it is annihilated. That is the whole principle of generalization and its entire process."[28] Such division would manifest openly in the twenty-first century after September 11, 2001. Like the moon landing, this mediated event—a global experience characterized by the stream of images showing the Twin Towers collapsing—produced

26 Bratton (see note 19).
27 Jennifer Gabrys, "Becoming Planetary," in *e-flux Architecture*, https://www.e-flux.com/architecture/accumulation/217051/ becoming-planetary/ (accessed November 10, 2019).
28 Glissant (see note 1), p. 49.

another world image beyond *Blue Marble*'s unifying view. George Bush, Jr. described that perspectival shift when he demanded the international community divide itself along an "Axis of Evil" as the United States laid the groundwork to invade Afghanistan and Iraq, proclaiming: you are with us or against us.[29]

Then came 2008, when Beijing used the Olympic Games to demonstrate China's emergence as a world power on the global stage, using the ominous tagline: "One World, One Dream." The function of this slogan is not dissimilar to the "globalized" perspective that *Blue Marble* constructed. To quote Gabrys, "The detached and distant view of Earth produces an entity that could seemingly be managed—or programmed," paving the way for "the rolling out of behemoth systems that hold the planet and all of its entities in a space of complete capture."[30] China declaring the world "one" in 2008 was enough to foreshadow a global campaign that would manifest as the Belt and Road initiative, launched in 2013 to create a global twenty-first century Silk Road across land and sea, with China reportedly signing a total of 174 cooperative documents with 134 countries and 29 international organizations across Asia, Europe, Africa, Oceania, and Latin America by the end of April 2019.[31] As historian Arif Dirlik observed, "Changing the global order has been a long-standing goal of the Chinese revolution."[32] Calling the world "one" is a step toward this ambition.

29 Transcript of President Bush's address, published on CNN.com on September 21, 2001, https://edition.cnn.com/2001/US/09/20/gen.bush.transcript (accessed November 20, 2019).
30 Gabrys (see note 26).
31 As reported by PricewaterhouseCoopers (PwC) PwC China Data Centre, https://www.pwccn.com/en/research-and-insights/belt-and-road/data.html (accessed January 24, 2020).
32 Arif Dirlik, *Complicities: The People's Republic of China in Global Capitalism* (Chicago, 2017), p. 128.

Interestingly, writes scholar Benjamin Lazier, philosopher (and Nazi) Martin Heidegger disapproved of the tendency in modern astronomical science to reduce "all natural bodies to specimens of a single kind."[33] More specifically, he objected to the reduction that made obsolete the distinction between earthly and celestial bodies, which brings to mind *Powers of Ten* and the equivalence it created between the opposing scales of infinite and infinitesimal. As Lazier writes, "To enter into a relation with something of such size ... demands a form of management and radical reduction, and a mode of being-human especially suited to the process: hence [Heidegger's] talk in a later essay of the 'planetary imperialism' of 'technologically organized man.'"[34]

Of course, there is a contradiction between Heidegger's ideas against planetary imperialism and his support of a nationalist movement that acted on imperialist ambitions. Perhaps the horror that Heidegger felt when viewing images of earth from space was driven by the prospect of becoming assimilated into an imposed world order—not simply a cognitive shift from local (national) to global (planetary), but an actual, geopolitical realignment. He described an acute sense of displacement when looking at the Apollo images, proclaiming in 1966 that man had become uprooted from an earth on which he no longer lives.[35] Later, Gayatri Chakravorty Spivak, who advocated for a definition of the planetary as a counterpoint to globalization's "imposition of the same system of exchange

33 Benjamin Lazier, "Earthrise; or, The Globalization of the World Picture," in *The American Historical Review*, Vol. 116, Issue 3, June 2011, p. 611.
34 Ibid.
35 Lazier (see note 32), p. 609.

everywhere," remarked: "The globe is on our computers. No one lives there."[36]

Indeed, "The terrestrial seems like a 'world' to us only when we can leave it," wrote Henri Lefebvre—"first in our imagination, and then by means of technology."[37] To picture the world is indeed to dream it—to simulate or engineer its image, which can be "cleansed of all contradictions, pristine and seamless, covering its crises up, or triumphing in them when and only when they can be usefully exploited."[38] To use Lazier's words, "What appears as the Whole Earth is in fact just another instance of the technological globe—and still worse, a technological globe that masks its fact."[39] In the case of the *Blue Marble*, this mask erased the material intricacy of the earth in order to reduce it to "one" without acknowledging the sheer complexity contained within the whole.

It is fitting, then, that 2019 brought about another first in space imagery, when an international network of scientists unveiled the first image of a black hole. The phenomenon was captured using an Event Horizon Telescope, a network of eight ground-based radio telescopes positioned at high-altitude sites around the world, from Antarctica to Spain, to form an earth-sized lens.[40] This array collected data that was delivered to two specialized computers known as correlators, which processed the information before the final image was constructed by four imaging

36 Gayatri Chakravorty Spivak, *Death of a Discipline* (New York, 2003), p. 72.
37 Henri Lefebvre, *Introduction to Modernity* (London, 1995), p. 188.
38 Ibid.
39 Lazier (see note 32), p. 614.
40 Event Horizon Telescope Press Release, "Astronomers Capture First Image of a Black Hole," April 10, 2019, https://eventhorizon telescope.org/press-release-april-10-2019-astronomers-capture-first-image-black-hole (accessed November 10, 2019).

teams.[41] Benjamin Bratton calls this a "world picture" —"crucially not a picture of our Earth, but rather a picture taken *by* the Earth."[42] It is the "opposite," he says, "of what they call a mirror," because it does not show humans in the world—rather, it shows "the abyss in which they can never be reflected."[43]

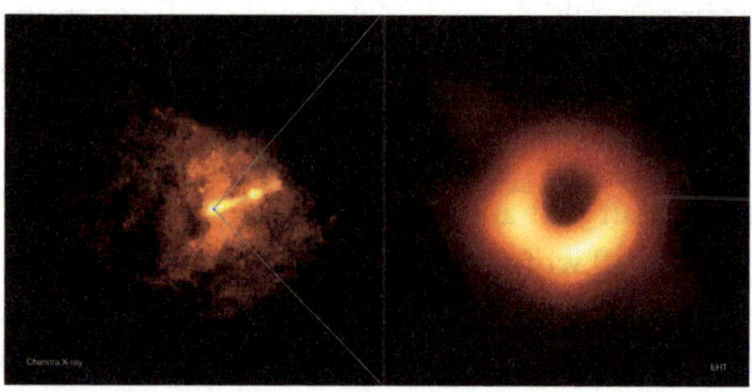

Black hole, Chandra X-ray, Villanova Event Horizon Telescope, 2019

While Bratton thinks this visualization is terrifying, it also holds potential. A black hole is a void that never stops accumulating, drawing everything in—its all-encompassing form brings to mind Glissant's description of the aesthetics of the *chaos-monde*, which "embraces all the elements and forms of expression of this totality within us."[44] As a world image constructed from a multipolar perspective, *Black Hole* echoes a worldview that Lefebvre gestured at when discussing the conflict between two principles. "We

41 "Event Horizon Telescope: The Black Hole Seen Round The World: Hearing Before Committee On Science, Space, And Technology, House Of Representatives, One Hundred Sixteenth Congress, First Session," May 16, 2019, Serial No. 116–19. Printed for the use of the Committee on Science, Space, and Technology, https://www.govinfo.gov/content/pkg/CHRG-116hhrg36301/pdf/CHRG-116hhrg36301.pdf (accessed January 20, 2020).
42 Benjamin Bratton, "Excerpt: 'The Terraforming,'" in *Strelka Mag*, September 18, 2019, https://strelkamag.com/en/article/excerpt-bratton-the-terraforming (accessed November 10, 2019).
43 Ibid.
44 Glissant (see note 1), p. 94.

have no more right to parenthesize unity or interaction than we have to think of progress as something with only one side to it," he wrote. "On the contrary, we should regard becoming in a polyscopic way."[45] It is at this point that the edge of understanding becomes visible; when the planetary as an all-encompassing and ever-evolving concept describing the interconnected material existence of life on earth (and beyond) comes into perspective. If, as Lefebvre said, it is ultimately "impossible to represent the 'world' as having a realizable structure and a possible stability," there is no better picture to reflect this common field than a vacuum that collapses everything into its intangible form.[46]

Lefebvre rejected the idea that a picture of the world could be simplified into a split between contrasting sides. He preferred "to seize the dramatic and conflictual interpretation of each 'side' of the picture" in the knowledge that "the picture is just a metaphor for a technical operation, itself abstract, by which the movement from one to another can be grasped."[47] But to grasp this movement, Lefebvre cautioned, is to kill it: a murder driven by modernity's craving for coherence and structure that only creates confusion, in which dialectical movements that are actually interconnected are separated and immobilized. What would happen if such movements occurred unhindered? To reach a point, quoting Glissant, at which "Relation is no longer expressed through a procession of trajectories, itineraries succeeding or thwarting one another, but explodes by itself and within itself, like a network, inscribed in the self-sufficient totality of the world"?[48]

45   Lefebvre (see note 36), p. 233.
46   Ibid, p. 188.
47   Ibid, p. 193.
48   Glissant (see note 1), p. 195.

To surrender the compulsion for order is to loosen the hard edges that border not only perspectives of the world and its geographies, but also the words that describe it as an all-encompassing "one"—whether "world," "earth," "global," or "planetary," these are open terms in popular parlance until they are claimed in theory or politics, after which they often take on an overbearing scale of immutable definition. At this juncture, I should clarify my understanding of borders, and the material and immaterial territories contained within them, because this understanding structures a general perspective when it comes to defined spaces and the politics that lie in their production. Just as a nation-state contains a population within its boundaries, and as a border functions as the edge of a delineated space, so words and the objects or subjects they define are spaces in which meaning has been contained and whose edges are solidified by its definitions. Words, and by association the ideas they represent, are like territories—sites of negotiation between stakeholders who have an interest in their usage. To quote G. L. Brook, they "are conventional symbols [that] bear [...] the meaning which the speakers of a language have at any given time tacitly agreed to assign to it."[49]

As such, words can mean at once too much and nothing at all. This is especially true when thinking about the multiplicity of perspectives that are articulated in spaces of global discussion, which draw from a broad field of references—and indeed individual and collective experiences—that are not always aligned, and which have often been occluded, suppressed, or omitted. Debates surrounding the meaning and usage of words that describe this planet,

49 G. L. Brook, *Words in Everyday Life* (London, 1983), p. 3.

for example, are all too often predicated on staking a claim—that is, to have the ultimate say on what it means to utter a term, or worse still, to argue for the negation of one term by another. While this might work in some disciplines, it seems counterproductive to apply such rigidity to the synonymous or related terms that describe this earth, where the words "we" and "our" are truly applicable, since it is absolutely shared by all who live and die on it.

Susan Buck-Morss describes the *Earthrise* and *Blue Marble* images as signals of a new, fragmented global era in her essay "Seeing Global." Exploded structures of history are "scattering fragments of the past forward into unanticipated locations," creating juxtapositions and affinities that offer "new readings of the past as a way of charting a different future."[50] Such fragmentation was encapsulated by the transformation of the earth's image into an icon, at once singular and multiple, reproducible and accessible—anyone could hold the planet in their hands, or at the very least hang its picture on their wall. "For the first time," Buck-Morss writes, "humanity sees its whole body reflected. It is a body in pieces."[51] She hints at what possible future lies ahead when mentioning "modernity's hoped-for 'Family of Man,'" concluding that "the history of humanity, far from over, may be just at the beginning."[52]

In 1991, Immanuel Wallerstein wrote about "the inescapably universal phenomenon" of the nation-state since 1945, an emergence that ran concurrent to developing world consciousness bound by a "universal persona" called "humanity."[53] The result of this "dual track," Wallerstein

---

50 Buck-Morss (see note 15).
51 Ibid.
52 Ibid.
53 Immanuel Wallerstein, "The National and the Universal: Can There Be Such a Thing as World Culture?" in *Culture, Globalization, and the World System*, ed. Anthony D. King (Minneapolis, 1997), p. 92.

observed, is an increasing resemblance between nation-states and their political and social forms, all fueled by the proximity and connections produced out of technological innovation and economic development. Even nationalism, Wallerstein stated, looks more identical when fervor intensifies—a process that highlights one of the fundamental contradictions of modernity as "inherently globalizing,"[54] in which the trends toward national autonomy and globalization "are deeply rooted."[55]

The nation-state is one of the most violent forms of definition there is, its name being the ultimate signifier of an immutable boundary applied to a complex and material space composed of living, breathing entities, some of whom have been subjugated under a definition (or many) that erases their own. "Australia" could mean anything to anyone depending on the frame of reference and the context—settler or aboriginal, for example—not to mention the conditions in which the word is articulated, mediated, and ultimately accepted or rejected. Perhaps it is this instability of meaning that the form of the nation-state—and by association, definitions in general—ultimately resists, especially when considering the political power that perspectives hold once they become entrenched as a collective position.

Hence, the subtitle of this text, "How to Dismantle Maps," which considers the act of defining as a form of mapping, and responds to this consideration by reframing the process of definition as a means to un-map: that is, to consider the act of definition as an opportunity to loosen the edges that mark out a word—and what it signifies—by acknowledging the possibility that a word's meaning

54 Anthony Giddens, *The Consequences of Modernity* (London 1990), p. 63.
55 Stuart Hall, "The Question of Cultural Identities: Globalization," in *Modernity and its Futures*, eds. Stuart Hall, David Held, Tony McGrew (London, 1992), p. 299.

belongs to an actual and material many. Here, the verb "dismantle" interprets the object of a map not as a navigational tool, nor as a collection of lines drawn in the dirt, but as a structure that produces hierarchical space, much like words themselves, particularly when thinking about the relationship between mapping and geopolitical naming, and by association world imaging, as instruments of power. Consider "The Middle East," coined in the late nineteenth century by colonialists seeking to claim the territories between the so-called Far East and Near East. The region's modern components were marked out by Western powers cutting artificial lines across a declining—and then collapsed—Ottoman Empire: a process so violent that one observer was reported to have said: "They are making a breeding place for future war."[56]

To dismantle the map, then, is to take apart an imposed structure that defines—and through that definition, contains—what are in fact fluid, intricate, and changeable inter-relational states, in order to create a greater, more palpable porosity between the edges of meaning, representation, and life itself. This is where the Samoan concept of *vā* feels especially relevant: a hyperactive and hyper-relational space that "encompasses multiple times and places," where "all aspects of temporality are present."[57]

56   Karl E. Meyer, "Editorial Notebook: How the Middle East Was Made," in *The New York Times*, March 13, 1991, https://www.nytimes.com/1991/03/13/opinion/editorial-notebook-how-the-middle-east-was-invented.html (accessed November 10, 2019).
57   Bernida Webb-Binder, "Pacific Identity Through Space And Time in Lily Laita's Va I Ta Taeao Lalata E Aunoa Ma Gagana," *The Space Between: Negotiating Culture, Place, and Identity in the Pacific*, ed. A. Marata Tamaira (Occasional Paper Series 44. Honolulu, Hawai'i: Center for Pacific Islands Studies, School of Pacific and Asian Studies, University of Hawai'i at Mānoa, 2009), p. 27. The concept was introduced to me by artist Rosanna Raymond during the *52 ARTISTS 52 ACTIONS* symposium organized by Artspace Sydney (July 20–21, 2019).

Samoan poet Albert Wendt describes *vā* as a relational space "that holds separate entities and things together in the Unity-that-is-All"—a place where the in-between is neither empty nor divisional but filled with contexts and meanings that change as relationships shift and evolve.[58] Located within this swirling rhizome of realms— "which composes the story of us in the ever-moving present"—are the maps and fictions that express "what we believe our cultures, our nations, ourselves were and are," Wendt explains. Maps that operate like reflections, in that we "read one another ... through the mirrors of who and what we are."[59]

Perhaps it is this shifting instability that truly defines the world as both planet and material earth: a sprawling and fragmented geography that is ultimately expressed and experienced by each living thing that constitutes it as the passage of time continues its course. In this messy, material multitude, words are worlds in their own right; to be navigated with others in order to further discover the complexities, nuances, and textures of their terrains. When we use them, we become cartographers of time and memory— inhabitants of a vast in-between where definitions are never solid but always negotiated, and where concepts intermingle, as they should. *Vā*, for instance, could relate to a plethora of concepts—*chaos-monde*, or thirdspace, maybe. Or perhaps, quoting Moraru's summation, what Derrida might call "a 'haptical' world in which most if not all of its parts touch one another, interact and modify each other, derive their meanings from other parts within the whole as well as from the whole itself, and otherwise

58 Wendt, quoted by Bernida Webb-Binder, ibid, p. 27.
59 Ibid.

hang together so much that the negotiation of their being together is an axial routine of the everyday."[60]

A word's function thus lies not in the absoluteness of its definition, but in the ability of those who wield it to express their understanding or interpretation of the term in use while engaging with the possibility that the word they are using (which extends to the concepts expressed) could mean something different to someone else. It might seem trivial, but Arif Dirlik summed up the importance of foregrounding the intricate web of subjective experience within the framework of geopolitical discussion when he wrote about "The complexity and fluidity of subjectivity that is implicit in the currently pervasive metaphor of 'borderlands,'" which he claimed "implies the 'overdetermination' of subjectivity"—a recognition that is "liberating, but only given the simultaneous recognition that an overdetermined subjectivity has contextual direction and preference."[61] "In other words," Dirlik said, "the subject is still a subject in everyday existence, regardless of what any wild theorizing may suggest."[62] Likewise, the world will always be one world, no matter what we agree (or disagree) to call it, or how it is divided, for that matter. (To quote the caption for an image of planet earth on the back page of *The Last Whole Earth Catalog* in 1971: "We can't put it together. It is together.")[63]

---

60 Christian Moraru, *Reading for the Planet: Toward a Geo-methodology* (Ann Arbor, 2015), p. 22.
61 Arif Dirlik, *After the Revolution: Waking to Global Capitalism* (Middletown, CT, 1994), p. 106.
62 Ibid.
63 *The Last Whole Earth Catalog* (Portola Institute/Random House, 1971), viewable on Internet Archive, https://archive.org/details/B-001-013-719/page/n1/mode/2up (accessed February 7, 2020).

That is not to say that the use of certain words is unhelpful in global discourse, or that historical ideas and discourses associated with them should be dismissed. But in the context of a global and yet still contested and asymmetrical sphere of art and visual culture, where English remains the lingua franca, there should be flexibility to untether words and their meanings from entrenched anchors—rooted, for example, in the "academy" or western-centered canons—in order to resist the violence of their imposition and make room for new, or less dominant, articulations. If the planetary discussion is indeed an earthly (and thus worldly and global) one that traverses registers and languages, then acknowledging the nuances and differences in understanding is to recognize that every individual is capable of speaking to the ideas that determine the world as a heterogenous complexity rather than a homogenous whole defined by compounds (or ivory towers) of power. To understand reality as a messy and unruly process mediated by constant and diligent negotiation—to give shape and meaning to it without reducing it to a set of rigid constructs—is to open pathways through that which is already defined.

This is where the Pacific concept of *Talanoa* seems helpful, especially when thinking about the question of defining a notion as broad and as all-encompassing as the planetary. *Talanoa* describes "a process of inclusive, participatory, and transparent dialogue," that builds empathy and seeks out "wise decisions for the collective good."[64] The concept was introduced to me by artist Shivanjani Lal in the context of *52 ARTISTS 52 ACTIONS*, a 2019 project

64 United Nations Climate Change Conference, Talanoa Dialogue Platform 2018, https://unfccc.int/process-and-meetings/the-paris-agreement/the-paris-agreement/2018-talanoa-dialogue-platform (accessed August 16, 2019).

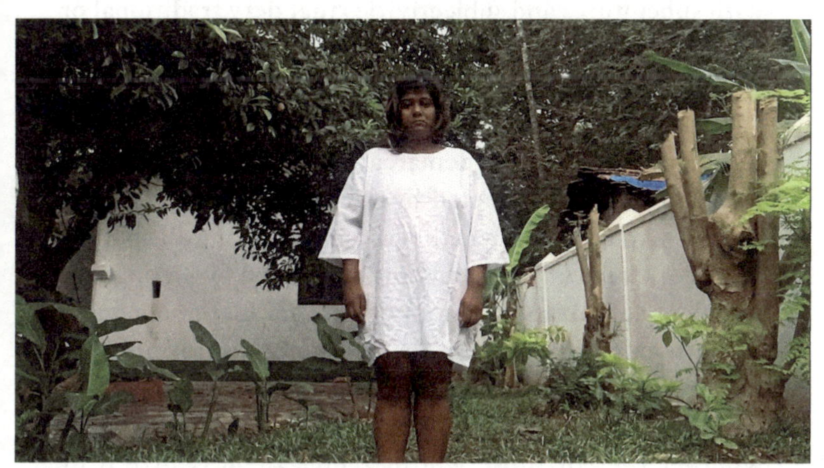

Shivanjani Lal, *Gesture*, 2018, performance still, from the exhibition
52 ARTISTS 52 ACTIONS

organized by Artspace Sydney engaging 52 artists and collectives throughout Asia that unfolded online before culminating in an exhibition in Sydney. The idea of *Talanoa* lent itself to the project's intentions, given the matrix of expressions that were brought together in terms of artworks, artists, approaches, and points of reference, particularly in relation to one of its aims: "to map and frame the region of Asia and its diaspora as endlessly evolving, with subcultures and subjectivities that defy traditional or rigid narratives."[65]

While Asia was named as an organizational frame, *52 ARTISTS 52 ACTIONS* was interested in unmapping the region as it is officially demarcated. It did so by bringing together artists connected by varied experiences of embodied displacement, whether as a member of a diaspora, a refugee, a subject whose history is marked by an ongoing legacy of colonization or geopolitical conflict or conquest, or quite simply as a body that does not conform to the terms and definitions that describe the status quo. In general, all of these conditions can apply to a single person, whether they or those who perceive them realize it or not. Everyone navigates the complexities of hybrid and cross-hatching heritages within the parameters of the modern world in some way (or many ways), defined as it is, according to one measure, by the nation-state—a form whose violence lies in the inflexible borders that outline the "unity" around which it is centered.

This unfolding relates back to the concept of *vā*, which allows for all possible existences to exist in a hyper-relational state that acknowledges time as a consistent

65 Introduction to the publication *52 Artists 52 Actions: Small Acts of Disobedience* (Artspace Sydney and Thames & Hudson Australia, 2019) published on Ocula.com, July 17, 2019, https://ocula.com/ magazine/insights/52-artists-52-actions/ (accessed July 17, 2019).

arbiter of change. Sina Va'ai, Professor of English in the Faculty of Arts at The National University of Samoa, locates this process within the postcolonial condition of Pacific Island peoples, for whom "*vā* operates nsot only at a physical and relational level but also metaphorically to describe" a negotiation of "spaces between and across different cultural worlds, redefining and repositioning themselves in the process."[66] This process of redefinition and repositioning, in which imposed definitions are transcended (or exploded) by evolving existences that problematize their frames, could well be visualized in the movement from *Blue Marble* to *Black Hole*—from a picture of "one" world to the polyscopic removal of its mask.

66 As quoted by Bernida Webb-Binder (see note 56), p. 28.

PAST

PAST

The Salzburg Summer Academy and its Early Transnational Relations

Simone Wille

Taking the early transnational connectedness of the Salzburg International Summer Academy of Fine Arts as a starting point, I would like to take a closer look at some of these connections and relate them to a selected, albeit larger, picture of postwar modernism that has its roots in both Western Europe and multiple locations around the world. In connection with the geographies I am most familiar with—parts of Asia, South Asia, and to a certain extent the Middle East—I primarily look at a handful of protagonists, teachers, and students who participated in the Salzburg Summer Academy between the nineteen-fifties and the nineteen-eighties. My focus lies in demonstrating that regardless of their national affiliation, artists came to participate in an increasing number of art schools across Europe in order to consciously take part in a trans-cultural project of modernism, thereby critically responding to a colonial diffusion of a particular concept of modernism. In this essay, the Salzburg Summer Academy is viewed against the backdrop and the significance of postwar artistic mobility and the dimensions of cultural transfer that came to shape modernism on a transnational scale.

The image on the following page is a starting point to elucidate my interest in the Salzburg Summer Academy's early transnational connection. In the image, dating to 1987, we see a group of artists from Japan, the Czech Republic or former Czechoslovakia, Italy, Slovenia or former Yugoslavia, and Austria. On the far left, we can see the

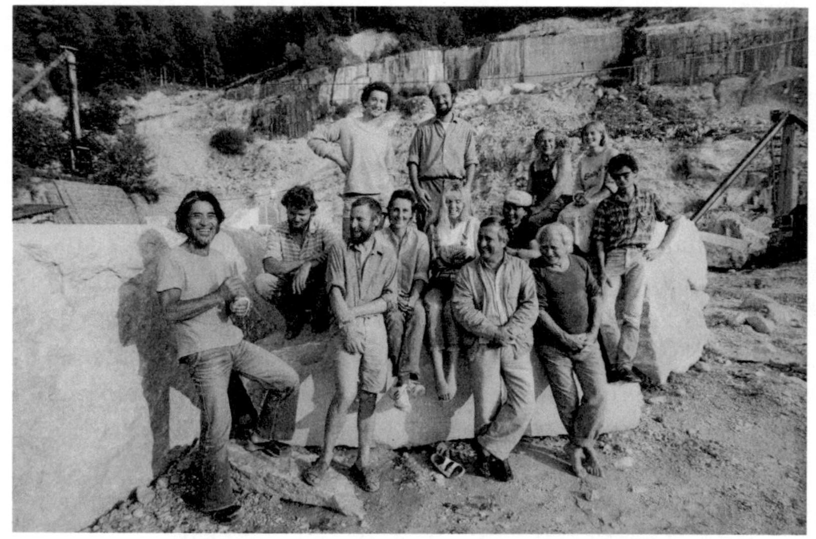

fig. 1—Makoto Fujiwara, Alois Lindenbauer, Janez Lenassi, Karl Prantl, Milos Chlupáč, and students; Sculptors' Symposium 1987; Kiefer Steinbruch Fürstenbrunn

artist Makoto Fujiwara (born in 1938), the second from the right is Karl Prantl (1923–2010). To his left is Janez Lenassi (1927–2008). And it seems to be Milos Chlupáč (1920–2008) seated next to the woman on the right. Furthermore, I suspect that the man wearing a hat behind Karl Prantl is Kengiro Azuma (1926–2016). The year 1987 was the second year of the Sculptors' Symposium within the Salzburg Summer Academy and it was precisely this core group of artists who, led by Karl Prantl, shaped the first years of this venture in Salzburg.[1]

I am familiar with these artists through my engagement with the Symposium of European Sculptors in St. Margarethen southeast of Vienna, established in 1959 through the initiative of Karl Prantl. St. Margarethen's story doesn't necessarily appear in mainstream art history; while researching postwar artistic routes between Bombay, Paris, Prague, and Lahore, roughly between the nineteen-forties and nineteen-seventies I literally stumbled over it. Some time ago, in an archive in Prague, I came across a postcard dated 1961, written by an Indian artist, addressed to a friend in Prague, informing him that his time in St. Margarethen had been very productive. This then instigated a search to find out what the Indian artist Ajit Chakravarti (1930–2005) was possibly doing in St. Margarethen. Not only did I find the sculpture he produced during the Sculptors' Symposium in 1961, I also found work by Krishna Reddy (1925–2018), a fellow Indian artist who participated in the symposium the following year (see the full-page image at the conclusion of this essay).

Both these artists' postwar and postcolonial journeys across nations, regions, and continents fall in line with my

1 Milos Chlupáč remained in Salzburg and directed the Salzburg Sculptors' Symposium almost uninterrupted for twenty years. He was celebrated for his work in Salzburg in 2006.

research. Their unexpected journeys to St. Margarethen also opened a perspective about regional, Central European connections with places such as Paris but even more so with their own regional geography; that is, Prague and St. Margarethen or Ljubljana and Graz, Klagenfurt, and Vienna.[2] Thus, when I discovered that some of the protagonists that I'd encountered in St. Margarethen appeared to be instrumental in establishing the Sculptors' Symposium in Salzburg in 1986, I approached Hildegund Amanshauser and asked her if I could access the Summer Academy's archive to perhaps find out about similar networks and connections with unexpected cultural geographies.

The protagonists in the photograph (see figure 1) participated in at least one edition of the Symposium of European Sculptors in St. Margarethen, and some attended several other sculptor symposia that occurred around the world and were closely connected with and in response to St. Margarethen. Makoto Fujiwara's collaborative work known as the *Japanese Line*—a site-specific project, immovably bound to St. Margarethen, which he realized with

2 Krishna Reddy came to Europe after having been trained in Shantiniketan, prior to the partition of India. He then studied in London with Henry Moore, in Paris with Ossip Zadkine, and subsequently in Milan with Marino Marini. Between 1957 and 1976 he worked with Stanley Hayter's pioneering Atelier 17 in Paris. In 1956 and 1965, he was included in the Biennial of Graphic Arts in Ljubljana. In 1958, his work was shown at the Biennale in Venice. In 1960, he attended the third general assembly meeting of the International Association of Plastic Arts in Vienna. In 1961, he had a solo exhibition at the Mala Galerija in Ljubljana and in 1961, he showed at the Galerie Würthle in Vienna. In 1962, he participated in the Sculpture Symposium in St. Margarethen and the same year he had a solo exhibition at Galerie 61 in Klagenfurt. In 1963, he exhibited at the Galerie im Griechenbeisl in Vienna, at the Forum Stadtpark in Graz, and at the Albertina in Vienna.

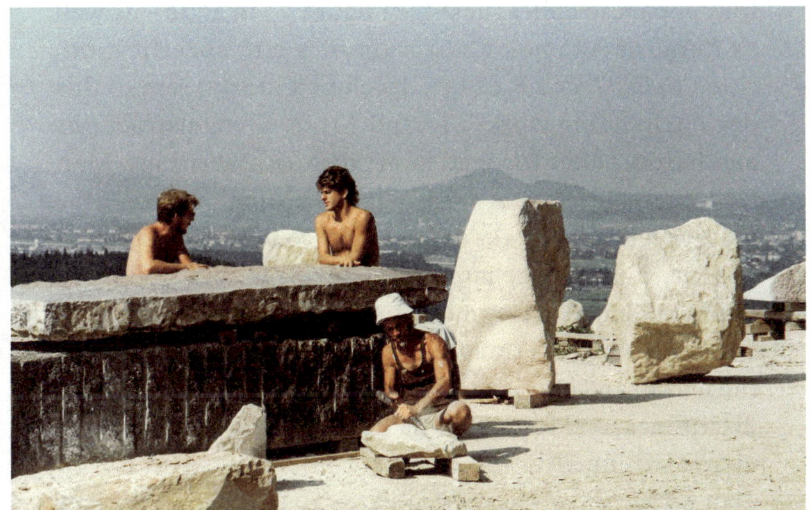

fig. 2—Sculptors' Symposium 1988, Fürstenbrunn quarry

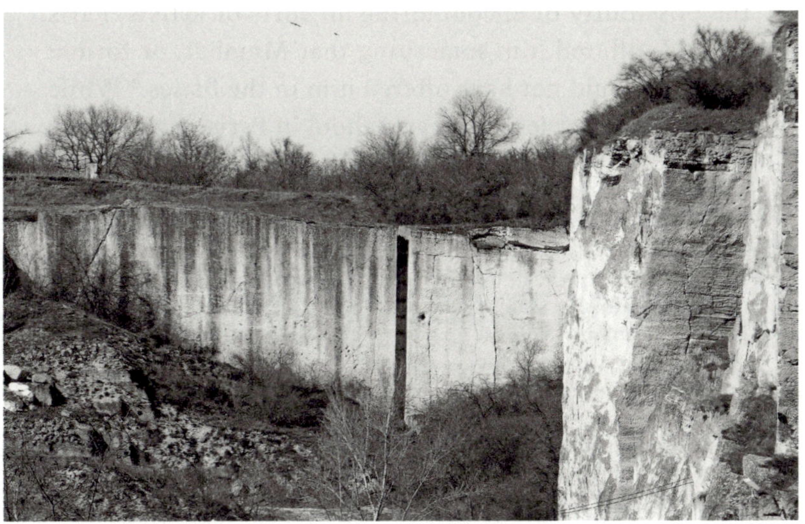

fig. 3—Makoto Fujiwara, Takao Hirose, Satoru Shoji, Tatsuzo Yamamoto, and Makio Yamaguchi, *Japanese Line* (1970); a collaborative, site-specific sculpture made at the Sculptors' Symposium in St. Margarethen.

four Japanese colleagues[3] (see figure 3) in 1970—as well
as Kengiro Azuma's realization of a site-specific work
titled *Cielo, Terra E Uomo*, developed in 1971, are to this
day outstanding works of Land Art or site constructions
and hardly acknowledged in art historical writings. Manfred Bauschulte refers to the *Japanese Line*[4] as one of the
most spectacular works of landscape sculpture in Europe.[5]

Yet, what may be more relevant are the artist's biographies, which are a testimony to artistic movement and circulation, of artists transcending the territorial borders of
the nation and seeking to connect with individuals, places,
disciplines, and ideas that lie outside their usual environment. I frequently return to my interview with the Indian artist Akbar Padamsee (1928–2020) who, like many
Indian artists, headed to Paris in the early nineteen-fifties
simply because he enjoyed the city's artistic freedom and
the possibility of encountering all sorts of artists. Paris,
he said, offered him something that Mumbai, or former
Bombay, could not have offered him in the fifties.[6] While
Padamsee never joined an art school in Paris, many of the

3 Makoto Fujiwara first met Karl Prantl during a sculptor symposium in Krastal in Carinthia in 1967, which is how he was
invited to St. Margarethen. For the *Japanese Line* Fujiwara collaborated with sculptors Takao Hirose, Satoru Shoji, Tetsuzo
Yamamoto, and Makio Yamaguchi.

4 The *Japanese Line* is 65.5 meters long, 80 centimeters deep,
and 70 centimeters wide. It starts at the bottom of the quarry,
climbing up the steep wall with slightly wavy stairs to reach the
hill, where it continues, with interruptions, until it reaches the
chapel at the area's highest point.

5 Manfred Bauschulte, *Versuch über die Festigkeit. Die Steinkunst
von Karl Prantl* (Vienna, 2014), p. 239. Translation from German
by the author.

6 From a personal interview with the artist in Mumbai, July
2018. See also Simone Wille, "Die künstlerische Moderne und ver-
nachlässigte Initiativen," in *Kunstforum International*, Bd. 252
(February–March 2018), p. 95.

artists who still flocked to Paris in the late forties and well into the sixties participated in one, often even more than one, of the many and mostly liberal art schools there.

The international character of the Salzburg International Summer Academy of Fine Arts was clear from the beginning, not least in its wording. Thus, German, English, French, and Italian were announced as "official" course languages already in 1953.[7] Martin Fritz, however, clarifies that "however diverse and international the Summer Academy's orientation, even after the opening and expansion of the eighties and nineties, the majority of participants came from the German-speaking region." Fritz elucidates that while the academy in its self-representations continuously points to its broad geographical spread over more than thirty nations, it has remained firmly anchored in Austria and Germany.[8] While Fritz clearly set out to mainly rate the time between the late eighties and the nineties, thus referring to the time of the directorship of Barbara Wally and Wieland Schmied, he emphasizes that, due to its geopolitical location, Austria and Salzburg are especially suited to creating connections. He continues to quote from the preface of the 1989 Summer Academy brochure, where it says that the location of Salzburg, "as a point of intersection between North and South, East and West, predestines the town and its cultural institutions for encounters and the forging of links."[9]

7 Martin Fritz, "Humanism, Pluralism, Globalisation: Six Decades of the Salzburg International Summer Academy of Fine Arts," in *The World's Finest Studio*, ed. Hildegund Amanshauser (Salzburg, Vienna 2013), p. 150 and note 150. See also the German version of the text, p. 37, which slightly deviates from its English translation.
8 Ibid., p. 37. Translation by the author.
9 Ibid., p. 37 and p. 159, note 149.

Enabling encounters and nurturing contacts was not only a declared principle for the Salzburg Summer Academy; it was also a guiding principle for the Sculpture Symposium in St. Margarethen. This may well be due to the fact that Austria was quite isolated in the immediate postwar era. The artistic scene in Austria between 1945 and well into the fifties had suffered from both material destruction as well as an absence of artists who, due to Nazi persecution, had to leave the country prior to the war and were not asked to return to Austria after 1945. The art historian Wieland Schmied wrote that in 1945 there was no tradition to which Austria could have connected, no development that could have continued organically.[10] While it took time to fill this void, a number of initiatives were born out of this situation and perhaps the more interesting ones happened not in the capital but in the provinces, thus on the periphery. Oskar Kokoschka was one of the artists who waited in vain for a request to return, and in 1947, he accepted British citizenship. In Vienna, the city councilor for culture, Viktor Matejka (1901–1993), was one of the very few who tried to bind Kokoschka closer to his homeland. In Salzburg, with Friedrich Welz (1903–1980) being the most instrumental, Kokoschka succeeded in establishing his own art school model, the School of Vision, the Salzburg Summer Academy of Fine Arts.

THE ART SCHOOL
AS A PLACE OF EXCHANGE

A look at Paris and the frequency of its many art schools during the late nineteenth and the twentieth centuries roughly into the sixties demonstrates clearly how artists

10 Wieland Schmied, *Malerei nach 1945. In Deutschland, Österreich und der Schweiz* (Frankfurt a. M. et al., 1974), p. 61. Translation by the author.

from around the world came to Paris with a desire to participate in the project of modernism. French art historian Claire Maingon, in her comparative study of two art schools, l'Académie André Lhote (1925–1962) and l'Atelier Léger,[11] points out some of the reasons that made artists opt for a particular art school in Paris. According to Maingon, especially between World War I and World War II, the French capital hosted an extraordinary number of foreign artists who generally gathered in the Paris's liberal academies as opposed to the celebrated ones. While the Montparnasse neighborhood generally reflected cosmopolitanism during that time, the liberal art schools such as those of André Lhote and Fernand Léger seem to have particularly strongly reflected this cosmopolitanism. As opposed to l'École des Beaux-Arts, the less formal admission procedure and the less academic teaching approach attracted a large amount of foreign and female artists to these more liberal art schools.

In a study about Paris and its cosmopolitanism between 1945 and 1989, Fanny Drugeon points to the importance of artistic movement in relation to the development of multiple aesthetics and the constitution of networks.[12] While Drugeon primarily calls for the investigation of the motifs, the conditions, and the consequences of foreign artists' sojourns in Paris, her study informs us that, contrary to common art historical narratives, Paris was still very much sought after by international artists in the postwar era. Drugeon points to the numerous well-known artists from the Middle East, Europe, Africa, Asia, from

11 Léger opened his atelier in 1933. It closed in 1940 when Léger left for the United States. His atelier was reopened in 1946 and ran until 1953.

12 Fanny Drugeon, *Paris cosmopolite? Artistes étrangers à Paris, parcours 1945–1989. Éléments d'une recherche en cours* (Paris, 2015), p. 161.

North to South America, and from Australia, drawing attention to their long Parisian stays, often in connection with developing key moments in their respective careers and, in many cases, resulting in the decision to remain in Paris.[13] Iftikhar Dadi, in his book on modernism in Muslim South Asia, has argued along a similar line, saying that Paris "... amid the general atmosphere of decolonization, had become an important meeting center for postcolonial artists and intellectuals."[14] This clearly contradicts mainstream art historical writing where, in keeping with Serge Guilbaut, it has been widely accepted that with the late forties, New York came to replace Paris as the center for artistic modernism.[15]

What these accounts by Maingon and Drugeon reveal, however, is that the choice made by artists to study at their chosen art schools was largely connected to the individual artists running the schools, their public profile, their ability to theorize in the form of published texts and books, along with the artistic style they came to teach and for which they were known.[16] This is precisely one of the main reasons that artists came to be attracted to the Salzburg Summer Academy. Oskar Kokoschka had an exceedingly high international profile. It was unmistakably his charismatic personality along with his stylistic orientation that made him "... the undisputed fascination of the school."[17] Ina Stegen summarizes what many others have

---

13 Ibid., p. 173.

14 Iftikhar Dadi, *Modernism and the Art of Muslim South Asia* (Chapel Hill, 2010), p. 161.

15 Serge Guilbaut, *How New York Stole the Idea of Modern Art. Abstract Expressionism, Freedom and the Cold War*, trans. Arthur Goldhammer (Chicago, 1983).

16 Drugeon 2015 (see note 12), p. 168; Maingon 2010 (see note 12), p. 220.

17 Ina Stegen, *Das schönste Atelier der Welt. 25 Jahre Internationale Sommerakademie für Bildende Kunst, Salzburg* (Salzburg, 1978), p. 225.

claimed to be the core qualities in Kokoschka's personality by speaking about "the kind of attraction which the name Kokoschka projected worldwide, the kind of human and artistic radiation which emanated from him, the kind of breathless concentration and readiness which streamed towards him when he entered a room,"[18] thereby referring to qualities that are in line with the two artists/teachers from Paris introduced earlier. From the beginning, the Summer Academy witnessed a mix of nationalities among its participants and teachers; a selected number of individuals are well-known artists but perhaps less known to a European audience.

SELECTED INTERNATIONAL ARTISTS AT THE SALZBURG SUMMER ACADEMY

In 1955, the artist Margo Veillon (1907–2003) participated in the Summer Academy. She took part in the lithography course led by Slavi Soucek.[19] Veillon was born in Egypt in 1907. Her father was a Swiss merchant and her mother Austrian. Veillon lived in Paris between 1929 and 1931. These two years can be considered her apprentice years where she experimented with a multitude of artistic styles, developing a special interest in Cubism. Veillon is considered an important artist in Egypt and forms part of a strong group of female artists of which Marguerite Nakhla (1908–1977), Effat Naghi (1905–1994), Tahia

18 Ibid.

19 In the Summer Academy archive, Margo Veillon is listed as having taken part in the lithography course in 1955. In her published biographies it frequently states that she studied lithography with Oskar Kokoschka that year. The lithography course was headed by Slavi Soucek but the naming of Kokoschka in her biography clearly indicates the degree of familiarity and fame that emanated from him. Archive ISBK, file "Teilnehmer Listen ISBK 1953–1959. 1014 TN."

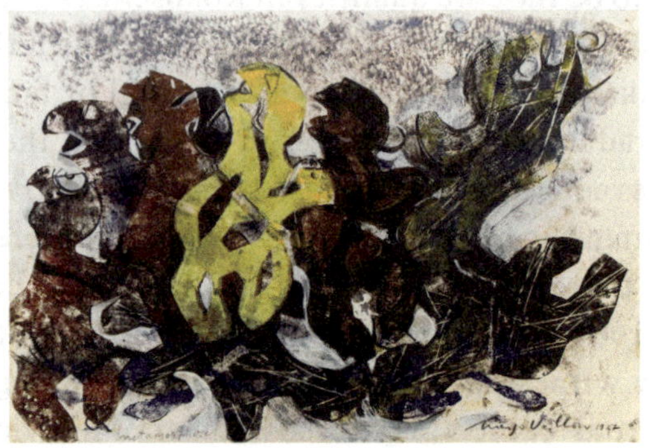

Margo Veillon, *Metamorphose*, 1967

Halim (1919–2003), Inji Efflatoun (1924–1989), Gazbia
Sirry (1925), and Zeinab Abdel Hamid (1919–2002) have
achieved international recognition through their pioneering stylistic aesthetics that were often paired with social
and political commentaries. While Veillon traveled extensively throughout her life—from 1960 she regularly spent
summers in Switzerland—she was considered a local artist who deeply engaged with Egypt. The largest body of
her work along with her archive is with the American
University in Cairo. Parts of her work are on permanent
display there.[20]

Kawkab Youssef El-Assal (1909–2009) is another
Egyptian artist who participated in the Summer Academy
in 1958 and in 1959.[21] In the early nineteen-thirties, she

20 See Bruno Ronfard, ed., *Margo Veillon. Painting Egypt.*
The Masterpiece Collection at the American University in Cairo
(Cairo and New York, 2003); Green Art Gallery, *Modernist*
Women of Egypt (Dubai, 2017).

21 The spelling of her name varies slightly in literature. In the
archive of the Summer Academy she is recorded as Youssef El Assal
Kawkab, see Archive ISBK file "Teilnehmer Listen ISBK 1953–1959.
1014 TN." The spelling here is based on what I found most frequently on various websites. See, for example http://www.fineart.
gov.eg/eng/cv/print_my_cv.asp?IDA=1690, (accessed August 3, 2019).

studied at the Hornsey School of Art in London and upon her return to Egypt became an art teacher. Like Veillon, Kawkab El-Assal spent summers in Europe, two of which took her to Salzburg. Reflecting on her life in a profile interview in 2001 for *Al-Ahram*, a weekly English online journal, she felt irritated by the fact that values that had been appreciated by her generation had become the reason for controversies. She reflects on the "… great expressionist Oskar Kokoshka [sic], with whom she studied" saying that "… art, Kokoshka would tell his students, is seeing with your eyes and not only an expression of emotion or of intellect."[22] This is clearly in line with Kokoschka's mission at his summer school to convey to his students from around the world to see the human being as central to all things.[23] According to participants listed in the archive of the Summer Academy, a few other artists from Egypt and Kuwait appear in these early years. In the late sixties, there is an increase in participants from non-European countries;[24] in the seventies, this trend intensified.

In 1970, the painter Zao Wou-Ki (1920–2013) came to teach at the Summer Academy. He was born, raised, and educated in China, moved to Paris in 1948 where he soon became well connected and represented in important exhibitions, biennales, galleries, and museums around the world. In 1965—by now a French national—Wou-Ki

22 Aziza Sami, Kawkab El-Assal: Lessons for life, http://www. fineart.gov.eg/eng/cv/print_my_cv.asp?IDA=1690 (accessed August 3, 2019).

23 Archive ISBK, Ordner "Oskar Kokoschka + Sommeradademie" where Kokoschka is quoted as saying, "Der Mensch als das Maß aller Dinge, dies ist meine Devise für die Sommerakademie in Salzburg" (The person as the measure of all things; this is my maxim for the Summer Academy in Salzburg).

24 See Archive ISBK file "Teilnehmer Listen ISBK 1968." On the lists are Lebanese, Indian, Columbian, South African, Israeli, Mexican, and Australian artists.

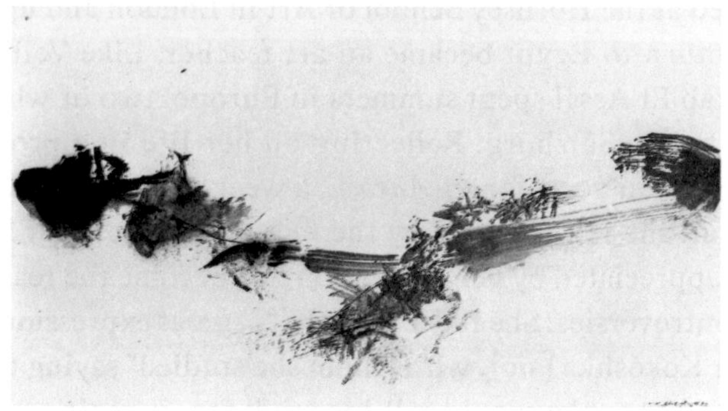

Zao Wou-Kui, *Untitled*, 1972

showed works on paper at the Graphische Sammlung Albertina, Vienna, in a solo exhibition in collaboration with the Forum Stadtpark in Graz. Walter Koschatzky, in his introduction text, speaks of the role of the institution to inform the public not only about art from the West but also from the Far East. He continues by emphasizing Austria's chance to extend its position as a bridge builder in the field of fine arts.[25] The exhibition at the Albertina and at the Forum Stadtpark in Graz showed more than seventy works by Zao Wou-Ki. What Koschatzky does not mention is that Zao Wou-Ki's work had already been seen at the Albertina in a group show in 1963. This was an exhibition titled *Graphik 63. Werke aus der Biennale Ljubljana*, organized by Koschatzky showing a selection of around 200 works from the 1963 Ljubljana Biennial of Graphic Art. Koschatzky's intention was to foster knowledge about graphic arts and encourage a collector culture in Vienna. Koschatzky admiringly speaks about the achievements of the Ljubljana Biennial and he praises the groundbreaking

25 Walter Koschatzky, "Zum Geleit," exh. cat. *Zao Wou-Ki. Aquarelle, Radierungen, Farblithographien*, Graphische Sammlung Albertina (Vienna, 1965), p. 3.

initiative of Slavi Soucek in Salzburg.[26] A series of works by Zao Wou-Ki are with the Albertina in Vienna. Some of these works were acquired as early as 1958.

While in Salzburg, Zao Wou-Ki showed his work at the Salzburger Kunstverein. In Paris he is remembered by friends as a spiritual master,[27] as an artist with great proficiency in informalism,[28] and as one of the first painters who dared to confront Chinese pictorial conceptions with Western techniques and materials.[29] Zao Wou-Ki's invitation to Salzburg must certainly be seen in line with a general opening of the Summer Academy toward contemporary tendencies. What took place with Emilio Vedova (1919–2006), as a representative of abstract painting between 1965 and 1969, seemed to have been carried on with the invitation of Zao Wou-Ki.

In 1975, the Iraqi artist Dia Al-Azzawi (born in 1939) participated in the workshop for lithography, led by the German artist Otto Eglau. It was his first introduction to lithography and is said to have sparked his ongoing engagement with image and text through a variety of formal possibilities offered by printmaking. In a recent large-scale retrospective about the artist's work in Doha[30] the catalogue references the Salzburg experience as having challenged his practice toward an exploration of form

26 Walter Koschatzky, "Vorwort," in *Graphik 63. Werke aus der Biennale Ljubljana*, exh. cat. Graphische Sammlung Albertina (Vienna, 1963), p. 6.
27 Richard Texier, "Zao Wou-Ki était un maître spiritual," in *Zao Wou-Ki. L'espace est silence*, exh. cat. Musée d'Art moderne (Paris, 2018), p. 24.
28 Stéphane Calais, ibid., p. 24.
29 Fabienne Verdier, ibid., p. 25.
30 *Dia Al-Azzawi: A Retrospective from 1963 until Tomorrow*, October 17, 2016 until April 16, 2017, Mathaf: Arab Museum of Modern Art, Doha. This was a two-part retrospective of which the second part took place at Qatar Museums Gallery Al Riwaq, Doha.

and color which eventually led to an understanding of image and text as a defining feature related to the history of Arab art.[31]

Suad Al-Attar (born 1942) took part in the lithography course in 1976. In the early nineteen-sixties, she participated in the important Baghdad Modern Art Group and her 1965 exhibition in Baghdad is referenced as one of the first solo exhibitions by an Iraqi woman. Her work is part of many major collections such as the Barjeel Art Foundation in Sharjah, Mathaf: Arab Museum of Modern Art in Doha, the British Museum in London, and the Gulbenkian Collection in Lisbon.[32]

CONCLUSION

In light of this account, how are we to read the Salzburg Summer Academy's early transnational connections? How are we to read "connections" of artists and the motives, conditions, and circumstances of their participation with the workshops at the Summer Academy in Salzburg? The postwar era is marked by an intensified engagement of artistic production across sites within newly created nation-states that followed with the decolonization of regions in Asia and Africa. While we have seen a welcome and increasing amount of research from several sites across the globe such as Mumbai, Lahore, Rio de Janeiro, Ljubljana, Cairo, Baghdad, and so on, work still needs to be done.[33]

31　Ibid., p. 46.

32　Some general information on the artist can be found on the official website of the Barjeel Art Foundation, https://www.barjeelartfoundation.org/artist/iraq/suad-al-attar/ (accessed August 5, 2019).

33　Some landmark works are by Kobena Mercer, ed., *Cosmopolitan Modernisms* (Cambridge, 2005); Kobena Mercer, ed., *Discrepant Abstraction* (Cambridge, 2006); Partha Mitter, *The Triumph of Modernism. India's Artists and the Avant-Garde 1922–1947* (London, 2007); Andreas Huyssen, "Geographies

Most of all, it remains to draw these "individual stories," in the words of Monica Juneja, "out of their isolated 'areas' and plot them on a common matrix that would show connections" but most of all it remains to "rewrite the story of European modernism by situating it within the larger, complex political and cultural determinations of colonialism and global connections that made its emergence possible."[34]

Following artists' routes also requires including the participation in off-center activities such as the Salzburg Academy and the artists' exhibitions along these regional journeys. The regional and international contacts made possible in Salzburg can then offer the opportunity to not only account for developments in this particular locality but more so to productively introduce this geographically peripheral milieu into mainstream art historical discourse. Reflecting on cross-cultural connections of artistic ventures will help to situate them in both regional and transnational art-historical writing.

of Modernism in a Globalizing World," in *New German Critique* 100, Vol. 34, No. 1 (Winter 2007), pp. 189–200; Iftikhar Dadi, *Modernism and the Art of Muslim South Asia* (Chapel Hill, 2010); Sonal Khullar, *Worldly Affiliations. Artistic Practice, National Identity, and Modernism in India*, 1930–1990 (Oakland, 2015); Sam Baradouil, *Surrealism in Egypt. Modernism and the Art and Liberty Group* (London, 2017); Michele Greet, *Transatlantic Encounters. Latin American Artists in Paris Between the Wars* (New Haven, 2018); Beáta Hock, Anu Allas, eds., *Gobalizing East European Art Histories. Past and Present* (London and New York, 2018).

34 Monica Juneja, ed., *Alternative, Peripheral or Cosmopolitan? Modernism as a Global Process* (Bielefeld, 2017), p. 93.

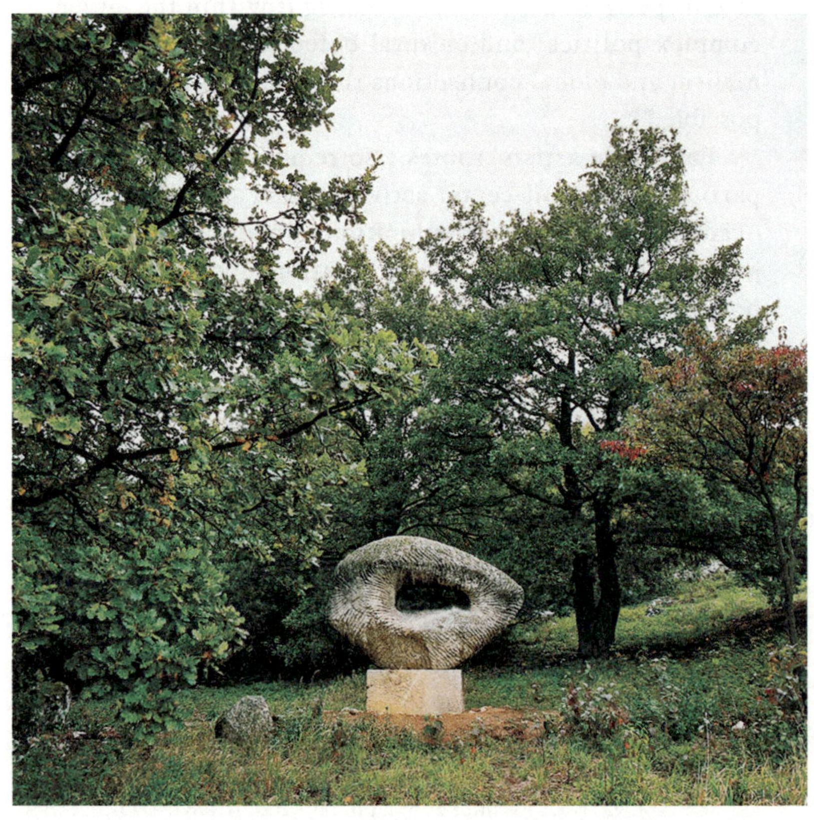

Krishna Reddy, *Two Forms in One*, 1962; a site-specific sculpture in the
St. Margarethen quarry

Geographies of the South: Unfolding Experiences and Narrative Territorialities

Fernando Resende

AN ONGOING PROCESS OF INVENTING GEOGRAPHIES

The fact that all territories are part of, and formed by, disputes should not undermine the fact that certain struggles, within clear contexts, differently configure specific territories. With this in mind, this essay understands that thinking about a "geography of the South" demands the exercise of first, working on a possible concept of "South"; and second, understanding how historical and temporal perspectives affect the formation of its geography. Only from this point, this essay suggests, can we consider and problematize the subjects (and objects) of such geography as part of a conflict that constantly produces contested regimes of subjectivities under the influence of forces that form the territories to which they are connected.

Dealing more specifically with the issue of visual culture and geography as instances of knowledge and spectatorship production, I suggest looking at two images, produced in different times and contexts, through which to read the inscription of the black body as part of a territory built in the "geography of the South." One is a 1912 photograph by Chichico Alkmim, a Brazilian autodidact; the other a still from a contemporary film by Afro-Brazilian director Yasmin Thainá. When connecting these two images, we are able to perceive the body as part of a narrative territoriality. And it is then, in the historical and temporal interval between these two images, that the expropriation of the Black body—one of the cruelest acts

promoted by the colonial system implemented in Brazil—
comes out as part of the ongoing conflict that marks the
territory we will be thinking about.

Produced within a complex of entangled temporalities
and disjunctive histories, the territory that we understand
as forming the geography of the South consists of a never-
ending asymmetrical conflict. The geography of the South
always fights against a "geography of power,"[1] and it
is within this process that other geographies must continuously be invented. Thus, the process of inventing
geographies, part of the work to which image producers
dedicate in the context of the conflicting narratives into
which we are all embedded, is fundamental. As our everyday experiences unfold throughout time and space—due
to the scars our bodies accumulate—the production of
aesthetic-political gestures is a significant instrument in
our ongoing struggle.

THE SOUTH AS THE REST

Either individually or collectively, we are all part of multiple territories, though we often insist on demarcating and
emphasizing our sense of belonging by claiming a particular territory to be ours. This essay takes as a starting point
this paradoxical way of triggering a discussion of what has
been called the Global South, a space of constant juxtaposed and conflicting histories and temporalities. Its main
aim, more than getting to a definition of the term, is to understand how an aesthetic dimension—a way of claiming

---

1 Fernando Resende, "The Global South: Conflicting Narratives
and the Invention of Geographies," in *Revista IBRAAZ—Contemporary Visual Culture in Northern Africa and the Middle East*,
November 6, 2014, www.ibraaz.org/essays/111 (accessed March 12,
2020).

and evoking experiences—ought to be considered, if the Global South is comprehended as a territory.

When referring to the "Global South" the first issue that comes to mind is a physical, fixed geography that identifies what and where this South would be; either where we could find poverty, economic problems, and inequalities as well as an exotic spontaneous happiness aligned with a freer way of moving the body. This physical geography would correspond exactly to the definition of *a* South. Yet we doubt that this can be taken as a simple truth. By questioning the simplicity of a thought that denies the complexity immersed in any territory, we expect to be confronted with the idea that certain geographies imply the apprehension of territorialities—constituted of aesthetic-political gestures—if the purpose is to think/work within *and* beyond physical borders.

In this sense, if we understand the Global South as an "ex-centric location,"[2] we can assume such a territory corresponds to what exists beyond the centers of legitimacy, knowledge, and power. From this perspective, the Global South is any way of being, thinking and/or living out of what is institutionally and geopolitically recognized as part of an "order." Caroline Levander and Walter Mignolo said that to explore the Global South is to investigate the "world dis/order."[3] We are then closely aligned with this thought, stating that the Global South, as a territory, is part of an expanded geography—the geography of the South—with its physically demarcated and affectively

2 Jean and John L. Comaroff, "Theory from the South: Or, how Euro-America is Evolving Toward Africa," in *Anthropological Forum*, vol. 22, no. 2, (June 2012), p. 12.
3 Caroline Levander and Walter Mignolo, "Introduction: The Global South and Dis/Order," in *The Global South*, vol. 5:1, (Spring 2011) pp. 1–11.

constructed terrains; all, at the same time, lived, imagined, and invented.

Therefore, far beyond what one could define as a place of emerging or decaying economies—a prevailing dichotomous discourse one might stick to as a prospect for reaching the center (or not)—the geography of the South is nevertheless affected by many conflicts of all kinds. A space of richness and strong processes of resistance also gives room to economic inequalities and starvation. "Latin America is not the West, but the rest," Octavio Paz said in 1993. This suggests that the geography of the South, also beyond what is called "Latin America," consists of this "rest" at which we constantly look and with which we permanently live.[4] In this sense, "the rest"—whatever is not part of what has been produced and legitimized as "the West"—forms the territoriality we are in search of.

CONFLICTING HISTORIES AND TEMPORALITIES

To apprehend the idea of the South in terms of its territorialities implies understanding it as a way of being and living beyond centers, mainly those imposed and legitimized by colonial projects, practices, and thoughts. In this sense, the challenge of thinking about (the Global) South as a territory reinforces the paradox of its constitution: it is, at the same time, part of a physical and symbolic dimension, exactly due to the fact that a territory is never fixed, but always in the state of being produced.

To this end, Milton Santos proposes the idea of territory from the perspective of its configuration.[5] For him,

4 See Octavio Paz, "America en plural y singular," in *Itinerario.* (Mexico City, 1993). Translation by the author.
5 See Milton Santos, *Metamorfoses do espaço habitado* (São Paulo, 1988).

territory is a "production of an inhabited space," where various technologies and techniques, means of production, objects, and subjects are constantly colliding and therefore always in charge of reinventing definite forms of living. Thus, as a decentered space and, at the same time, part of an ongoing construction, the geography of the South consists of a structured and structuring process of constant dispute and production of imaginaries and histories that coexist within disjunctive times; a process built throughout negotiations and conflicts.

From this perspective, what we propose here to understand as "the rest," in opposition to "the West," is a territory that encompasses "sub-territories," which are in constant conflict with any legitimized power. Such an approach leads us to understand the ex-colonies and other decentered locations—in South America, Africa, or any other continent—as part of an ongoing internal dispute. What collide in these localities, following Santos's definition of a territory, are the entangled histories that are part of a distinct geography. It is not, or at least not only, a matter of considering these ex-colonies' struggle against the power of the Other (an external colonialist agent), but of mostly taking into consideration an internal dispute among definite forms of being that coexist in that one territory. In other words, "the Other"—that can in fact, and many times, be a projection of the colonizer—forms part of the multiterritoriality within which that territory is built.

We notice, in this sense, the fundamental recognition that within a territory there are multiple forms of being—a nonharmonious conjunction of multiterritorialities,[6] due

6 See Rogério Haesbaert, *O mito da desterritorialização: do 'fim dos territórios' à multiterritorialidade* (Rio de Janeiro, 2016).

to the basic fact that a territory is made of conflicting histories. Carlos Zambrano gives us the most exact definition on this point: a territory is "a sort of palimpsest of representations that stratifies histories, which are conflictingly juxtaposed."[7] Being aware that power is a keyword, we understand that in any territory, as it is constituted by juxtaposed histories, the things that conflict are related to a flow of tense negotiations. We are speaking of wills and desires as part of a power game that very much follows the demarcation of what, or which, history is or is not legitimate.

Besides (or because of) all that, temporalities are also colliding forces in this same territory. When describing and discussing experiences of being part of postcolonial societies, Achille Mbembe places the issue of power in close connection with what he calls "entangled temporalities." His aim is to denounce power by rehabilitating the two notions of age and *durée*:

> By age is meant not a simple category of time, but a number of relationships and a configuration of events often visible and perceptible, sometimes diffuse, 'hydra-headed,' but to which contemporaries could testify since very aware of them. As an age, the post colony encloses multiple durées made up of discontinuities, reversals, inertias, and swings that overlay one another, interpenetrate one another, and envelope one another: an entanglement.[8]

In other words, entangling temporalities evoke and produce layers of power that not only structure what we conceptualize as "South," but also enhance the conflicts and

---

7 Carlos Zambrano, "Territorios plurales: cambio sociopolitico y gobernabilidad cultural," in *Boletim Goiano de Geografia*, Vol. 21, No. 1 (January 2001), p. 31. Translation by the author.

8 Achille Mbembe, *On the Postcolony* (Los Angeles, 2001), p. 14.

disputes one notices in this territory. Senses and values of progress, development, binary perceptions of what is more or less civilized, for instance, structure these fights, giving room to processes of identity and, many times, territorial disputes. And in the geographies of the South, one always knows that those who are able to keep the system rolling by tying themselves to hegemonic alliances and interests are quite often the winners.

We thus also understand the Global South as part of an exhausted geography,[9] a territory that has long lived through a type of a conflicting situation that, due to its long duration, has produced (and is then constituted by) distinct and all the same conflicting subjectivities; ways of being that, more than ever, require other or at least clear ways of thinking. In order to pervade this game or system, the challenge of resisting—or (re)existing, as it is stated by José Celso Martinez Corrêa[10]—requires not only the production of aesthetic gestures that reverberate the cruelty of the game, but also the political action of inventing other geographies from and within the terrain from which these gestures and actions emerge.

Besides working on how this configured territory is formed, the challenge we face requires positing certain fundamental questions. Being aware of the fact that one is thinking from a terrain built under asymmetric disputes, we should ask: how can images contribute to making the complexity inscribed in such territories visible? Which elements would we need to look at in order to produce a possible critique of the formation of this territory and the struggle in which images of the South are immersed?

9 See Irit Rogoff, *Terra infirma: Geography's Visual Culture* (New York, 2006).

10 Zé Celso, as he is also known, is a very important octogenarian Brazilian anthropophagist thinker and playwright. He is director of Teatro Oficina, one of the most prolific theater companies in Brazil, which dates from the sixties and is still very active.

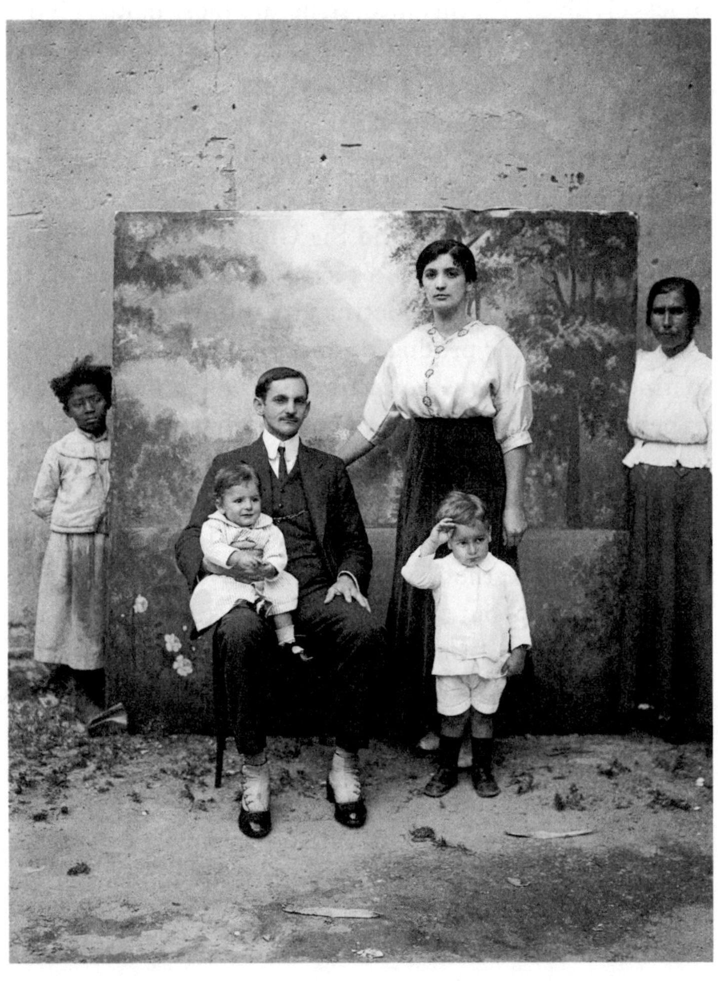

Photograph of a family portrait session by Chichico Alkmim, Diamantina, Brazil, around 1910. The woman to the far right, holding the backdrop, is Miquita, Alkmim's wife.

NO PACIFYING CONFLICTS

The work of Chichico Alkmim, a Brazilian photographer from the late nineteenth and the early twentieth century, might help us go deeper into these matters.[11] Notice how layers of territories—multiterritorialities, constituted by entangling times and histories—lie in the image on the previous page.

Taken in the first decade of the twentieth century, when the abolishment of slavery in Brazil was still recent,[12] this photo not only takes us back in time, but also takes us through layers of conflicting historical, political, and cultural perspectives. By contrasting hierarchical positions among Black and White people, and juxtaposing several temporalities (territories of power), Alkmim postulates the existence of distinct times and experiences of the ones being photographed. Moreover, as if this were not sufficient to allow the viewer to be in touch with the intermingling territorialities present in that geography, Alkmim allows us to awkwardly confront frames of power, all part of that same space.

Irit Rogoff contributes to reading Alkmim's photograph, by saying that "geography [if perceived within cultural studies] can be viewed as the relation between subjects and places refracted through orders of knowledge, state structures, and national cultures." If it is so, such a relation is "produced as social-cultural narratives which are geographically emplotted."[13] From this perspective, what one sees in the image produced by Alkmim is a nonpacified geography.

11 Chichico Alkmim (1886–1978) established himself in Diamantina, Minas Gerais, in 1912. He was a self-taught photographer who took pictures of religious and popular festivities, streets, landscapes, and people.

12 Slavery in Brazil was formally abolished in 1888.

13 Rogoff (see note 9), p. 22.

We see an ongoing conflict between a geography of power built within the frame (and painted landscape) where the white family is inscribed, and what is meant to be out-of-the-frame context, in which we see the Black woman and girl. The central and tricky point in Alkmim's image is that he not only frames what would be the "official framing," but also what isn't. His photograph, in this sense, is what was not supposed to be. In the image, we understand, if the painted landscape serves as a setting for the dominant power, it is the old and scrawled wall in the background that sustains the landscape, held by the hands and bodies of the Black woman and child, which supports the whole colonial system.

Thinking from the perspective of a South, whose geography has served as the basis for implementing the project of objectifying and expropriating the Other, it is the colonial system that comes to the fore in Alkmim's image. And being so, it must be emphasized, we end up dealing not only with an issue of representation: what grabs our attention more is that it reveals and lets us see its conflicting parts (en)acting together. In this sense, the geography emplotted in Alkmim's photograph turns out to be a possible image—never a mirror—of the context and disputes of a specific time period in Brazil. What is also suggested is that this photograph contains a substantial part of the history of a country.

This might sound like too much, after all it is "only an image," but if an image, according to Georges Didi-Huberman, is either everything or nothing, there is always a chance that it carries some significant part of the whole. Didi-Huberman developed his argument on the basis of four photographs that came from the deep horrors of the

Holocaust.[14] These photos were taken by members of the *Sonderkommando*, the special unit of Jews from the camp whose job was to take care of the gas chamber and dispose of the corpses. Having been "snatched from hell," in Didi-Huberman's words, these photos give body to the unimaginable: the gas chamber and furnaces in full operation. According to him, "the photographic image appears from the fold between the imminent obliterations of the witness and the unpresentability of the testimony: to snatch an image from that real."[15] Where there should be no image, he argues, these photographs came to be. Formed in the interval between what is somehow left in time, an image, for that reason, is an in-between space that depends not only on the arrangements of these remains and traces, but also on how one faces the ashes of history. Taking this into consideration, where should we head once this image we are looking at emerges from the "rest" we refer to here?

THE BODY
AS A SOURCE FOR
NARRATIVE TERRITORIALITIES

The expropriation of the body of the Other—the basis for the colonial system implemented in the Americas—has strongly contributed to an ongoing production of a non-pacified territory we apprehend as "the South." From this viewpoint, the ashes of the history of slavery in Brazil (and in the Americas) keep burning. Memory, which is the fuel that maintains the embers, is, after all, an issue of the present, located within the same intermingling and

---

14 See Georges Didi-Huberman, *Imagens, apesar de tudo* (Lisbon, 2012). English edition: *Images in Spite of it All: Four Photographs from Auschwitz* (Chicago, 2008).

15 Didi-Huberman, p. 19 (Portuguese edition), introduction (English edition ibid).

conflicting times and histories to which we have been referring. Thus, contested regimes of subjectivities, entangled temporalities and disjunctive histories, along with the work of memory, are part of these territories.

It is in this sense that the geography of what we here propose to understand as "South" is always part of a process of reconfiguration. It is never done; it is never there. It burns, dries, starves, brightens; it constantly dies of and springs within and from the remains left by the colonial projects and long-lasting unequal power disputes. It is a type of geography that requires permanent attention so as to be lived and read anew. There is no peace in the geographies of the South. And, one should also notice, there is no peace in Alkmim's image.

By framing and juxtaposing what is in and out of the frame, Alkmim allows us to recognize that time is not serial, but an interlocking of presents, pasts, and futures that retain their depths of other presents, pasts, and futures, each age bearing, altering, and maintaining the previous ones.[16] The understanding of this fact, particularly in postcolonial societies, cannot only mean accepting the existence of layers of time, but most of all, it should help us be aware of the fact that these layers only exist in the context of power disputes. This way, Alkmim also activates the presence of contesting regimes of subjectivities, which here are the result of processes of subjectivation that not only subjugate people, but also give them the chance of positioning themselves, once this same zone of dispute, although asymmetric, is also where the unpredictable lies. Once again, Mbembe helps clarify this point: this time is made up of disturbances, of a bundle of unforeseen events, of more or less regular fluctuations and oscillations, not necessarily resulting in chaos and anarchy (although

16 Mbembe, (see note 8), p. 16.

that sometimes is the case); moreover, instabilities, unforeseen events, and oscillations do not always lead to erratic and unpredictable behaviors on the actors' part (although that happens, too).[17]

It is from this perspective that the questions one asks and the gestures (images) one produces cannot disregard the geography from which they emerge. The asymmetries, fluctuations, and oscillations most of all produce gestures and unfold experiences that cross times and spaces. Issues related to race and gender seem to appear nowadays as part of the ashes that keep burning in Brazil. In spite of the fact that these are contemporaneous issues one notices as problems in and from geographies, in the context of the geographies of the South, they inevitably evoke problems triggered by the implementation of the colonial system.

In the case of Brazil, in particular, many films (images) made today by young Afro-Brazilian women touch both race and gender issues from the perspective of a body that needs to be reorganized within the postcolonial context in which it exists. An imagined Africa, the one that has been invented exclusively due to the expropriation of her bodies (a result of slavery and colonial enterprises), has become a solid territory built within the bodies of women who need to fight against everyday racism.[18] Let us take a close look at the image below and see how it can help us delve into these points.

From the very beginning of her debut film *Kbela* (2015), Yasmin Thainá, an Afro-Brazilian filmmaker, shows the dismembered bodies that inhabit her images. In the frame shown, we see a head without a body and a body without a head. Although head and body are both lively,

17 Ibid.
18 See Grada Kilomba, *Memórias da Plantação—episódios de racismo cotidiano* (Rio de Janeiro, 2019).

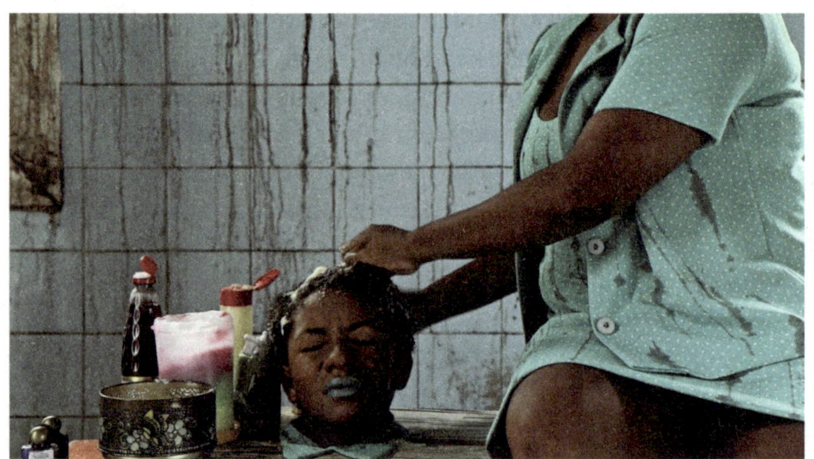

Yasmin Thainá, *Kbela*, 2015, film still

holding contrasting and brilliant colors, they are inevitably dissociated. The gesture of trying to chemically "shape" the curly hair of this head with no body holds aggression, for it reiterates the break: the absence of the body, and, in the body, the absence of the head. In the geographies of the South, due to power struggles, these are bodies whose heads have been set aside, and excluded from standard norms. The opposite is also true: in the geographies of the South, these are heads barely anchored by their bodies, which are meant to give support.

Most notably present in the favelas, where the majority of the population is Black, the traces of the Brazilian slave project are also present in the low representation of Black women and men in spaces of power (in the business and political spheres, for instance). Afro-descendants in Brazil, who according to the last demographic census make up approximately fifty-four percent of the population, are treated and recognized as a minority, often being subordinated and relegated to poor living conditions. As part of the geography of the South, it is not possible to look at these lives—these bodies without heads and/or heads with no bodies—without turning to the slavery project, and the process of delegitimizing Black bodies. Activating the objectification of the Other[19] is no doubt a scar the global colonialist power has left on the Black body.

Not even time can erase a deep scar. In the body on which it appears, a scar is always a reminder of its cause. And being so, it becomes itself a constitutive part of the territory that same body occupies, helping build territorialities. According to Zambrano, a territoriality is "a phenomenon that is similar to the imagined community, a symbolic connection with the territory, which is capable

19 See Achille Mbembe, *Critique of Black Reason* (Chapel Hill, 2017).

of generating identification among distinct perceptions."[20]
If we return to Alkmim's image, made in the first decade of
the past century, we notice that expropriated Black bodies,
as "supporters" of the colonial system, are already there.
And in an image produced in the second decade of the
twenty-first century, another one—but the same expropriated Black body—insists upon being seen. It is from this
perspective that, in the case we examine, expropriated
bodies evoke or produce a territoriality within the thread
of an image that crosses time and space.

Fundamental to the process of comprehending the
social and cultural construction of the territory, this
territoriality, built throughout narratives—images, in this
case—is not only the affirmation of the territory itself—
it is "my body"; it is "my South"—but also the evocation
of the experience of being part of it. In other words, the
image itself produces this territoriality—a shared and
collective experience—thus building what I suggest to
be understood as an expanded territory from where the
geographies of the South emerge.

The ongoing conflicts the geography of the South is
confronted with, exactly because of its asymmetric entangled temporalities and disjunctive histories, constantly
colliding in a certain physical territory, weave aesthetic-
political gestures and give place to a "narrative territoriality": an aesthetically built territoriality that, by crossing
times and spaces, and carrying along a palimpsest of representations, evoke experiences that produce identifications
and commonalities.

In the favelas of Rio, the banlieues of Paris; in the
besieged city of Gaza, in a square in Marrakesh or in
the deserts of Jordan; either in one century, one decade

20 Zambrano (see note 7), p. 32.

or another, these produced narrative territorialities are somehow part of the modes of being South.[21] From this perspective, one can take the Global South as part of a complex spatiality, and thus the *gesture of reading a certain geography* of such expanded territory is not only the act of mapping existences, pointing out similarities and differences, but also of producing cartographies of the lives and experiences of those who are in constant disputes in the South. The unfolded experiences these cartographies elucidate are, most of all, the ashes of history that keep us all alive, giving us the chance to be part of the continuous (re)existing process of inventing (other) geographies.

21 See see Fernando Resende et al., *Modos de Ser Sul: territorialidades, afetos e poderes* (Rio de Janeiro, 2020).

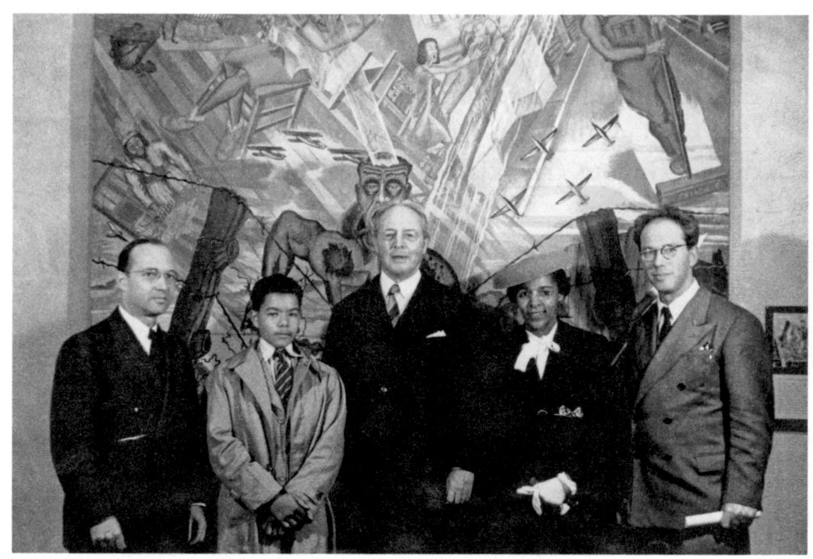

Guests shown at the private preview of the exhibition *Young Negro Art*, the work of students at Hampton Institute, in the Young People's Gallery in the Museum of Modern Art, 11 West 53rd St., New York, October 5, 1943. From left to right: Dr. Ralph Bridgman, President Elect of Hampton Institute; Ludlow Werner, son of the editor of *New York Age*; Dr. William Jay Schieffelin, oldest trustee of Hampton Institute; Miss Flemmie P. Kittrell, Dean of Women, Hampton Institute; Dr. Viktor Lowenfeld, Head of the Art Department at Hampton Institute and psychologist.

The Art of Liberation: Viktor Lowenfeld and African American Modernism

Christian Kravagna

The case of Austrian art educator Viktor Lowenfeld, who after fleeing to the United States from Nazi persecution became an important figure in the development of African American modernism through his work at a Black college in Virginia, can be seen as an example of productive transculturation of artistic ideas and educational concepts in a political context of anti-racist alliances.[1] My choice of Lowenfeld's work as the subject of my current research—besides two further case studies on relations between Austrian and African American protagonists during the interwar years—is due to a specific navigation through the history of modernism in art. In my book on transmodernism,[2] I sketched an alternative landscape of modern art by tracing transcultural modernisms in various parts of the world along the encounters of artists and intellectuals.

1 Lowenfeld and African American modernism form a case study of Austrian/African American relations during the interwar years in the book *Die Kunst der Befreiung/The Art of Liberation,* currently in preparation. Research was supported by the Dietrich W. Botstiber Foundation. This paper was first presented at the conference *The Routes of Modernism: Artistic Mobility, Protagonists, Platforms, Networks,* organized by Christian Kravagna and Simone Wille, Academy of Fine Arts and Museum of Modern Art, Vienna, November 23–24, 2018.

2 Christian Kravagna, *Transmoderne: Eine Kunstgeschichte des Kontakts/Transmodernism and the art history of contact* (Berlin, 2017). See also Christian Kravagna, "Toward a Postcolonial Art History of Contact," in *Texte zur Kunst,* 91 (September 2013), pp. 110–131.

This art history of contact focuses on the development of transcultural modernisms in the context of twentieth-century anticolonial and antiracist liberation movements. The perspective of liberation is also a determining factor in the most recent relocalization of my transcultural research horizon in aspects of emancipatory Austrian, or rather Viennese, cultural history.

MAKING A U-TURN IN NAVIGATING THE ROUTES OF MODERNISM

This "return" to Vienna was a result of years spent studying African American modernism and its complicated relations with both the concurrent dominant White modernism and the Black struggle for equality in a racist society. Several years ago, at a certain point in my work on the art of the Harlem Renaissance and African American representatives of Abstract Expressionism, I could not help wondering when the Museum of Modern Art in New York—as *the* definitive institution in the American modern art scene—mounted the first exhibition of works by African American artists. In the context of an art world largely segregated until well into the sixties, which differentiated between exhibitions of modern art and exhibitions of Black art, this question is of no little importance, for during the first decades of the twentieth century, Black artists generally showed their work in exhibitions arranged by relevant organizations, such as the Harmon Foundation, or held by Black universities, such as the Atlanta University Annual Exhibition founded by Hale Woodruff in 1942.[3] The MoMA archive lists *Young Negro*

3 Christian Kravagna, "Painting the Global History of Art: Hale Woodruff's *The Art of the Negro*," in *Tate Papers*, no. 30 (August 2018).

Art, which opened in October 1943, as the first exhibition of works by contemporary African American artists.[4] The corresponding press release mentions the curator as Lowenfeld—an Austrian-sounding name that caught my attention. This unexpected encounter with Austrian history in the context of African American modernism triggered a change of direction in navigation through art history, which, after wide but necessary detours, now focused more strongly on my home port. Anyone looking at the history of their own country or city from the perspective of a different and distant political and cultural region can develop a stereoscopic view of historical phenomena, combining complementary or contrapuntal observations from two points of view. This kind of (re-)localization of the "global" research horizon may help to counteract the danger of a certain fragmentation that hangs over "planetary" research perspectives.[5]

Young Negro Art presented approximately fifty works by eight students at the Hampton Institute in Hampton, Virginia. The school is one of the first historically Black colleges and universities founded after the Civil War to train formerly enslaved and future generations of African Americans barred from access to White institutions of higher education. In the year of the MoMA exhibition, the

4 In 1937, the Museum had already held an exhibition of gravestones by Black Folk Artist William Edmondson from Tennessee. In 1935, MoMA organized *African Negro Art*, the first representative exhibition of classical African art in an American museum of art.

5 According to Mary Louise Pratt, planetary consciousness originated in colonialist-based eighteenth-century circumnavigation of the world and research projects. In 2008, with reference to Pratt's book *Imperial Eyes: Travel Writing and Transculturation* (London and New York, 1992), I curated the exhibition *Planetary Consciousness* in the art space of Leuphana University, Lüneburg. See: Stefan Römer, "Planetary Consciousness," in *springerin,* issue 4 (2008).

Hampton Institute celebrated the seventy-fifth anniversary of its foundation in 1868. Lowenfeld had been appointed assistant professor of industrial arts in 1939. Until then, the school had offered no program for art training. Within a short time, the Austrian refugee (who at the time hardly spoke English) managed to create an environment of learning and artistic expression that was to have an enormous influence on several African American artists who would later achieve prominence, including John Biggers, Samella Lewis, and Elizabeth Catlett. It is important to note that the Hampton Institute was not an art school, since most of the young people who would attend Lowenfeld's newly-established art class came to Hampton to learn a craft or a trade. The sixteen-year-old John Biggers, for instance, came to the school from North Carolina, intending to train as a plumber. Although Lowenfeld's art program was initially classified as an elective, many students were soon taking part in the evening class.

The photographs of the opening of *Young Negro Art* preserved in the MoMA archive show none of the exhibiting artists, since most of them had been conscripted into the Army when the United States entered World War II. In the immediate neighborhood of the Hampton Institute was a naval base, for which Lowenfeld and his students produced teaching materials for training soldiers in language and writing. The photographs do, however, show some of the works, including *Night Scene* (1941) by Junius Redwood, which was purchased by the museum, and *Dying Soldier* (1942) by John Biggers, which may be seen as the young painter's way of coming to terms with his fears in the face of his conscription into the Navy. While (most of) the young artists were evidently unable to take part in the opening in New York, one photograph shows MoMA

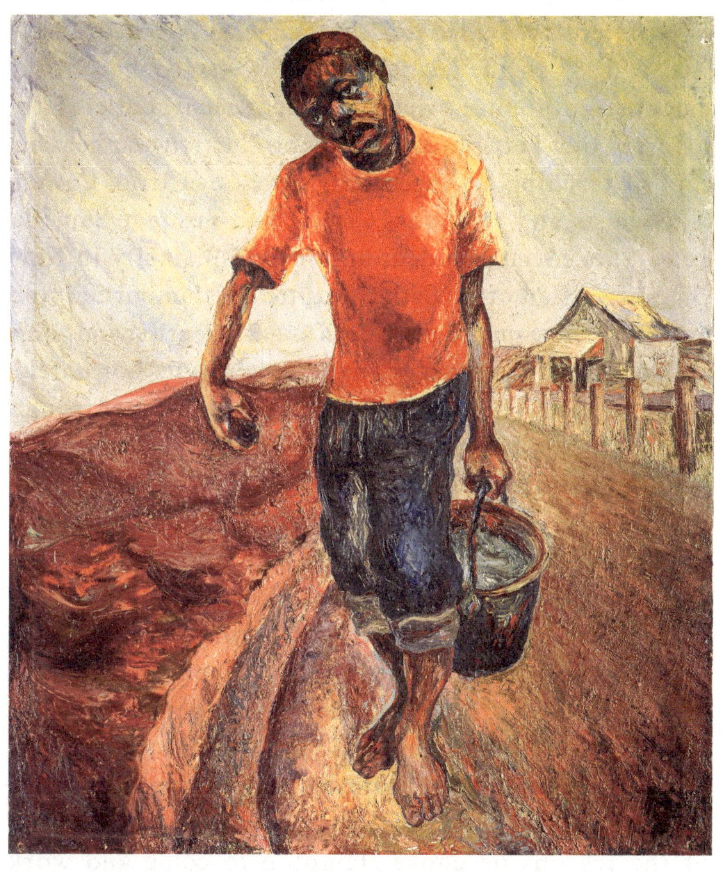

Samella Lewis, *Waterboy*, 1944, Hampton University Museum

director Alfred H. Barr, Jr. drinking tea with the more established artists Charles White and Elizabeth Catlett, both of whom had spent six months at the Hampton Institute from January 1943. White executed his mural *The Contribution of the Negro to Democracy in America* (1943) (see p. 108) in the institute's Clarke Hall, and Catlett taught sculpture in Lowenfeld's department. Catlett later reported that her approach to art production and her concept of teaching art essentially developed from Lowenfeld's ideas and methods. Catlett had brought Samella Lewis, her former student at Dillard University in New Orleans, to Hampton. Catlett was the most important role model for the young Lewis, both as a Black artist and as an anti-racist activist—and right after her came Lowenfeld. "Lowenfeld did a lot to help me approach my art from a point of view where I was working from experience," said Lewis in an interview.[6]

Then there was John Biggers, who came to Hampton in 1941 and had a close relationship with his mentor almost until Lowenfeld's death in 1960. "Man, I'm telling you," Biggers remembers, "that Lowenfeld turned me on!" Biggers describes his encounter with Lowenfeld as a rare experience of a productive relationship between Blacks and Whites in the segregated South. "Viktor was entirely different from white Americans. He was completely untypical of any white person I'd ever met … He said to us one of the reasons he chose Hampton to come and work in was because the African American people are socially

6 "Image and Belief: Samella Lewis Interviewed by Richard Cándida Smith," in *Art History Oral Documentation Project*, compiled under the auspices of the Getty Research Institute for the History of Art and the Humanities, The J. Paul Getty Trust 1999, p. 59.

handicapped and he felt a kinship because of his own struggles in Germany (Austria) and what he had just endured there."[7]

VIENNESE ROOTS

To understand what in Lowenfeld's manner "turned on" Biggers and other students, we have to look back at his years in Vienna. Here are the roots of his later role in the development of African American art. In interwar Vienna, Lowenfeld developed his understanding of art as a liberating practice and his teaching methods, based on stimulation and support of the students rather than on specific requirements and training. During the nineteen-twenties he also developed his interest in non-visual forms of artistic expression. Finally, it was his experience of anti-Semitism in Vienna that equipped him with an acute sense for discrimination, which was to guide his work with racially oppressed young people in the American South.

Born in Linz in 1903, Lowenfeld moved to Vienna in the early twenties to study painting. From 1923, during his studies at the School of Arts and Crafts, he taught mathematics and art at the Jewish Chajes High School, and worked at the Jewish Institute for the Blind, for blind and partially-sighted young people. In his first book, *Plastische Arbeiten Blinder* (sculptures by blind people) written in collaboration with art historian Ludwig Münz in 1936, Lowenfeld wrote on the basis of his ten years of work with blind people: "Basically, we do not begin with form, but with expressive content. A false critique of form

7 John Biggers in conversation with Gabrielle Simon Edgcomb, *From Swastika to Jim Crow: Refugee Scholars at Black Colleges* (Malabar, Florida, 1993), p. 98.

can spoil forever the creative joy of the blind. For what might appear as 'wrong' to the sighted, often can be caused by particular expressive intentions."[8]

For blind people, sculptural expression is based not simply on the sense of touch that replaces the visual sense in the sighted. Rather, the creative act is based on bodily awareness and the artist's kinetic perception. Although haptic perception is very important, Lowenfeld emphasizes the more comprehensive experience of the body in motion and in its relation to the spatial environment. The creative process, he says, is primarily a matter of expressing feelings and ideas, not of rendering forms "correctly." Lowenfeld differentiated his own approach to art education from that of Franz Čižek, Viennese pioneer in child art, and considered it incorrect to impede the act of free expression by imposing any rules. Lowenfeld avoided demonstrating how one should draw or model; instead, he observed the efforts of individual students and supported them with technical suggestions or examples of solutions to similar problems by other artists. As some former high school students remember, he often used stories and non-visual prompts to inspire artistic creativity.[9] In his book *The Nature of Creative Activity* (1939), published shortly after he fled Vienna, Lowenfeld summarizes his concept of art: "Art consists in depicting the relations of the artist to the world of his experiences, that is, in depicting his experience with objects and not the objects themselves."[10]

8 Viktor Lowenfeld, "Vom Entstehen der Plastiken," in Ludwig Münz, Viktor Lowenfeld, *Plastische Arbeiten Blinder* (Brünn, 1934), p. 101.
9 Susan K. Leshnoff, "Viktor Lowenfeld: Portrait of a Young Teacher in Vienna in the 1930s," in *Studies in Art Education*, vol. 54, no. 2, 2013, pp. 158–170.
10 Viktor Lowenfeld, *The Nature of Creative Activity* (New York, 1939), p. 132.

Besides his fifteen years of working with young and blind people, Lowenfeld's ideas on art and creative expression were also influenced by the expressionism of Oskar Kokoschka and the art-historical concepts of Alois Riegl. Lowenfeld adopted Riegl's concept of the haptic and the optical as two different approaches to representation and expression; he took from Kokoschka the emphasis on physical sensations as a determining factor in artistic creativity.[11] Shortly after completing the German manuscript of *The Nature of Creative Activity*,[12] Lowenfeld was forced to flee the Nazis, who soon took over the Jewish Institute for the Blind and consigned his students to concentration camps.

Lowenfeld fled to England with the help of Herbert Read, and then arrived in New York in late 1938, finding accommodation in a Jewish refugee hostel on 69th Street. The Viennese art educator, whose book on creative activity—which later became enormously influential—had just appeared in England, trod the streets of Manhattan, penniless and practically without a word of English. After visiting an exhibition on child art, he met Victor D'Amico, director of the Department of Education of the Museum of Modern Art, with whom he would later realize the *Young Negro Art* exhibition. After a four-month teaching post at Harvard University in spring 1939, Lowenfeld accepted the offer from the Hampton Institute in Virginia. Only a few months after his move south, Lowenfeld's first exhibition in the Young People's Gallery at MoMA opened in

11 An initial survey of Viennese influences was attempted by Peter Smith, "Lowenfeld in a Viennese Perspective," in *Studies in Art Education*, vol. 30, no. 2 (1989), pp. 104–114.
12 A German edition was not published until the year of the author's death. Viktor Lowenfeld, *Vom Wesen schöpferischen Gestaltens* (Frankfurt am Main, 1960).

March 1940. *Visual and Non-Visual Art Expression* was based on photographs of clay sculptures from Lowenfeld's creative work with blind and partially sighted people in Vienna. With the *Young Negro Art* exhibition in 1943, D'Amico and Lowenfeld continued their collaboration in the field of African American art.

THE PROBLEM OF THE VISUAL IN A RACIST SOCIETY

When Lowenfeld started work at the Black college in the segregated South in 1939, his educational intervention came at a point in the development of American modernism when the ideology of the separation of the senses in art and the dogma of "pure opticality" in the theory of painting was established. Critics like Clement Greenberg saw the "essence" of each artistic genre as consisting of a reflection of "what is unique and irreducible in every single art."[13] The central task of the individual arts was declared to be their self-definition, that is, the determination of what was intrinsic to them and the exclusion (as far as possible) of anything alien to that essence. According to Greenberg, the increasing awareness and acceptance of "the original flatness of the stretched canvas" and painting's pure visuality must necessarily result in the exclusion of everything not in keeping with the particular medium.[14]

The discourse on purity in art and the dogma of the separation of the arts must be understood in the context of racial segregation and White contempt for everything

13 Clement Greenberg, "Modernist Painting," in *The Collected Essays and Criticism*, vol. 4, ed. John O'Brian (Chicago, 1993), pp. 85–93.
14 Clement Greenberg, "Towards a Newer Laocoon," in Pollock and After: *The Critical Debate*, ed. Francis Frascina (London, 1985), pp. 60–70.

mixed. Regarding the purity of art, Barnett Newman's position was close to Greenberg's: "Art is a realm of pure thought. As such, it, like other realms of pure thought, must be concerned with its own problems. Art is self-contained. Politics is not only unnecessary, it is irrelevant."[15]

What meaning could such a statement have for a Black artist living and working under the conditions of Jim Crow racism? There is in fact a complicated relationship between African American artists and the claim of Abstract Expressionism to represent the aesthetic embodiment of the universal.[16] Around 1940, white and Black artists in the United States looked back on—or were in the process of constructing—their own lines of tradition in modern art. White American modernism, particularly the New York School, saw itself at the progressive end of a development in European modernism in which abstraction was accorded a high standing. At the same time, the representatives of the New York School drew on Indigenous North American art to underpin the "American" identity of their version of modernism. African American art, on the other hand, had been concerned since the early twentieth century and the Harlem Renaissance with the elaboration of an artistic idiom to express the experiences and ambitions of an oppressed people. In addition to Social Realist styles, the most advanced artists of the 1920s–1950s period—including Aaron Douglas, Jacob Lawrence, Hale Woodruff, and Norman Lewis—are distinguished

15　Barnett Newman, "The Painting of Tamayo and Gottlieb," in *Selected Writings and Interviews*, ed., John P. O'Neill (New York, 1990), p. 72.
16　I deal with the problem in the chapter "Reinheit der Kunst in Zeiten der Transkulturalität: Modernistische Kunsttheorie und die Kultur der Dekolonisation," in *Transmoderne: Eine Kunstgeschichte des Kontakts*, pp. 173–213.

primarily by their ability to combine elements of European modernism with elements of African "ancestral arts" and the Black cultures in America.[17]

As a refugee from racist persecution in Europe, Lowenfeld developed in Hampton a form of art instruction that understood artistic expression as a means of liberation from negative self-images and as a way of empowering young African Americans.[18] Founded in 1868, concurrently with the school, the Hampton Institute's museum provided a perfect place for this, having always collected both African and African American art.[19] Lowenfeld considered the African collection particularly important for his teaching. As Ira Dworkin wrote, Lowenfeld situated the African collection more strongly in a modern discourse, based on his European experience with the reception of African art among the avant-garde of the early twentieth century.[20] John Biggers repeatedly commented on the mind-altering nature of his confrontation with African

17 The aims of African American artists' reflection on the ancestral African arts were represented from the 1920s primarily by Alain Locke. See Alain Locke, "The Legacy of the Ancestral Arts," in *The New Negro: Voices of the Harlem Renaissance*, (New York, 1997), pp. 254–267.

18 Ann Holt, "Lowenfeld at Hampton (1939–1946): Empowerment, Resistance, Activism, and Pedagogy," in *Studies in Art Education*, vol. 54, no. 1 (2012), pp. 6–20.

19 See the chapter "Hampton — Der Geist der Befreiung: Sammeln, emanzipatorische Bildung und die Rückeroberung von Geschichte" in Cornelia Kogoj, Christian Kravagna, *Das amerikanische Museum: Sklaverei, Schwarze Geschichte und der Kampf um Gerechtigkeit in Museen der Südstaaten* (Vienna, Berlin, 2019); Kravagna, "The Museum of Liberation: An Excursion into the Early History of Reconquest," in *How to move on with Humboldt's legacy: Rethinking ethnographic collections*, blog, University of Cologne 2018, https://blog.uni-koeln.de/gssc-humboldt/en/the-museum-of-liberation/ (accessed January 23, 2020).

20 Ira Dworkin, *Congo Love Song: African American Culture and the Crisis of the Colonial State* (Chapel Hill, 2017), p. 183.

art under the conditions of emancipatory teaching. The general education system and the political climate in the racist South, he said, had caused everything African to seem base and ugly, even in the eyes of young Blacks. Thus

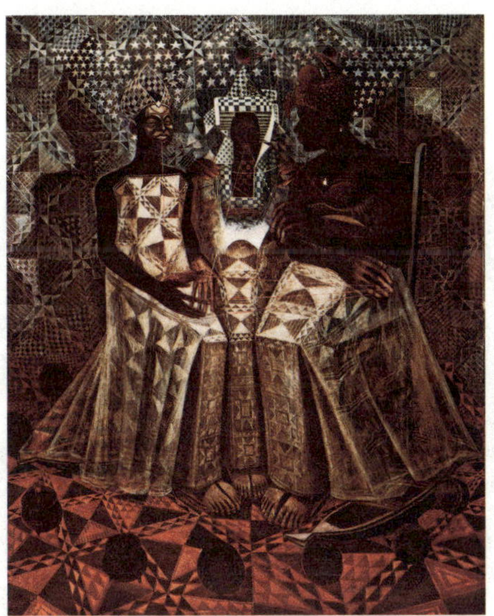

John Biggers, *Starry Crown*, 1987, Dallas Museum of Art

to the young Biggers who—as he himself said—had entered the school with a "stereotyped concept" of Africa, the African artifacts in the Hampton Museum looked at first "ugly, unlike anything I had seen before."[21] In the ensuing years, under Lowenfeld's tutelage, Biggers came to recognize African motifs and design principles as an essential source for the development of his own distinctive style of painting.

21 John Biggers, 1988, in conversation with Alvia J. Wardlaw, as cited in "A Spiritual Libation: Promoting an African Heritage in Black Colleges," in *Black Art—Ancestral Legacy: The African Impulse in African-American Art* (Dallas Museum of Art, 1988), p. 57.

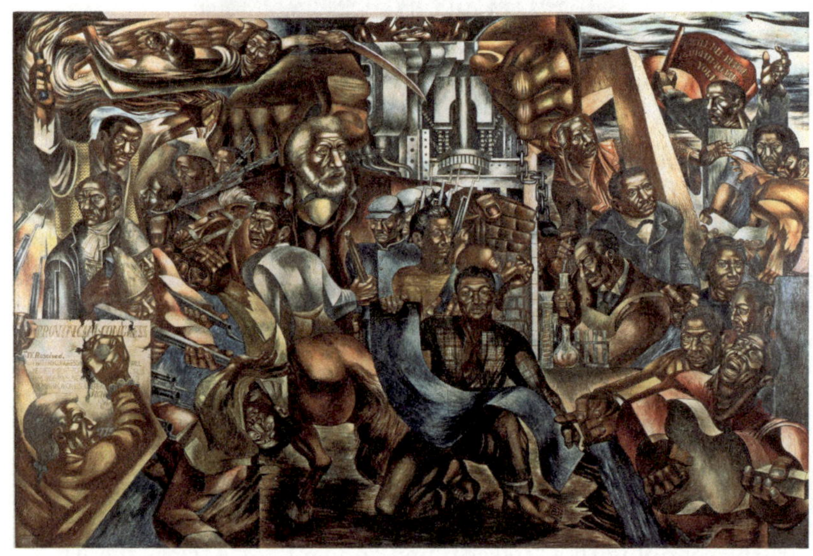

Charles White, *The Contribution of the Negro to Democracy in America*, Mural Clarke Hall, Hampton University, 1943

Two points should be mentioned here. First, it was not Lowenfeld alone who gave the Hampton art students self-confidence and new prospects for the future. Guest artists such as Charles White and Elizabeth Catlett also made important contributions, even if they worked only briefly with the students. John Biggers assisted his role model White in creating the mural *The Contribution of the Negro to Democracy in America*, and Samella Lewis benefited particularly from the strong position of a female Black artist in Catlett. Second, the relationship between the white teacher and his Black students should not be seen as a one-way influence of the older teacher on his students. Unquestionably, the theory and education practice of the Austrian Jew had a great impact on the development of these African American artists; but Lowenfeld's approach to art education and his concept of the creative act benefited from his students in Hampton. During his years there, Lowenfeld wrote his book *Creative and Mental Growth*, published in 1947,[22] and he managed to translate the insights gained from his work with physically handicapped people in Vienna into the political context of a group subjected to racial discrimination in the United States. Lowenfeld's understanding of artistic expression— neither as reproduction of external reality nor as a product of specific stylistic conventions, but rather as the expression of the experience of subjects in their specific social worlds—encouraged an artistic development linking the formation of Black identity in the segregationist United States with the awareness of the history and culture of the African diaspora. Lowenfeld had never had ambitions to produce great artists; his artistic work always focused on

---

22 See Viktor Lowenfeld, *Creative and Mental Growth* (New York, 1947).

the creative process as a method of self-expression and, as far as possible, of the free development of the individual.

Samella Lewis, who apart from her artistic work later became an influential historian of African American art, recalled the political aspect of Lowenfeld's pedagogy: "It was a great cause for him, to work against segregation, prejudice ... In a way he encouraged us to use art as an instrument or tool to combat serious deprivation and prejudice, and the evils of discrimination. He forced us to take a position in relation to humanity and inhumane treatment of other peoples."[23]

At the time of the *Young Negro Art* MoMA exhibition, Lowenfeld published two articles on Black art. In "Negro Art Expression in America" he wrote: "If we would like to learn to understand Negro art we have to try to analyze the forces which determine his experiences with the world which surrounds him."[24] Among the striking achievements of Lowenfeld's intervention in a segment of African American modernism is how he adapted Alois Riegl's concept of the visual and the haptic and Oskar Kokoschka's emphasis on physical sensations for the hard reality of the nexus of race and art in the American South. In an era when the cult of pure vision dominated White American modernism, Lowenfeld recognized that Black Americans were historically and socially not positioned on the side of the viewer, and thus had a problematic relationship with the primacy of visual perception: "New Negro art is not the art of visually-minded people who feel as spectators.

23 "An interview with Samella Lewis/Interviewer: Harry Henderson," Henderson Papers, Penn State University Archives, University Park, PA, as cited in Ann Holt, "Lowenfeld at Hampton (1939–1946): Empowerment, Resistance, Activism, and Pedagogy," in *Studies in Art Education*, vol. 54, no. 1 (2012), p. 12.
24 Viktor Lowenfeld, "Negro Art Expression in America," in *The Madison Quarterly*, vol. 5, no. 11 (1945), p. 27.

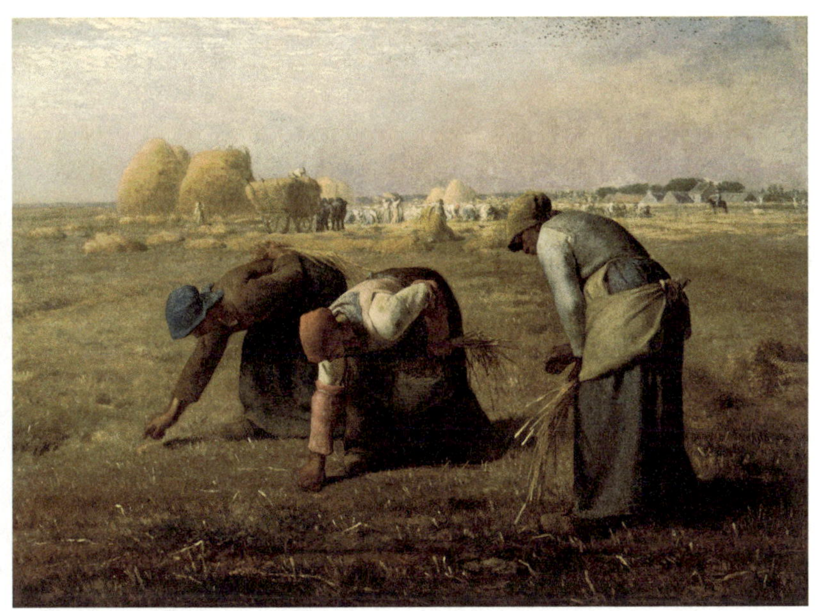

Jean-François Millet, *The Gleaners*, 1857

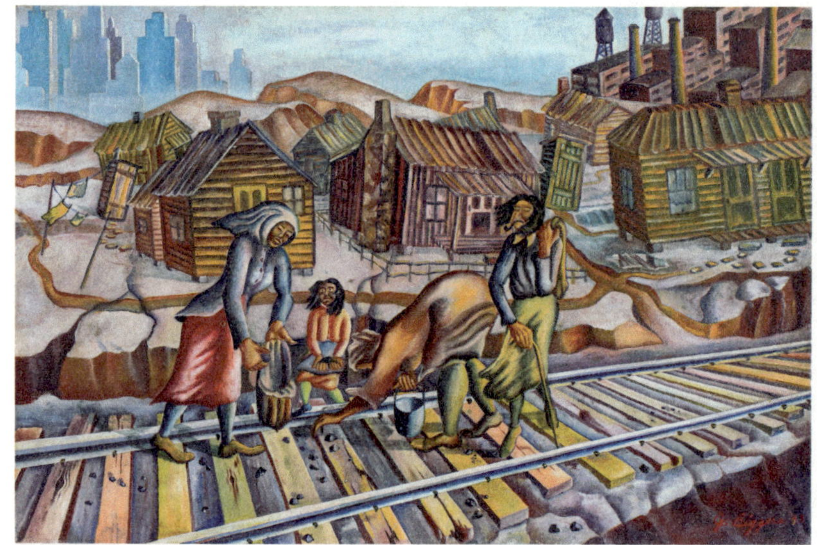

John Biggers, *The Gleaners*, 1943, Michael Rosenfeld Gallery, New York

It is the art of people who feel involved in their own struggle. In this art the self is projected as the true actor of the picture whose formal characteristics are the result of a synthesis of bodily, emotional, and intellectual apprehension of shape and form."[25]

In this connection, we can actually speak of a context-sensitive reinterpretation of Riegl's concept of the visual and the haptic experience of the world, which lends it a new political dimension. Just as certain concepts developed in Viennese art and art history underwent a process of transculturation when transferred by a Jewish refugee into an African American context, familiar motifs of European painting were appropriated and modified by Lowenfeld's Black students to articulate their own experiences in a racist society. An example is *The Gleaners* by Jean-François Millet (1857) as interpreted by John Biggers in 1943 in the setting of a poor black neighborhood by the railroad tracks, which often marked the dividing line between the White and the Black sides of a segregated American city.

One aim of my current project is to more accurately record such translation processes with reference to their stylistic transformations and semantic shifts in their motifs. This inevitably entails taking a closer look at the ambivalences involved in an exhibition like *Young Negro Art*. While it was unquestionably an achievement to put the artistic production of young African American artists up

---

25 Viktor Lowenfeld, "Negro Art Expression in America," in *The Madison Quarterly*, vol. 5, no. 11, 1945, p. 30. A classic text on the problem of the visual in African American culture is: Michelle Wallace, "Modernism, Postmodernism, and the Problem of the Visual in Afro-American Culture," in *Out There: Marginalization and Contemporary Cultures*, eds. Russel Ferguson et al. (London and New York 1990), pp. 39–50.

for discussion for the first time in the Museum of Modern Art, the presentation in the Gallery for Art Education (Young People's Gallery) also points to an institutional marginalization of this art. In many museums this continues until today. It is only with recent efforts to reconsider the racial politics of collecting and exhibiting modern art in major museums that cases like the Lowenfeld school and its MoMA presentation in 1943 attract attention anew.[26]

Translated from German by Gail Schamberger

26 In autumn 2019, shortly before the museum reopened its revised display of the permanent collection which now includes significantly more African American art than ever before, MoMA published the book *Among Others: Blackness at MoMA*. It critically explores the museum's dealing with Black artists and Black subjects in art since its founding days. *Young Negro Art*, organized by Lowenfeld and D'Amico, is briefly discussed in an essay: Darby English and Charlotte Barat, "Blackness at MoMA: A Legacy of Deficit," in *Among Others: Blackness at MoMA*, eds. Darby English and Charlotte Barat (New York, 2019).

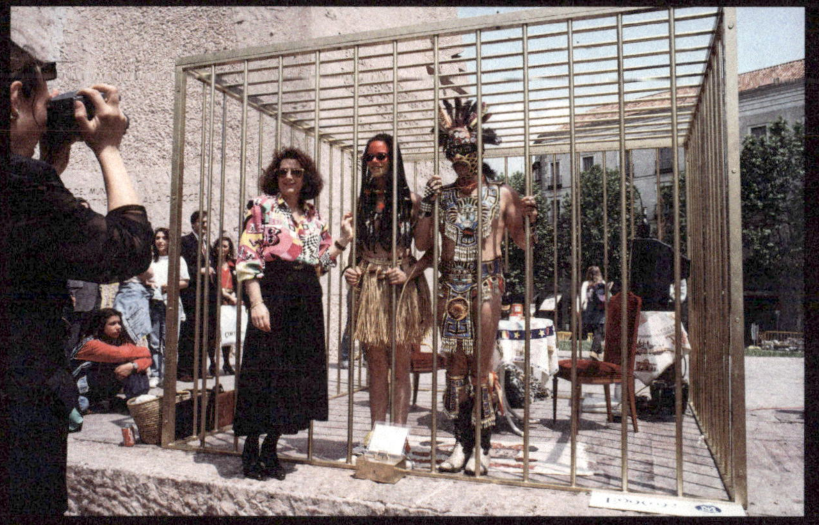

Guillermo Gómez-Peña and Coco Fusco, *Two Undiscovered Amerindians Visit Madrid*, 1992

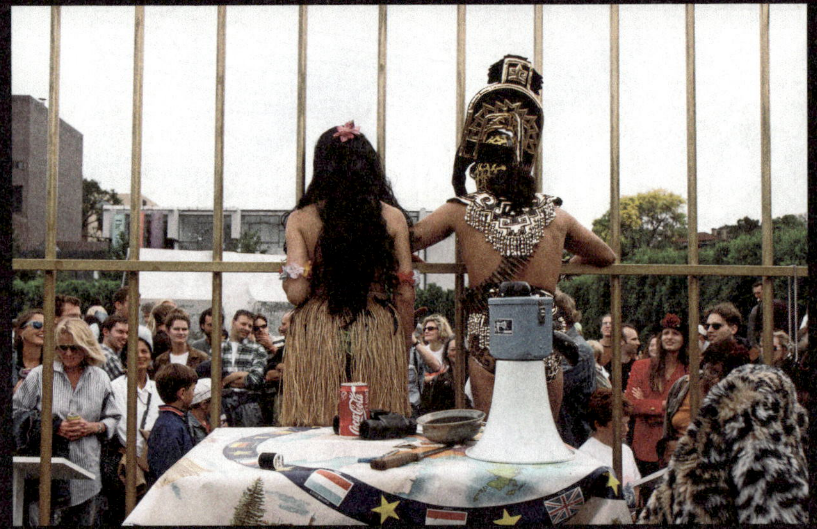

Guillermo Gómez-Peña and Coco Fusco, *Performance of Original Aboriginals*, Minneapolis Sculpture Garden, 1992

Case Study:
The Couple in a Cage:
Two Amerindians
Visit the West

Kate Sutton

"What you lookn at?" These were the words spray-painted across Pat Ward Williams's eponymous 1993 billboard-sized photograph of five black youth, sitting passively on a stoop. The image debuted in the foyer of the Whitney Museum, hung just above the restaurant as part of the institution's notorious 1993 biennial. Curated by Elisabeth Sussman in collaboration with Thelma Golden, John G. Hanhardt, and Lisa Phillips, the show was widely reviled for its overt political stance and provocations like the inclusion of footage of Rodney King's 1991 beating by the Los Angeles Police Department amid works by Jimmie Durham, Lorna Simpson, Renée Green, Fred Wilson, Glenn Ligon, Janine Antoni, and Matthew Barney.

In one of the more generous reviews of the time (history has been kinder to the exhibition than its contemporaries were), *The New York Times*'s critic Roberta Smith hailed the show as a "watershed" that was "less about the art of our time than about the times themselves."[1] While acknowledging the presence of "unusually large numbers of nonwhite artists, artists whose work is openly gay, and women"—a curious phrasing—Smith then contrasted the contributions of those participants against those by White male artists, lamenting that "the unfortunate impression created is that to succeed, the art of minority artists and women must be closely tied to their personal

1 Roberta Smith, "At the Whitney, a Biennial With a Social Conscience," in *The New York Times*, March 5, 1993, Section C, p. 1.

situation, preferably to their sense of victimization."[2] In a 2016 *Artforum* column, Sussman countered this reading, instead tying the exhibition's mission to a quote from Homi K. Bhabha's catalogue essay: "to think beyond narratives of origin and initiatory, initial subjects and to focus on those moments or processes that are produced in the articulation of 'differences.'"[3]

There is a thin line between an "articulation of 'differences'"and the performance (burlesque, even) of a marginalized identity. The potential for slippage was made all the more clear in one of the biennial's opening day performances, when artists and educators Coco Fusco and Guillermo Gómez-Peña appeared in a gilded cage in the guise of "Guatinauis," hailing from the fictional island of "Guatinau" (the name a garbled riff on Guanahani, the site of Columbus's first landing, and the phrase "What now?"), as part of their ongoing piece, *The Couple in a Cage: Two Amerindians Visit the West*. Within their cage, the "noble savages" were done up like the Village People, with flamboyantly outré costumes—Gómez-Peña in a feathered headdress, Fusco in a grass skirt and a leopard-print bikini top—offset by designer shades and Converse sneakers. For added effect, guards would feed the artists through the cage's bars and lead them on leashes to the bathroom. In exchange for donations, Gómez-Peña would share "authentic" stories in a nonsense babble, shot through with brand names, while Fusco would exuberantly bop to hip-hop music. Otherwise, the couple entertained themselves in their moderately-furnished digs, lounging with their early-model laptops, stitching up voodoo dolls at the table, perusing tomes of postmodern theory, or posing for

2 Ibid.
3 Elizabeth Sussmann, "The 1993 Whitney Biennial," in *Artforum* (Summer 2016).

Polaroids with visitors who coughed up a nominal fee. For the Whitney performance, the artists upped the ante by offering a glimpse of real Guatinauis genitals for the bargain price of five dollars. It was a tease, as those who paid would find out; Gómez-Peña lifted his grass skirt, but he kept the main attraction tucked between his legs. The disjuncture between Gómez-Peña's macho theatrics and this dainty, feminized pose was jarring; but what *did* his audience expect?

The Couple in the Cage had originally been conceived to mark the 500th anniversary of Christopher Columbus's landing in the New World, an event now strategically strewn with misconceptions, misinformation, and mythologization to mask the Eurocentric framing of the explorer's encounter of an existing continent and its existing civilizations as a "discovery." Fusco and Gómez-Peña's collaboration was first performed in 1992 as part of the Edge 92 Biennial in Madrid, when, for three days, the artists offered themselves up in a public square as a kind of unclaimed New World bounty, ripe for the taking (or at least the photographing).

Between its debut in Madrid and its final iteration at the Whitney, *The Couple in a Cage* would be staged in five other sites: London's Covent Garden; the Walker Art Center in Minneapolis; the Smithsonian National Museum of Natural History in Washington, D.C.; the Australian Museum of National History in Sydney; and the Field Museum of Natural History in Chicago, a city that had its own troubled history of putting humans on display as host to the World's Columbian Exposition in 1893.[4] Each location lent its own nuances to the project. It was

---

4 The artists performed a modified test run of the work at the University of California, Irvine, in 1992. The performance would be also enacted at Fundación Banco Patricios in Buenos Aires in 1994. This latter rendition was slightly removed from the others

arguably in the natural history museums that the performance had the most resonance, as it demonstrated just how easily one could unsettle grand guiding narratives à la "Manifest Destiny."[5] In a text titled "The Other History of Intercultural Performance," published a year after the Whitney performance, Fusco catalogued various audience responses —from the moral outrage of an English gentleman, traumatized guards, sympathetic schoolchildren, and befuddled foreign tourists, to a curator distraught at how little criticality her audience exhibited in consuming the spectacle.[6] In comparison, the iteration within the Whitney was probably the least interesting, because it clearly sited the project within the burgeoning discourse of identity politics, trimming the productive ambiguities of the performance's more public settings. In the sanitized space of art-as-critique, the piece functioned not as an articulation of difference, but its caricature. To that extent, *The Couple in a Cage* paled alongside more provocative interventions, like Daniel Joseph Martinez's contribution, which made presumptions of its own by branding the mandatory Whitney visitor tags with the statement "I can't imagine ever wanting to be white."

As a self-described "satiric spectacle," *The Couple in the Cage* aimed to push at what Fusco calls "the happy multiculturalism" at work in exhibitions like the Centre Pompidou's 1989 *Magiciens de la Terre*, which, in the name of correcting the art world's reigning Eurocentrism,

in intention, and took place a year after Coco Fusco wrote the official history of the piece. Except where specified, the discussion of the performance will draw upon the iterations included in that history.

5 A phrase coined in 1845, meaning that the United States is divinely destined to spread democracy and capitalism across the North American continent.

6 Coco Fusco, "The Other History of Intercultural Performance," in *TDR: The Drama Review (1988–)*, Vol. 38, No. 1 (Spring 1994).

elevated Eurocentric notions of authenticity to counter-productive levels.[7] (In her reflections, Fusco derisively recalls the account of the French curators demanding to see Cuban artist José Bedia's shrine to confirm that he actually practiced Santería and was thus truly "authentic" in borrowing its forms.)[8] *The Couple in the Cage* turned these well-intentioned notions on their heads. As Fusco observed, "Our cage became a metaphor for our condition, linking the racism implicit in ethnographic paradigms of discovery with the exoticizing rhetoric of 'world beat' multiculturalism."[9] In other words, in their exuberance to prove their embrace of diversity, institutions were inadvertently repeating the acts of Othering, only now not as the shadow of a shameful past, but as a proud part of the mission statement. The museums were not the sole targets here, however; one of the true surprises for the artists was how ready audiences were to buy into the act.

On that note, it needs to be said that *The Couple in the Cage* could not function the same way today. It would take mere seconds on a smartphone to establish that the performers were not who they claimed to be. In 1992, however, long before the reign of Fake News, Fusco and Gómez-Peña came brandishing their own back-up, supplementing the performance with an informative panel on Guatinau, purportedly drawn from an entry in *Encyclopedia Britannica*. The pseudo-scholarly description of the "specimens" lists their average heights and weights before adding, "The Male ... likes spicy food, burritos and Diet Coke, and his favorite cigarette brand is Marlboro." The "Female," meanwhile, "is fond of sandwiches, pad thai, and herb tea."[10] Corroborating these "facts" was a guide

7　Ibid, p. 145.
8　Ibid, pp. 151–152.
9　Ibid, p. 145.
10　Ibid, pp. 164–165.

sporting an ask me! button, as well as another assistant who would take souvenir Polaroids of the couple with visitors (reiterating that not only were these people worth *seeing*, they were worth *photographing*).

A second set of accompanying panels provided a loose chronology of "intercultural performances," instances of humans on display, compiled by Fusco.[11] Dating from the Caribbean native that Columbus supposedly brought back as a gift to the Spanish court (said to have later died of sadness) to "Tiny Teesha, the Island Princess," an attraction at the 1992 Minnesota State Fair, the timeline makes it clear that these exhibited humans were, in fact, *performing* (a point taken further in Barbara Kirshenblatt-Gimblett's essay, "The Ethnographic Burlesque").[12] The identity they were acting out was not their own, but rather one projected upon them by the expectant audience. Fusco spells this out in the final paragraph of her chronology, which could not help but feel like a swing at some of her colleagues: "The contemporary tourist industries and cultural ministries of several countries around the world still perpetrate the illusion of authenticity to cater to the Western fascination with otherness. So do many artists."[13]

In this sense, any blame laid at the foot of the institution of the museum also belonged to the viewers. For all its jocularity, *The Couple in the Cage* took no mercy on their audience and its willingness to engage with the spectacle—an aspect of the performance ground home by the 1993 single-channel video, *The Couple in the Cage: A Guatinaui Odyssey*,[14] produced by Fusco and Paula Heredia as

11 Reprinted in ibid., pp. 146–147.
12 Barbara Kirshenblatt-Gimblett, "The Ethnographic Burlesque," in *TDR The Drama Review: A Journal of Performance Studies* Vol. 42, No. 2 (Summer 1998).
13 Fusco (see note 6), p. 147.
14 Available online at https://www.artandeducation.net/

documentation of the project. As Fusco argues in "The Other History," ethnological displays were never *that* educational; rather, they were tailor-made to reinforce notions on the supremacy of the (most often European) audience, bolstering the logic of cultural imperialism under the banners of Manifest Destiny. Accuracy was of secondary concern. As Kirshenblatt-Gimlett notes, "The foreign villages at world's fairs included not only performers from Turkey, Egypt, Ireland, and Germany, among others, but also college students, immigrants, and other employees, who stood in for Turks, Egyptians, Irish, and Germans."[15] When addressing Fusco and Gómez-Peña specifically, the author picks up Steven Mullaney's term, "rehearsal of culture": "While *The Couple in the Cage* purports to rehearse a putative ethnographic reality, what it actually rehearses is a mode of encounter. Audiences assuming the former get caught in the latter."[16]

"Caught" is a key word here. According to scholar Diana Taylor, it was also a primary flaw of the spectacle: the audience could not win; there was no "correct" response to the performance. She writes, "Fusco and Gómez-Peña enacted the various economies of the object … the body as cultural artifact, as sexual object, as threatening alterity, as scientific specimen, as living proof of radical difference. They were anything the spectator wanted them to be, except human."[17] Fusco described this mode of encounter more poetically, shifting the onus of the

classroom/video/244623/coco-fusco-and-guillermo-gmez-pea-the-couple-in-the-cage-two-undiscovered-amerindians-visit-the-west (accessed on March 1, 2020).
15 Kirshenblatt-Gimblett (see note 12), p. 176.
16 Ibid.
17 Diana Taylor, "A Savage Performance," in *TDR*, Vol. 42, No. 2 (Summer, 1998).

responsibility to the audience, and not to the stimulus they were provided:

> The cage became a blank screen onto which audiences projected their fantasies of who and what we are. As we assumed the stereotypical role of the domesticated savage, many audience members felt entitled to assume the role of the colonizer, only to find themselves uncomfortable with the implications of the game.[18]

The spectacle of Otherness, as Fusco constructs it, is predicated on the presumption of a white audience. The artist does, however, acknowledge the complexities of responses from people of color, whether in London, Madrid, or the States, noting the influence of class:

> Many upper-class Latin American tourists in Spain and Washington, D.C., voiced disgust that their part of the world should be represented in such a debased manner. Many other Latin Americans and Native Americans immediately recognized the symbolic significance of the piece, expressing solidarity with us, analyzing articles in the cage for other audience members, and showing their approval to us by holding our hands as they posed for photographs. Regardless of whether they have believed or not, Latinos and Native Americans have not criticized the hybridity of the cage environment and our costumes for being "unauthentic." One Pueblo elder from Arizona who saw us in the Smithsonian went so far as to say that our display was more "real" than any other statement about the condition of Native peoples in the museum. "I see the faces

18 Fusco (see note 6) p. 152.

of my grandchildren in that cage," he told a museum representative.[19]

And yet, prosaic as this moment of encounter and identification may have been (keeping in mind that this account is coming from the perspective of the performer, and was in many ways limited to the self-selected survey pool of those willing to speak about their experience on camera), Taylor would argue that it was the cage that would keep things comfortable for the viewer by providing the "the security of partial recognition," thus shielding the audience from having to face the ramifications of colonialism as it continued to shape their present.[20] Pointing to Fusco's Cuban heritage and Gómez-Peña's own move from Mexico City, Taylor concludes that they "really are Guatanauis, of sorts, though not in the way their spectators are being asked to believe." She writes:

> For all the trappings of difference, the subjects and objects may be more similar than one imagines. For some viewers, then, the bars of the cage actually protected against that realization, marking the radical boundary between the "here" and the "there," the "us" and the "them," allowing for no intra-, no cross-, no transcultural nada. Precolonial subjects, frozen in static essence, didn't experience today's hybrid ethnic and racial identities. The native body was believable, then, not because it was "real" but precisely because it wasn't. It served to maintain a distance between the pre- and the post-: precolonial to postcolonial; premodern to postmodern. Rather than challenging us to more fully acknowledge the racial and cultural heterogeneity of

19 Ibid, p. 162.
20 Taylor (see note 17), p. 168.

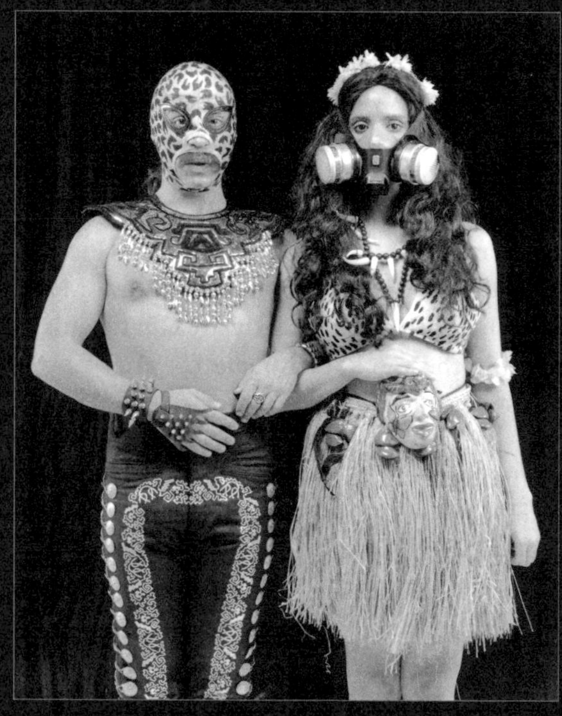

Portrait of Guillermo Gómez-Peña and Coco Fusco, for the exhibition
The Year of the White Bear, Walker Art Center, 1992

societies such as Latin America's in which very real indígenas continue to live in or alongside industrial centers, the "pre"/"post" hammers in distinct and identifiable boundaries.[21]

In short, the cage wasn't keeping the artists in so much as it was keeping the audience out of a reality in which colonial interests still determined their day-to-day lives.

A year after its publication, Fusco added an afterword to "The Other History," detailing the artists' experience touring the piece to Buenos Aires. There, she recalls, audience members were not so much dismayed at the *light*ness of the artists' skin (a complaint frequently registered in Madrid), but rather its *dark*ness: "We were not *real* American artists, meaning that we were not white." Once more, Fusco observed class distinctions in her audience: "Scores of mestizos and indigenous immigrants to the city from Bolivia, Peru and Argentina's northern regions watched us evening after evening with extraordinary sadness in their eyes. Meanwhile, dozens of Argentinian intellectuals sat sipping coffee in the bar directly behind us, often pretending to ignore the scene unfolding before them."[22] Fusco also recounts an episode of violence, in which someone douses Gómez-Peña with acid, as well as several accounts of sexual harassment. The latter had been a recurring theme in her observations of the earlier iterations of the performance. Perhaps one of her most insightful commentaries was that the first few days in the cage were harder on Gómez-Peña: "my experiences as a woman had prepared

21 Ibid.
22 Afterword to Fusco, "The Other History of Intercultural Performance," reprinted in Joanne Morra and Marquard Smith, eds., *Visual Culture: Critical Concepts in Media and Cultural Studies* (London, 2006), p. 217.

me to shield myself psychologically from the violence of public objectification."[23]

This becomes a curious sticking point for Fusco. In the film, she pulls a quotation from a tongue-in-cheek account of the Whitney performance that appeared in *Artforum*.[24] Writer Jan Avgikos (a woman, incidentally) comments on the distraction of Fusco's beautiful, "scantily-clad body." Fusco touts the quote as if proof of the intellectual failings of the "educated" art crowd. And yet, her body was—*is*—beautiful, and she willingly put it on display. She even riffed on this situation in the spoof *National Enquirer* cover produced for the film, which featured a side-story about Hollywood wanting a contract with the "female specimen only." If anything, *The Couple in the Cage* relied on outdated gender roles as part of its appeal toward verification. The presiding heteronormativity—hypersexualized though it may have been, with the didactic panels assuring visitors the specimens copulated twice a day, even repurposing some of the objects in the cage "into makeshift sex toys by night"[25]—was palliative, making the spectacle easier for their audience to swallow. Why fault them when they did?

Herein lies the real problem. In calling out "the violence of public objectification," Fusco subjects her audience members to it. And while she may have set the conditions for her own display, her viewers did not, particularly where the documentary was concerned. As Taylor observes, "Though it might have been the artists' intention to create a pause for reflection, this is the space that the video does not allow for. Quite the opposite, it freezes that immediate response. Before the spectator can digest and come to

<hr>

23 Fusco, (see note 6), p. 162.
24 Jan Avgkios, "Whitney Biennial 1993," in *Artforum* (May 1993).
25 Fusco (see note 6), p. 145.

terms with the show, that response is turned into show for someone else."[26] In this reversal of the "ethnographic lens," the critic sees a violence akin to the ethnographic practices supposedly targeted: "the video 'captures' or 'cages' the viewer."[27] This isn't liberation; it only begs the question: what are you looking at?

POSTSCRIPT

The 1993 Whitney Biennial was hailed as part of a sea change, the arrival of the incoming biennial tide, which would accord a touristic virtue to geographic Otherness, even while universalizing certain narratives, clearing the way for the decade or so of identity politics that would follow. In a roundtable discussion on the biennial,[28] curator Thelma Golden says that the measure of the exhibition's success should be the extent to which the biennial transformed the institution. In a 2012 essay in *Modern Painters*, Fusco mulls this very point:

Twenty years later, I still think about an unanswered question that led me into the cage. Is there anyone who really believes that we could be "post-racial" in a culture that fetishizes black athletes, equates black style with rebelliousness, pillages indigenous belief systems for pithy profundities to satisfy the spiritual cravings of secular materialists, and then depends on cheap immigrant labor, redlining, and mass incarceration to safeguard class hierarchies that are obviously racialized?[29]

26 Taylor (see note 17), p. 169.
27 Ibid, p. 170.
28 Available online at https://charlierose.com/videos/15655 (accessed March 3, 2020).
29 Coco Fusco, "Still in the Cage: Thoughts on 'Two Undiscovered Amerindians,' 20 Years Later" in *Modern Painters* (February 2012),

In 2020, it's hard to look at images of *The Couple in the Cage* without considering the state of politics in the United States, where right now kids—the majority coming from South and Central America—are sleeping in cages at detention facilities along the United States-Mexican border. If Fusco and Gómez-Peña were gesturing toward a continued readiness to exoticize the Other under the false flag of tolerance, fast-forward twenty-five years and that Other has already been openly vilified, with terrifying repercussions. Instead of loosening the ties of false narratives like Manifest Destiny, we have watched these fictions grow increasingly stronger and more resilient, in ways that demand more than a quirky photo-op. The question today seems not what are we looking at, but what are we still not acknowledging.

https://www.blouinartinfo.com/news/story/760842/still-in-the-cage-thoughts-on-two-undiscovered-amerindians-20-years-later (accessed February 26, 2020).

Trans-Imaginaries of Decolonization: Three Frames for the Art of *Lotus: Afro-Asian Writings*

Sanjukta Sunderason

AN UNMOORED AESTHETIC

As part of a wider project on connected histories of postcolonial art across India and Pakistan between 1947 and 1971, I have been developing the concept of the "aesthetics of decolonization."[1] So far it has been focusing on displacements as a trope for reading how artists, displaced or migrating under the shadow of the partition of the Indian subcontinent in 1947, reoriented their practice, and reimagined new cultural institutions and sovereignties. Such locational dynamics and formations allude to the creative cultures of decolonization despite its corrosive trails of wars, partitions, and genocides; yet, they have only partially addressed the imaginational mechanisms that decolonization generated. Imagination, it can be

1 Further to a European Commission Marie Curie project, *Aesthetics of Decolonization: Artists, Modernisms and Nation-States in India, East and West Pakistan, 1947–1971* (2013–2017), I have elaborated on the idea in Sanjukta Sunderason, "Aesthetics of Decolonisation in South Asia," in David Ludden ed. *Oxford Research Encyclopedia of Asian History*, 2020. The idea of "aesthetics of decolonization" had been used in the context of postcolonial literatures by Ngugi wa Thiong'o in the context of George Lamming's writings, see Anthony Bogues ed., *The George Lamming Reader: The Aesthetics of Decolonization* (Kingston and Miami, 2011). The concept has also appeared later in the context of studies on art, periodicals, and decolonization, for instance, in Marion von Osten's 2016 article, "Aesthetics of Decolonization— The Magazine *Souffles (1966–1972),*" in *ASIA 2016*; 70 (4), pp. 1265–84.

argued by echoing Reinhart Koselleck, connects "spaces of experience" with "horizons of expectations,"[2] imagination forges "imaginary futures"[3] and "affective communities"[4] of sentiment, what Sonal Khullar, following Edward Said, has called the worldly affiliations, in her study of post-colonial artists.[5]

A wider unmoored aesthetic of creative work inhabits the decades of political decolonization—the nineteen-forties to the nineteen-seventies—ones that cannot be harnessed, essentially, to nation-states, locational histories, defined institutions, or iconic collectives. This imaginational work gains body *in transit,* becoming concrete only in sites that capture and frame such transits. Perhaps then, we (also) need conceptual tools to understand this sense of transit in understanding the aesthetics of decolonization. Such understandings of cultures *in motion*, echoing concerns raised by Daniel Rogers, need, however, to move beyond "hydraulic rhetoric" of flows and networks; they must proceed instead through "stories of intrusion, translation, resistance, and adaptation,"[6] whereby ideas, images, and idioms *in transit* get intertwined or framed—as collage, or as I will show here, as illustrations.

2 Reinhart Koselleck, *Futures Past: On the Semantics of Historical Time*, trans. and introduced by Keith Tribe (New York, 2004), pp. 258–59.
3 Manu Goswami, "Imaginary Futures and Colonial Internationalisms," in *The American Historical Review*, Vol. 117, No. 5 (December 2012), p. 1463.
4 Leela Gandhi, *Affective Communities: Anticolonial Thought, Fin-de-Siècle Radicalism, and the Politics of Friendship* (Durham and London, 2006).
5 Sonal Khullar, *Worldly Affiliations: Artistic Practice, National Identity, and Modernism in India, 1930–1990* (Berkeley, 2015).
6 Daniel T. Rodgers, "Cultures in Motion, An Introduction," in *Cultures in Motion*, eds. Daniel T. Rogers et al. (Princeton, 2013), p. 3.

In this essay, I am adding another layer to my formulation of the aesthetics of decolonization, by taking on board the momentum of transit, and foregrounding in particular, the dynamic contained in the prefix *trans*. I am turning to *Lotus: Afro-Asian Writings* (begun in 1967 as *Afro-Asian Writings*), the trilingual mouthpiece periodical of the Afro-Asian Peoples' Solidarity Organization (AAPSO) and Afro-Asian Writers' Association (AAWA)—both front organizations set up in the mid to late nineteen-fifties and active across Bandung, Delhi, Colombo, Tashkent, and Cairo. My focus, more specifically, is on illustrations in *Lotus*, a journal not known in particular for its visuals, but rather for its texts—prose, poems, reports, and essays.

Illustrations in *Lotus* offer, I will propose, critical entry points into understanding what I will venture to call *trans-imaginaries* of decolonization. Trans- here is not a passive prefix, but an agent that activates particular historicities of the aesthetics of decolonization, by framing particular imaginaries. Imaginaries, Henri Lefebvre and others have argued, are collective imaginations and cognitive frameworks that are complex yet unstructured and unarticulated.[7] I am interested in asking how the in-transit dynamic of the prefix trans frames the multi-dimensional imaginaries of decolonization, and how *Lotus* becomes a site for framing such trans-imaginaries. In what is essentially my first entry into studying *Lotus* more broadly, I am introducing here, albeit in rudimentary forms, three frames that constitute trans-imaginaries of decolonization.[8]

---

7 See Henri Lefebvre, *The Production of Space,* trans. Donald Nicholson-Smith (Oxford 1991). See also Charles Taylor et al., eds., *Modern Social Imaginaries* (Durham and London, 2004).
8 This brief essay is the first from a larger piece I am developing on the arts of solidarity in *Lotus*, parts of which were presented at, and will appear in volume tied to, the conference *Axis of*

TRANS-IMAGINARIES
OF DECOLONIZATION

Lotus was published in three languages—English, Arabic, and French, its Arabic edition published from its headquarters in Cairo; and the English and the French editions published by the German Democratic Republic. A limited yet rich body of scholarship on *Lotus* reveals multiple drifts of questions: from thinking through cultures and methodologies of translation in world literature,[9] to activist and artistic retellings of the conjunctural solidarities of the nineteen-seventies,[10] as well as histories of transnational solidarities of the progressive left.[11] Art in *Lotus* has eluded the attention of scholars—both within the overtly literary focus of postcolonial cultural studies, and in modernist studies in visual art where focus has remained more often than not on individuals, movements, and iconic sites of modernism in the post-colonies—framed almost always by national or nation-statist grids, even while challenging the hegemonic gaze of Eurocentric modernisms. Indeed, in *Lotus,* texts are more active than

Solidarity: Landmarks, Platforms, Futures, organized in February 2019 by Tate Modern's Hyundai Tate Research Centre: Transnational, and the Institute of Comparative Modernities at Cornell University and the Africa Institute, Sharjah.

9 Hala Halim, "Lotus, the Afro-Asian Nexus, and Global South Comparatism," in *Comparative Studies of South Asia, Africa, and the Middle East,* Vol. 32, No. 3, (2012), pp. 563–83.

10 Nida Ghouse, "Lotus: Notes," in *After Year Zero: Geographies of Collaboration,* exh. cat., Museum of Modern Art (Warsaw, 2015).

11 I am referring here to Maia Ramnath's ongoing work on *Lotus,* parts of which I encountered as part of the larger *Forms of The Left: Activist Art & Left-Wing Aesthetics in Postcolonial South Asia* that I co-organized with Dr. Lotte Hoek, University of Edinburgh. I have benefited in particular from Ramnath's paper, "Lotus Roots: Transposing a Political-Aesthetic Agenda from South Asia to Afro-Asia," presented as part of the panels and workshops organized under the project.

the images themselves. Images are mostly illustrative; they either reflect directly the texts—stories, poems, or essays—or appear as freestanding artworks that complement the periodical's Afro-Asian themes. Many of the illustrations are anonymous. Apart from baffling a scholar studying such images, anonymity reinforces rather productively a wider, unnamed field of visual culture both embedded in and independent from the text. Anonymity also gives the images a more sovereign status in the context of the periodical itself. The illustrational work of such images makes them arts *of* the periodical. Seen thus, they become a parallel site for generating narrative-visual imaginaries—both expansive and collective—rather being marginal to the texts in the foreground.

Illustrations in *Lotus* activate three dynamics of what I have called trans-imaginaries of decolonization. The first, temporal, one is the *transitional* nature of these decades of the nineteen-fifties to the nineteen-seventies. This transitional dynamic was active both as simultaneities: as struggles for freedom some countries in Africa and Asia were being paralleled by or followed similar struggles in others; and also as continuum: as freedom was being imagined and debated as a continued struggle despite political independence. The transitional nature of these decades made freedom itself imaginaries-in-transition rather than (postcolonial) resolutions. A second, spatial dynamic lies in the *transnational* footprints that retreating colonial empires produced as they entangled with the Cold War's geopolitical grids. Decolonization thus generated new connected geographies that both echoed and subverted the geopolitics of colonialism. A third, idiomatic dynamic lies in the *transcultural* nature of cultural production during these decades where artists, activists, and political workers formed forums and fronts that thrived on collaboration, translation, and montage—and at the same time negotiated the alienations that resulted from the failures of such transcultural initiatives. I will elaborate via select illustrations in *Lotus*.

TRANSITIONAL VISIONS

Lotus was initiated in 1967, fairly late into the formations of Afro-Asian solidarity movements, most of which were formed in the mid-fifties, and at the tip of the formation of the Tricontinental—the anti-colonial, anti-imperial front of Latin America, Africa, and Asia. As such, the periodical, known to have drawn funds from the Soviet Union, appears as a forum for capturing the transitional visions of decolonization: ideas that were typically attuned to imagining continued struggles for independence, whether entangled with battlegrounds of the Cold War, or national and regional political negotiations. As an Afro-Asian forum, *Lotus* captures multiple temporalities of the transitional decades, from the postcolonial temporalities of the South Asian countries of India and Pakistan to the ongoing freedom struggles in African nations, the theaters of the Cold War in Vietnam, and the shifting contours of Arab resistance in Palestine or Lebanon. The visual imaginaries in *Lotus* are attuned to these multiple transitional temporalities, and allow for a dialectical reading of both modernism, as imagined via artistic forms and idioms; and freedom, as driving the ideological and imaginational thrust of such forms. As "transitional visions," art in *Lotus* can help us understand *historically*, the more granular cultural formations of decolonization.

I read art in *Lotus* as visions of a braided double movement: the retreat of colonial empires and simultaneous arrivals of postcolonial independence. The question of freedom active throughout *Lotus* needs to be read through the dialectics of these contradictory momentums—rife with the corrosive trails of war, genocide, partitions, and displacements, as well as the utopic visions of hope and solidarity. As *Lotus* attempted to forge conversations across a newly morphing "Third World," it grappled with the tensions of plural languages, affiliations, and visualizations. It carried emotive and intellectual negotiations around the idea and limits of freedom across Asian and African contexts and peoples. The question of freedom appears in multiple modalities—as a vision yet unrealized (figure 1); the promise of an impending unshackling (figure 2), as well as in images of grassroots guerilla war ongoing in Vietnam or Palestine (figure 3). There is an idealization of guerilla war, steeped in the texts around Vietnam and Arab resistance and Palestinian struggle. Epistemological and popular-political resistance runs through *Lotus,* and the illustrations—while not forged in modernist forms as in the Tricontinental posters of the seventies—were nonetheless illustrative acts in capturing visions of resistance, real or idealized.

Through the late sixties and seventies, *Lotus* reproduced visual reportage from Vietnam—for instance, in works of an artist like Huynh Phuong Dong, one of the country's most esteemed political artists, described also as a noted "combat artist." Regular visual reportage—reminiscent of this late-colonial, anti-imperialist genre—appeared in *Lotus* in drawings of battle scenes, troops in action, and daily life in the guerrilla bases, along with portraits of his comrades, both leaders and ordinary soldiers. Also striking are reproductions of the works of the Palestinian artist Ismail Shammout, who also drew refugee camps: "Shammout is an artist from Palestine," *Lotus* notes, "he has succeeded in forging a new style which combines both the realism of national resistance and poetic

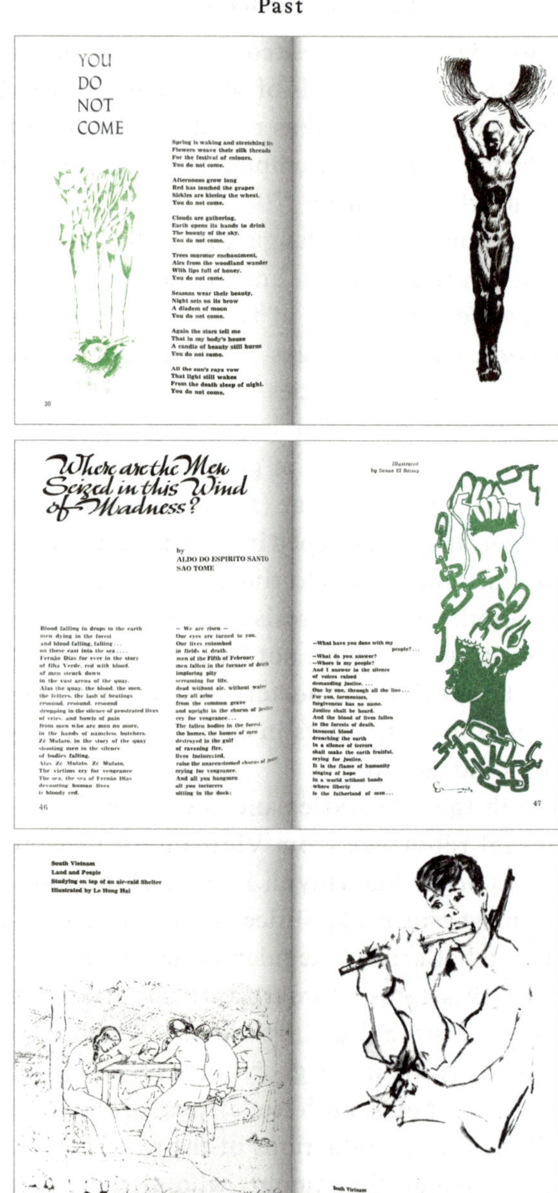

From top to bottom: Images from *Lotus: Afro-Asian Writings*; fig. 1—July 1973, fig. 2—January 1974, and fig. 3—March 1967

vision. He has been able, more than any other artist, to depict on canvas, the plight of Arab refugees" (*Lotus*, January 1970, Vol. 1, Issue 4).

Artworks in *Lotus* did not *reflect* the political agendas and rationalities of meta-political mechanisms of decolonization or Cold War. They offered, rather, another temporality—a horizon of imagination that could capture the more graduated, bottom-up negotiations of such geopolitics as they left a global trail, whether through struggles of independence, partitions of nations at the arrivals of independence, strategic alignments of culture with political ideologies, and indeed transnational forums that emerged at the crossroads these political processes.

The transitional vision in the illustrations of *Lotus* are narrative, non-abstract, with deeply allegorical echoes, with citations of soil, sun, frontal images of "man," harvest. They suggest time and again that freedoms can and should be read as ideas in progress: not (political) resolutions, but (artistic) searches. While echoing a visible Socialist figuration with an emancipatory late-colonial and postcolonial vision, such works were still a far cry from an official Soviet Socialist realist art, and captured rather a transnational footprint of socialist iconography typical to these transitional decades, one that was almost consciously open-ended to allow fresh entwinements with new political ends.

TRANSNATIONAL FRAMES

If colonialism produced an imperial aesthetic that cut across colonial empires, the aesthetic forms of decolonization, too, were transnational. The middling decades of the twentieth century are dominated with a geopolitical reorganization that was both triggered by or entangled with the retreats of British, French, Dutch, Portuguese, and German colonial empires over vast swathes of territories across Asia and Africa. Such retreats left trails of wars, genocides, famines, partitions, and displacements in the former colonies. At the same time they entangled many of those post/late colonial nations in the new post—1945 political and geographical hierarchies of a Cold War world, polarized between the contesting, hegemonic forces of the capitalist First World dominated by the United States, and the socialist Second World under the Soviet Union's spheres of influence. Many Afro-Asian nations, as is well known, formed the "Third World" and the "Non-Aligned" movement to both articulate their political identities at a global scale, and intervene in the new political doxa of the Cold War. Decolonization, it can thus be assumed, produced geopolitical frames that contained newly emerging nation-states enmeshed with mid-twentieth-century political and ideological geographies. If empire and its capitalist underpinnings thrived on transnational enterprises, decolonization both spoke from and challenged the organizing principles of such structures. It generated, in other words, its own transnational frames with their peculiar spatial imaginaries.

For *Lotus*, being the mouthpiece of the Afro-Asian People's Solidarity Organization necessitated the task of imagining an Afro-Asian composite that would visualize solidarity. This idea is visible in the intertwining of black and white—as colors—in producing a racialized imagery of Afro-Asian cohesion and united identity, imagination, and action. From the insignia of *Lotus* that visualized Afro-Asian Writers (figure 4), to depictions of entangled bodies of servitude (figure 5) and illustrations of essays like "Afro-Asian personality"—illustrations in *Lotus* reveal an art of visualizing a collective. Such images sought to symbolize universalism of solidarity through composite

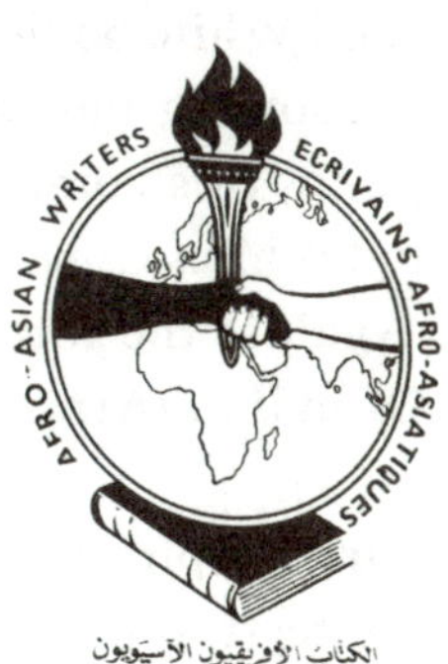

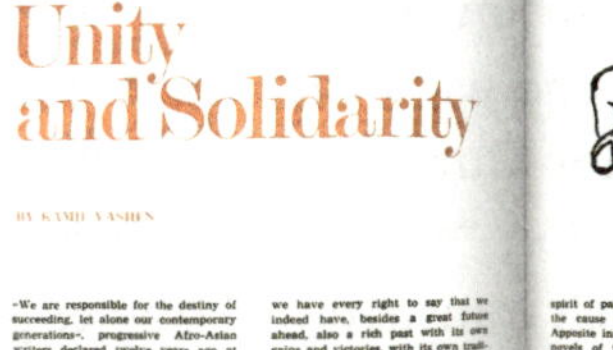

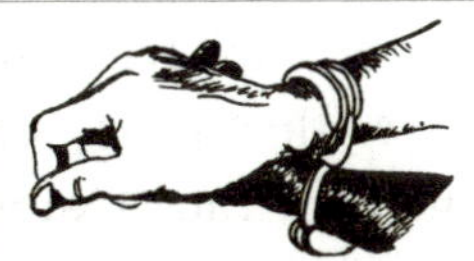

From top to bottom: fig. 4—*Lotus*'s insignia, fig. 5—spread from *Lotus*, July 1971, fig. 6—poem from *Lotus*, April 1970

particulars—of Black and White bodies—as well as in generative acts of collective sowing and harvest. In a poem by Vincent Tsoungui-Ngono, this composite was imagined as "Afrasia": "Blacks and Whites / A new humanity / On the march / Irresistibly / Against the forces / Of destruction Against the forces / Of evil … / Afrasia: Sun of freedom" (figure 6).

Such illustrations draw aspirational, tentative, or utopian lines between contesting political geographies of a decolonizing, Cold War world. By producing new transnational frames within the pages of the periodical, they seem to traverse the Iron Curtain dictated by the post-1945 realpolitik of the "West," and what Richard Wright called after Bandung, the "Color Curtain"—from W. E. B. Du Bois's use of the expression "color line" to describe a racially charged world. Such transnational frames generate new composite iconographic subjectivities—both racialized in visualization, and transcending race. I place *Lotus* within the aesthetic field of "drawing lines" between political geographies and cultural geographies of the post World War II, decolonizing decades, thus creating new "affective geographies" through postcolonial print cultures.[12] As the periodical generated transnational frames where these alternative geographies could be imagined and illustrated, new dynamics of transcultural montages could be articulated.

TRANSCULTURAL MONTAGES

Visualizing an Afro-Asian aesthetic and politics in *Lotus* was an act of transcultural imagination. While *Lotus* forms a hallmark site for translation and world literature

---

12 I will be developing this strain of argumentation further in the piece "Drawing Lines: Arts of Solidarity in *Lotus*," forthcoming 2020–21.

with iconic names of postcolonial literature appearing in three languages—a point highlighted by Hala Halim in her exhaustive study of the periodical—illustrations in *Lotus* reveal a different transcultural mechanism. A decolonial montage, I would argue, is attempted—albeit without expressed agenda—in combining translated texts, already bilingual and binational, with a third layer as it were, of drawings from different cultural and intellectual contexts—the act of illustration, in other words, was also an act of transcultural montage. Examples thrive across *Lotus* where poems on one site of struggle would be staged with images from another site: a poem on the Vietnam war framed together with art on Palestinian refugees (figure 7), or poems dedicated to the Congolese leader Patrice Lumumba from poets from India and Japan illustrated by Egyptian artists (figure 8). Later volumes of *Lotus* attempted more expressly the representation of modern art from Asia and Africa (figure 9).

While written pieces in *Lotus* ranged from short stories and poems from Africa, Asia, or Latin America, reports on the conferences of the AAPSO or AAWA, or essays on freedom, solidarity, expressionism, or militancy in cultural production, the illustrations—often anonymous—were often limited to artists emerging from Arab contexts, as evident in the list of illustrators at the end of each volume. There were a mixed bag of modernist graphic artists and committed political artists primarily from Egypt, where *Lotus* was based in the sixties and seventies, and Palestine. They spanned Egyptian surrealists, book illustrators, and poster artists, from Ramses Younan—the founding member of the Egyptian Surrealist movement; iconic artist, critic, and poet Ahmed Morsi; Abdel Hadi El-Gazzar—one of the most noted postwar

Past

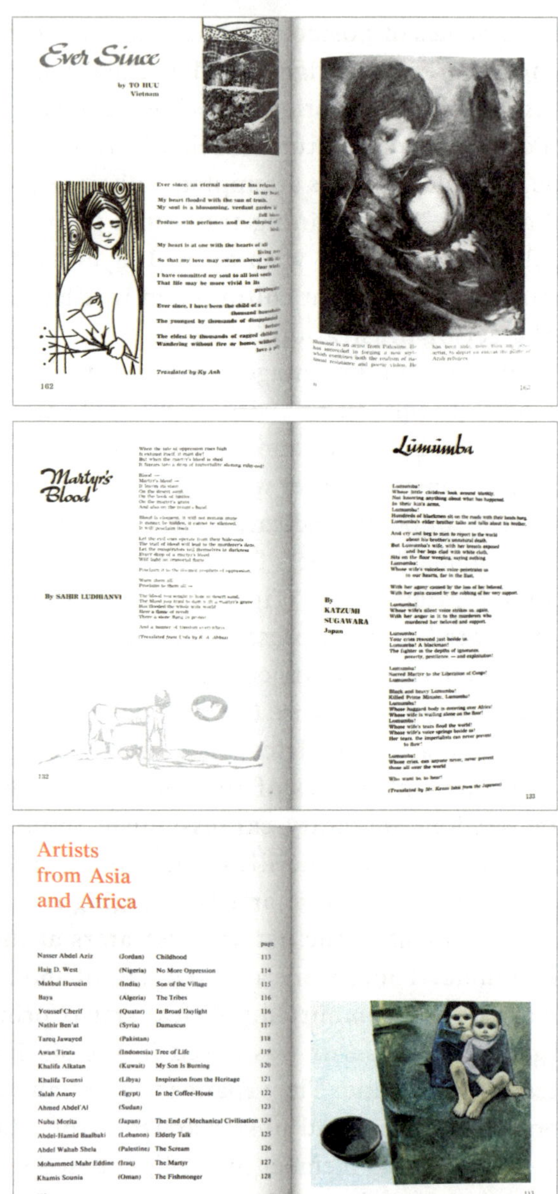

From top to bottom: Images from *Lotus*; fig. 7—January 1970, fig. 8—Volume 1, March 1967, and fig. 9—Volume 59, 1988

painters in Egypt; alongside Egyptian illustrators like Gamal Kotb (famed for his book covers for the writer Naguib Mahfouz); and poster maker Heba Enayat—who was part of the cultural mission of Arab artists who had in 1962 traveled to China as members of the UAR (United Arab Republic) cultural mission. There were noted Palestinian painters such as Mustafa Al Hallaj and Ismail Shammout. There were also iconic Afro-Arab artists with complex lineages, for instance, Uche Okeke and Ben Enwonwu of Nigeria; Ibrahim el Salahi of Sudan, the French-Senegalese painter Iba N'Diaye—each artist carrying by the late-sixties iconic status as "national artists" of their respective contexts as institution-makers and intellectual drivers.

Parsed closely, illustrations in *Lotus* reveal transcultural montage of multiple lineages of art and politics. Alongside Pan-Africanism and Négritude, and Pan Arabism, there are active traces of the progressive cultural movement of South Asia. This was revealed consistently in the poems and essays published from key national figures of movement like Faiz Ahmed Faiz from Pakistan—who eventually became the editor of *Lotus*—and Mulk Raj Anand and Sajjad Zaheer from India; as well as in regional figures like the radical poets Amrita Pritam from Indian Punjab, and Subhash Mukhopadhyay from Indian Bengal.

What connected this diverse spread? A vision of the political in art, the idea of artist as activist and shaper of politics, to name a few. In the very first volume, a poem by Ousmane Sembène, the Senegalese auteur and filmmaker, made a bid to capture the unifying drive connecting the fingers of "artists," the fingers of "land tillers," the "finger holding a trigger," and the "finger of a soldier," appealing: "Across the rivers and languages / Of Europe and Asia, / Of China and Africa, / Of India and the Oceans, / Let us join our fingers to take away / All power of this finger / Which keeps in mourning" (*Lotus,* Vol. 1, No. 1, March 1967).

BEYOND CLOSURES

"The modernities of today," Susan Friedman has argued in her theorization of planetary modernisms, "compel a rethinking of the modernities of the past."[13] Twentieth-century decolonization, it can be argued, produced its own modernity, one that entangled political and cultural sovereignty and generated visual forms that combined utopic visions with both lived and negotiated realities. If modernity, as Friedman argues, is read as a "geohistorical condition"—plural, recurring, global, relational, contradictory, utopic as well as dystopic—as she proposes,[14] a periodical like *Lotus* can be read as a concrete frame that sought to capture such "planetarity." While solidarity, translation, and transnational composition are foundational to this planetarity—generating foundational movements of what Hala Halim has called South-South comparativism—art in *Lotus,* I propose, visualizes possibilities of putting art and text from diverse contexts *in dialogue*, illustrating in the process a utopic cosmopolitanism *despite* differences of national histories.

In the eighties, *Lotus* shifted base to Beirut, and back to Cairo after a brief stint in Tunis, where it continued until the outbreak of the civil war. In 2016, *Lotus* was revived after many deliberations, with the Afro-Asian Writers' Association being renamed as the Writers' Union of Africa, Asia, and Latin America. It continues to carry short stories, poems, and essays that span from the Global

13 Susan Friedman, *Planetary Modernisms: Provocations on Modernity Across Time* (New York, 2016), p. 2.
14 Friedman, ibid., p. 4.

South, with the occasional illustration, with themes that echo former concerns of nationalism, identity, and freedom. The new *Lotus*, as Halim notes, seems to lack any "ideological orientation or conceptual coherence," even as it operates still with avowed goals of "tolerance, fraternity, and peace."[15] As growing scholarship on *Lotus* (this brief essay being a humble addition) reveal multiple historical impulses at play—activist, archival, or artistic—a wider historiographical impetus is being generated, perhaps like *Lotus* itself, towards writing/curating histories of hope, solidarity, and activism. It remains to be seen how scholarship itself can generate new trans-imaginaries—for capturing revivals of the projects of solidarity as well as assimilate multipolar questions that can truly capture the momentum of the *trans* in the radically altered conditions and stakes of the twenty-first century.

15 Hala Halim, "Afro-Asian Third-Worldism into the Global South: The Case of Lotus Journal," *Global South Studies,* https://globalsouthstudies.as.virginia.edu/key-moments/afro-asian-third-worldism-global-south-case-lotus-journal (accessed May 1, 2020).

PRESENT

PRESENT

Dis-Othering as Method: Leh Zo, A Me Ke Nde Za*

Bonaventure Soh Bejeng Ndikung

I dislike interviews. I'm often asked the same question: What in your work comes from your own culture? As if I have a recipe and I can actually isolate the Arab ingredient, the woman ingredient, the Palestinian ingredient. People often expect tidy definitions of otherness, as if identity is something fixed and easily definable. Mona Hatoum, interview with Janine Antoni[1]

Just in the nick of time when we, by repetition and re-iteration, start believing our own concepts that we have postulated and disseminated. Just at that point in time—t—when we think that notion of Post-Otherness,[2] which we have reflected upon for years in reference to that double moment of awareness and transition, we seem to be experiencing a quake that pushes us to reconsider, but not reject, the paradoxicality of the Post-Other moment,[3] reconsider who and how one bears historical

* Ngemba for "Keep yours, and I keep mine."
1 Janine Antoni, "Mona Hatoum," in *Bomb* (April 1, 1998).
2 Regina Römhild and Bonaventure Ndikung, "The Post-Other as Avant-Garde" in *We Roma: A Critical Reader in Contemporary Art*, Daniel Baker, Maria Hlavajova eds. (Amsterdam, 2013).
3 In the aforementioned article, we discuss the concept and moment of Post-Otherness as follows: "In that paradoxical moment, the figure of the 'Post-Other' emerges, a figure still bearing the signs of historical Othering while at the same time representing and experimenting with unknown futures beyond it. In the shadow of the dominant political imagination a cosmopolitanized reality of convivial struggles unfolds, speaking and acting against that imagery. The moment of the 'Post-Other,' however, is still in the state of emergence: it unfolds in the everyday practices of the

Othering, reconsider the mechanisms of rendering Other, as well as reconsidering who represents whom or who tries to shape whose future in contemporary societies and discourses. This quake has spurred the necessity to drop off prefixes and concentrate on root words. It seems as if to be able to do these reconsiderations, one needs to, at least temporarily, abrogate "Post-" to be able to situate "Otherness" within our day's context. Especially, taking into account that the "Post-" in Post-Otherness might be dangling on a cliff, threatening to fall either on the side of the "post-" in "postcolonial"—which doesn't imply an aftermath but rather intends to announce a continuity of an era shaped by its colonial past—or drop on the side of "post-racial," which tends to be a distraction from metamorphosed formats and technologies of racisms. At any rate, this proposal announces the descaling of the prefix in order to properly scrutinize "Otherness."

This quake has been prompted by two random observations. First, if one, even with a minimum of sensitivity, took a glance at some current political highlights, one is likely to hear the reverberations of discourses ranging from building walls to separate nations, "bad hombres" to the Islamification of the Occident. As Sasha Polakow-Suransky put it in his article "The Ruthlessly Effective Rebranding of Europe's New Far Right":

They [the Right] have effectively claimed the progressive causes of the left—from gay rights to women's equality and protecting Jews from antisemitism—as

'unconscious' kind when, e.g., the anonymity of urban life allows or infinite examples of everyday cosmopolitan interactions. [...] Such practices are still waiting to be united and made visible."

their own, by depicting Muslim immigrants as the primary threat to all three groups. As fear of Islam has spread, with their encouragement, they have presented themselves as the only true defenders of western identity and western liberties—the last bulwark protecting a besieged Judeo-Christian civilisation from the barbarians at the gates.[4]

This becomes interesting as one observes the efforts of the right to co-opt certain historically "Othered" others within their political strategies, brewing new alliances and forging common denominators that were once regarded contradictory, while constructing other "Others" on which long cultivated angst, prejudices, and resentments could be projected upon. This process should be understood as a cannibalization of "Otherness" and a subsequent regurgitation of "Otherness." For some historically "Othered," the only thing that has changed is the mechanisms and methodologies through which they are objectified and Othered. So, in our sociopolitical contemporary, one can observe an intensification in the construction and cultivation of "Otherness," morphing old conceptions of the "Other" to clothe new groups of people, while at the same the appropriation of the "Other" for purposes profitable to the privileged and powerful.

Second, another tendency, especially within the context of the cultural industry, is the resurfacing of what one might call "geographical specification-ing," which is the need to spotlight certain geographical regions. This is, of

4 Sasha Polakow-Suransky, "The Ruthlessly Effective Rebranding of Europe's New Far Right," in *The Guardian,* November 1, 2016, www.theguardian.com/world/2016/nov/01/the-ruthlessly-effective-rebranding-of-europes-new-far-right (accessed January 24, 2020).

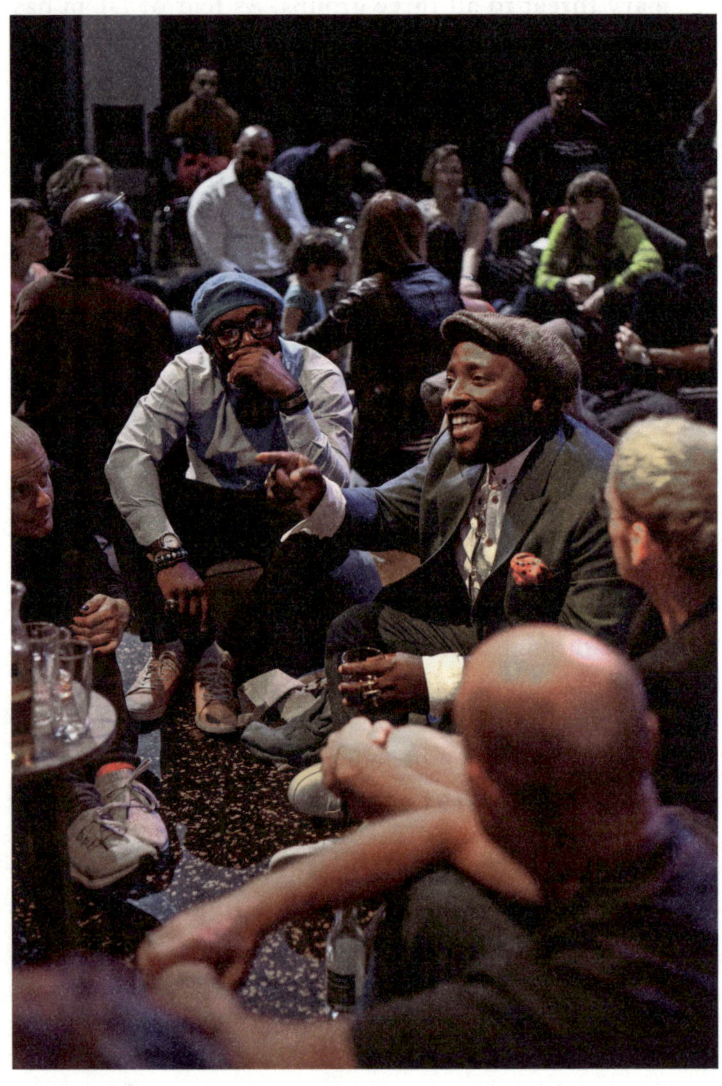

Author Bonaventure Ndikung (center) and others at the invocation
Dis-Othering as a Method, Savvy Contemporary, Berlin, 2018

course, not a new phenomenon, especially within Western museum institutions, or other cultural infrastructures in which, based on certain culture-political agendas or strategies, certain geographical regions are put in and out of focus as they like. Some have seen this practice as part of "soft power," whereby culture is used as a means to gently exercise political power on certain cultural and social groups. Take for example a museum or library in France that chooses to highlight Algeria, in the hope that it would thereby appease the Algerian community in an effort to soothe or clean the wounds of its colonial past. Or take for example the British Council, Goethe-Institut, Institut Français et al., opening cultural centers around the world to "promote culture." Soft power.

This "geographical specification-ing" is not always a bad thing. The long list of, for example, "African shows" or "Arab world shows"[5] around the world did indeed do a

5 *Contemporary African Art*, Studio International, London & New York, Camden Arts Centre, London, 1969; *African Contemporary Art,* The Gallery, Washington D.C., 1977; *Moderne Kunst aus Afrika* in the framework of the West Berlin Horizonte Festival der Weltkulturen (Nr. 1, 1979); *Art contemporain arabe: collection du Musée du l'Institut du Monde Arabe*, Paris, 1988; *The Other Story: Afro-Asian Artists in Post-War Britain*, Hayward Gallery, London, 1989; New York, *Fusion: West African Artists at the Venice Biennale*, Museum for African Art, New York, 1993; *Rencontres Africaines: Exposition d'Art Actuel*, Musée de l'Institut du Monde Arabe, Paris, 1994; *An Inside Story: African Art of Our Time*, The Yomiuri Shimbun, Japan Association of Art Museums, Tokyo, 1995; *Africa by Africa: A Photographic View*, Barbican Centre, London, 1999; *Authentic/Ex-Centric, Forum For African Arts*, Ithaca (NY), 2001; *The Short Century: Independence and Liberation Movements in Africa 1945–1994,* curated by Okwui Enwezor, Villa Stuck, Munich; Haus der Kulturen der Welt, Berlin; Museum of Contemporary Art, Chicago; P.S.1 Contemporary Art Center & The Museum of Modern Art, New York, 2001–02; *Africa Remix*, Museum Kunst Palast, Düsseldorf; Hayward Gallery, London; Centre Georges Pompidou, Paris; Mori Art Museum, Tokyo, 2004–2006, to mention only a few.

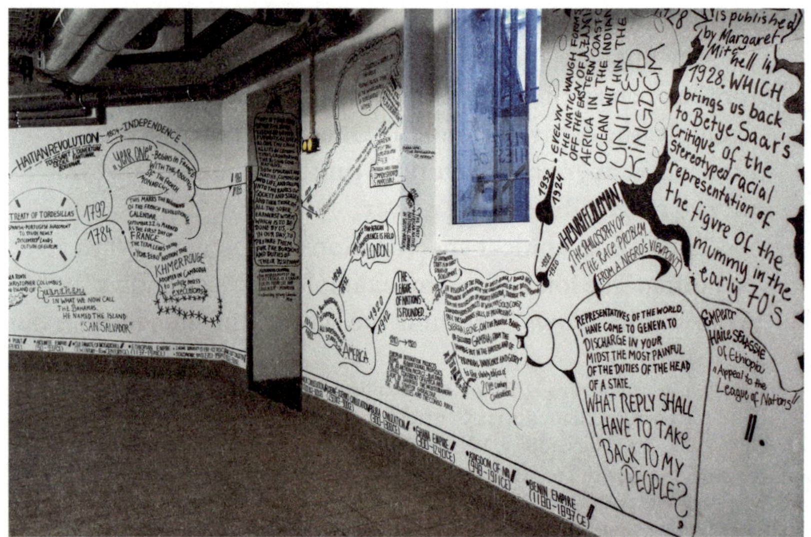

Boris Dewjatkin and Christopher Krauser, *Timeline*, 2018, installation view from the exhibition *Geographies of the Imagination*, Savvy Contemporary, Berlin

great deal in presenting to the world what an African or Arab contemporary could be. That said and that done, one must now take a stance to ask: what does it mean to put together an "Africa exhibition" or an "Arab exhibition" today, as we see in the New Museum, MMK Frankfurt, BOZAR Brussels, Fondation Louis Vuitton, and many other museums in the West? What does it mean to make geography the subject matter rather than some other conceptual or philosophical discourses of relevance? What about issues of representation if one really wishes to make a geographical exhibition, i.e. how would one represent the fifty-four African countries, thousands of African languages, and communities within such an exhibition? These issues necessitate requestioning and reconsidering.

What prompts this reflection now are the following suspicions: While the "geographical specification-ing" might be well-intentioned, one can't avoid thinking that the occasional presentation of an Africa, Arab, Asia, or similar shows is another, and for that matter, a reinforced act of "Othering." This suspicion is brought about by the fact that institutions tend to content themselves with having done an "Africa show" and therefore do not necessarily need to include other artists of African origin in their regular program. Such "geographical specification-ing" projects then tend to become a compensation for a lack of proper engagement with issues of diversity at the levels of program, personnel and public, and also tend to thrust the "Other" they construct into the "savage slot," as Michel-Rolph Trouillot would put it.[6]

6 Michel-Rolph Trouillot, "Anthropology and the Savage Slot: The Poetics and Politics of Otherness," in *Global Transformations* Palgrave Macmillan, (New York, 2003).

Additionally, there is something about the rhetoric in which such "geographical specification-ing" projects are accommodated. With this I mean the rhetoric of "giving a voice to," "giving space to," "making visible," "taking care of," and "making heard" the African, Asian, Arab, or whomever in question. These phenomena, which could be likened to a paternalization and infantilization strategies, push us to think of Gayatri Chakravorty Spivak's pertinent question, "Can the Sub-altern Speak?" But since Spivak, we have learned that the issue at stake is not whether the subaltern can speak, but rather looking at the twist Seloua Luste Boulbina gave with her question, "Can the non-subaltern hear and read?"[7]

The crucial question is whether these geo-social groups stereotypically put together in such shows, especially in Western museums, actually wish to be given a voice, space, or otherwise? And under whose terms? Don't they already have their spaces and voices? Again, the issue at stake is the agenda behind such rhetoric, and the fact that this rhetoric is indeed an important part in the process of constructing and cultivating "Otherness" within a bubble, i.e. unnecessarily and unwantedly. Which is to say that the exclusive mechanism in relation to such projects marks a difference between a constructed "norm" and the constructed "anomaly," which is the one-off, spaceship-like project that lands and then disappears.

It is equally important to point out the capitalist economic model behind such "geographical specification-ing" projects. The use of slogans, captions, and simplifications is the epitome of neoliberal economic practice. This goes hand in hand with the concept of soft power, wherein

---

7 Seloua Luste Boulbina, "Being Inside and Outside Simultaneously. Exile, Literature, and the Postcolony: On Assia Djebar," *Eurozine*, November 2, 2007, www.eurozine.com/being-inside-and-outside-simultaneously (accessed January 26, 2020).

culture is not only used for political aims, but also suits well as an entry into economic spheres. In the past years, we have heard from philosophers, economists, and politicians that the future of the world as we know it will be determined in Africa. Prompt was the reaction from the cultural sector, with projects like "African Futures," "Africa is the Future," and various sorts of "Afrofuturisms," as tags and labels well packaged for easy sales. It all becomes a commodity. The commodification of the "Other" and "Otherness."

> Where had they learned to converse and to dance? I couldn't converse or dance. Everybody knew something I didn't know. The girls looked so good, the boys so handsome. I would be too terrified to even look at one of those girls, let alone be close to one. To look into her eyes or dance with her would be beyond me. And yet I know that what I saw wasn't as simple and good as it appeared. There was a price to be paid for it all, a general falsity, that could be easily believed, and could be the first step down a dead-end street.
> Charles Bukowski[8]

It is worth taking a few steps back to reflect. Otherness as a phenomenon seems to have always existed in many societies all over, and rendering "Other" as a process is said to be inherent in processes of identity formation of individuals and societies. In Bill Ashcroft, Gareth Griffiths, and Helen Tiffin's *Key Concepts in Post-Colonial Studies* (1998), it is reiterated that: "the existence of others is crucial in defining what is 'normal' and in locating one's own place

8 Charles Bukowski, *Ham on Rye* (Los Angeles, 1982).

in the world."[9] That is to say, for an individual or society to know or define themselves or itself, it needs to define another individual or society with regards to what the former individual or society is not or doesn't wish to be. Often the "Other" then becomes that projection screen for all sorts of unwanted identitarian characteristics. That is then the thin line that separates the mere wish to "Other" in order to find one's own identity, and the othering that is discriminatory and segregational. But if one is the Other, then who is another?

Ashcroft, Griffiths, and Tiffin are fast to point out that it is often an interchangeable position of Other and Othering counterparts, where power probably determines who objectifies at what time. One is tempted to think that "geographical specification-ing" projects are then vehicles through which such power gradients are defined, and through which binaries of norm and anomaly, or self and other are defined. This of course applies to all sections to which majority and minority identities are defined and cultivated in relation to political, economic, and social power and how they come to define race, cultural, gender, and class identities, geographies, geopolitics, and economics.

From a feminist discourse and practice vantage point, Cherríe Moraga pointed out in her essay "La Guera" that "what the oppressor often succeeds in doing is simply externalizing his fears, projecting them into the bodies of women, Asians, gays, disabled folks, whoever seems most 'other.'"[10] Without wanting to equate the "Otherer," i.e. the one enjoying the privilege of making another "Other," with the oppressor, Moraga's argument holds ground with the tendency of the "Otherer" externalizing and projecting

9 Bill Ashcroft et al., *Key Concepts in Post-Colonial Studies* (Abingdon, 1998), p. 6.
10 Cherríe Moraga, "La Guera," in *This Bridge Called My Back*, Cherríe Moraga and Gloria E. Anzaldúa, eds. (London, 1981), p. 27.

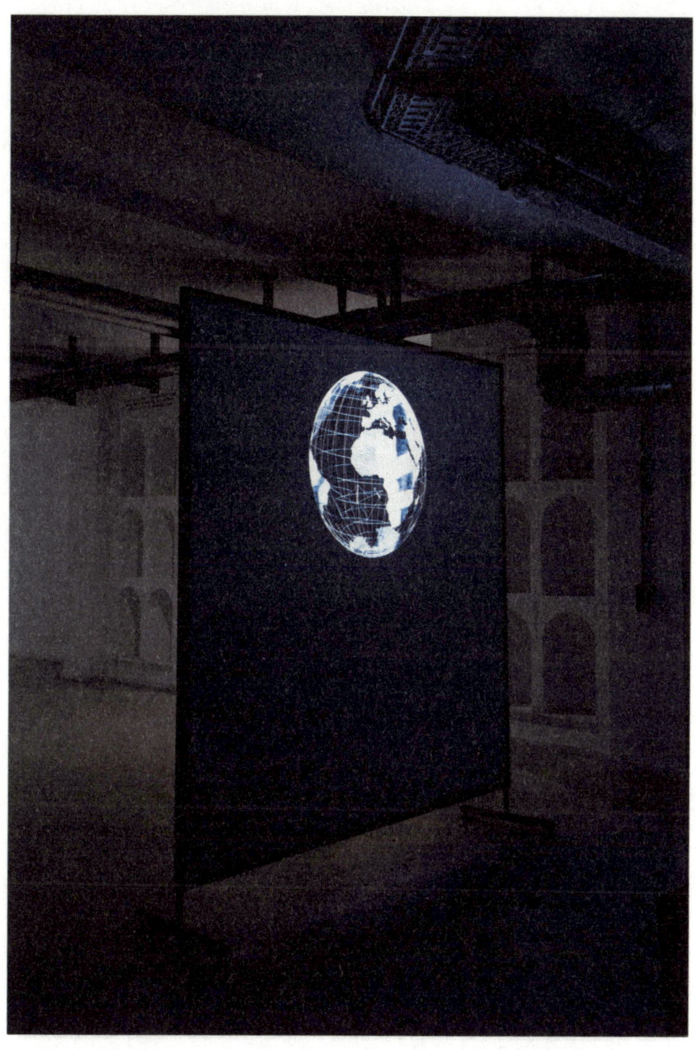

Jackie Karuti, *The planets-chapter*, 2018, installation view, *Geographies of Imagination*, Savvy Contemporary, Berlin

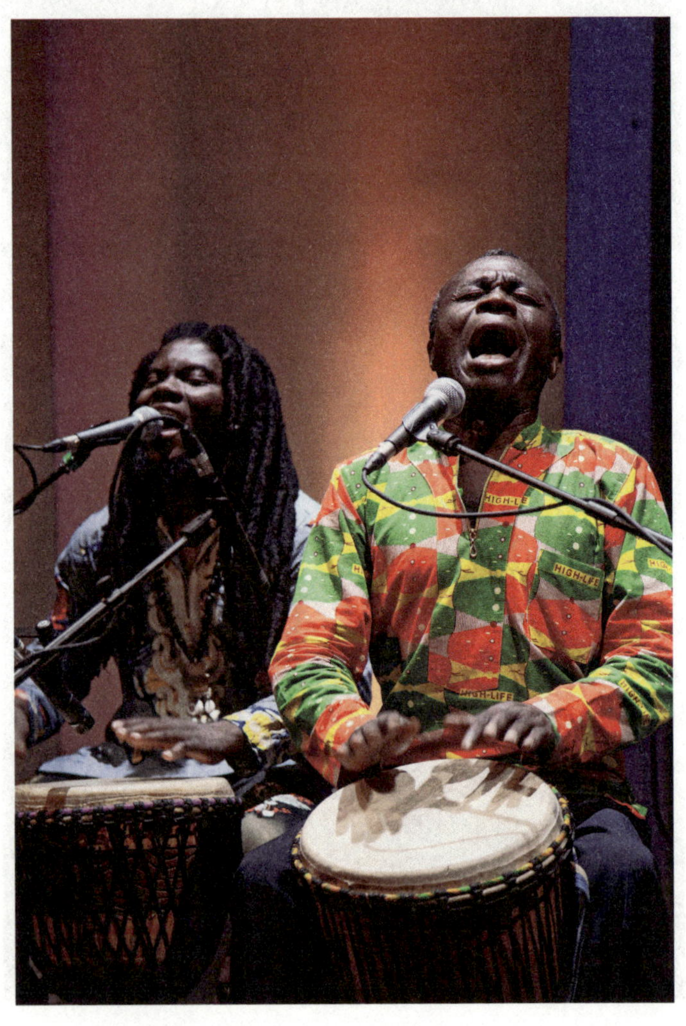

Drummers of Joy perform at the *Dis-Othering as a Method* invocation, Savvy Contemporary, Berlin, 2018

his/her fears on another in the enactment of Othering. Moraga proceeds with an expatiation on the phenomenon:

> But it is not really difference the oppressor fears so much as similarity. He fears he will discover in himself the same aches, the same longings as those of the people he has shitted on. He fears the immobilization threatened by his own incipient guilt. He fears he will have to change his life once he has seen himself in the bodies of the people he has called different. He fears the hatred, anger, and vengeance of those he has hurt.[11]

Taking this into consideration, what could "Dis-Othering" possibly imply?

First, Dis-Othering starts with the recognition of the acts and processes of Othering. With the revelation of the undercurrents that feed, justify, enable, and maintain acts and processes of Othering. It is in and upon this awareness and consciousness of and towards these acts and processes of Othering that one might be able to build resistance and protect oneself both from being Othered and from the urge to Other. Which is to say, it is in this recognition of the mechanism or technology of Othering that a circumventing of the embodiments of both noun and verb, the Othered and Othering, respectively, can be achieved.

Second, Dis-Othering could imply any effort to resist the internalization of those constructs that are said to make one that "Other." The tendency is to see oneself through the prism of the constructor of otherness or the oppressor, which is to say that faced with the violence of continuous belittling or jammed in that space of the savage slot in which one has been thrusted, the psyche of the

11 Ibid.

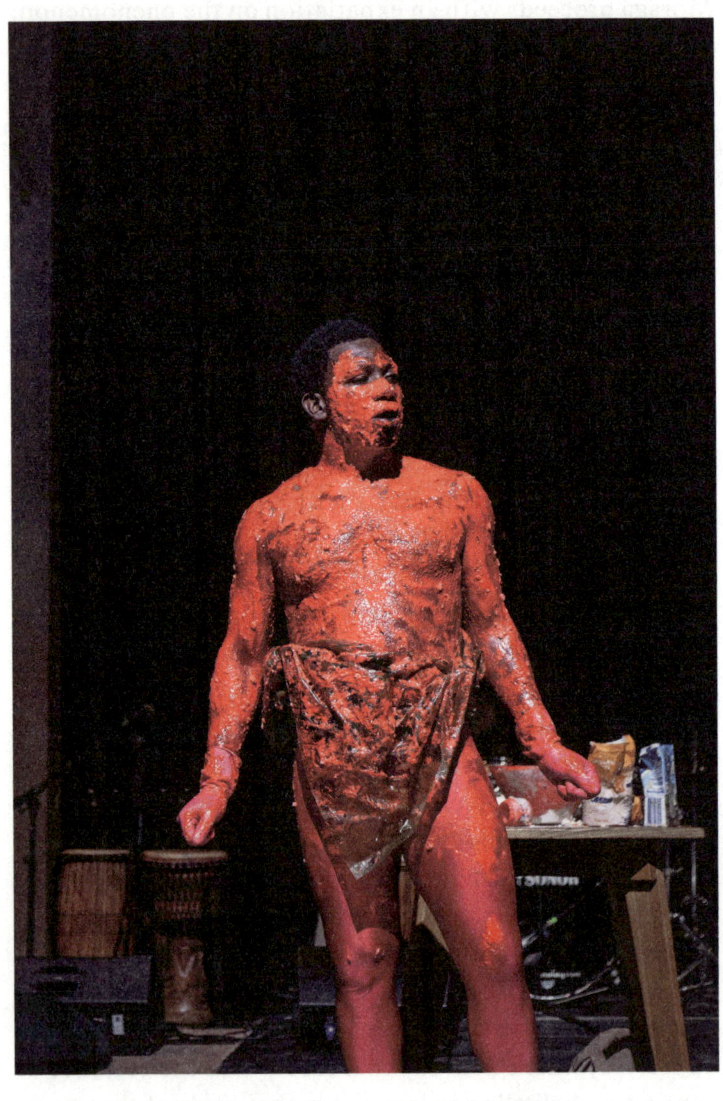

Hector Thami Manekekhla, *My Body is My Politics*, from the *Dis-Othering as a Method* invocation, Savvy Contemporary, Berlin, 2018

"Othered" forces that being to accept an existence within that marginal and liminal space.

Third, in relation to Moraga and complementary to point two, Dis-othering must be a self-made break, a self resistance by the "Otherer" to externalize his/her fears, aches, and longings to being considered a possible recipient. Therefore, with Dis-Othering I wish to propose the phenomenon in which social identity building is not made by projecting on the so-called "Other," but rather a projection towards the self. A self-reflection. A boomerang. That is to say instead of looking for or deflecting one's faults, fantasies, angst on some Other, one could embody them and live them. It is about acknowledging and embodying the plethora of variables that make us be.

Fourth, Dis-Othering has to do with the realization or the putting in practice of what bell hooks calls "The Oppositional Gaze,"[12] which is to say the possibility of interrogating the gaze of the "Otherer," but also the importance of looking back at and against the "Otherer," and looking at one another in that space of the "Othered."

Fifth, Dis-Othering must be a deeply non-capitalist, non-exploitative, and non-profit oriented act, wherein the principle of "what goes round, comes around" reigns. This is to say that if geopolitical, geo-economic, and neo-liberal capitalist economic goals of "profit, come what may" are catalysts to acts and processes of othering, then Dis-Othering must mean a negation and exemption from relations based on such principles.

Sixth, Dis-Othering must mean getting out of the cul-de-sac of power relations as the basis of being in the world. Dis-Othering is a call for an exploration of the cosmic

12 bell hooks, "The Oppositional Gaze," in bell hooks, *Black Looks: Race and Representation* (Boston, 1992).

vastness of the imagination of new futures, identities, ways of being, and ways of living together in the world based on and not despite our differences, but because of the importance and richness of our differences. Dis-Othering is a pledge for a reimagination, as much as a dismantling of cartographies of power, and a reinvention of geographies. Dis-Othering is a recalibration of human and non-human, spacial and social relations independent of the given powers, but based on an interdependency of all—animate and inanimate—that co-habit this world.

Seventh, Dis-Othering is the practicing of what Sara Ahmed calls the "feminist killjoy,"[13] which is the act of resisting the joy or taking part in the joy of laughing at or mocking or belittling or denigrating or othering someone. A refusal to accept the comfort of societal status quos in relation to misogyny, patriarchy, racism, classism, and genderism. Dis-Othering will have to mean speaking up, pointing out, calling out inequities, as much as proposing alternative ways of being in and perceiving a world of justice and justness.

This essay first appeared in a publication project under the auspices of *Dis-Othering as a Method, Leh Zo, A Me Ke Nde Za*, a collaborative project between BOZAR—Centre for Fine Arts, Brussels; Kulturen in Bewegung, Vienna, and SAVVY Contemporary, Berlin, on the necessary deconstruction of "Othering" practices in European cultural institutions.

13　See Sara Ahmet, *Living a Feminist Life* (Durham, 2017).

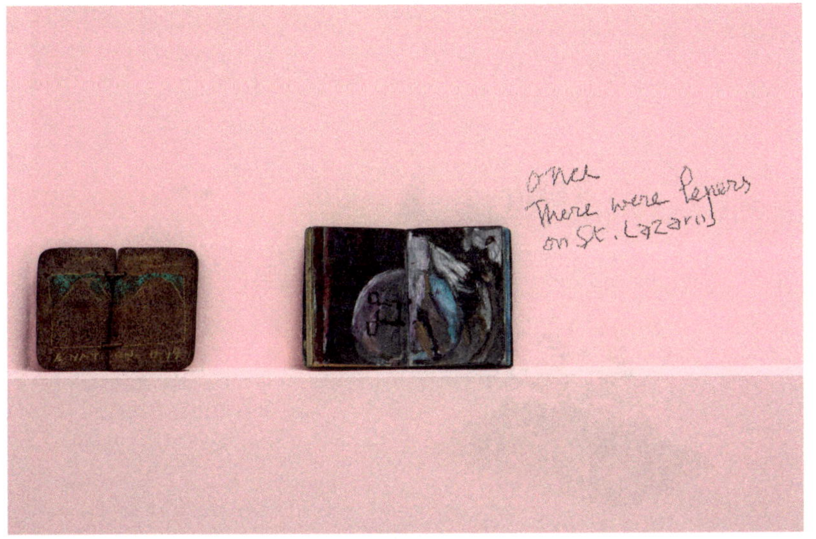

Here and next page, installation views of works by Anna Boghiguian in *Positions 2*,
Van Abbemuseum Eindhoven

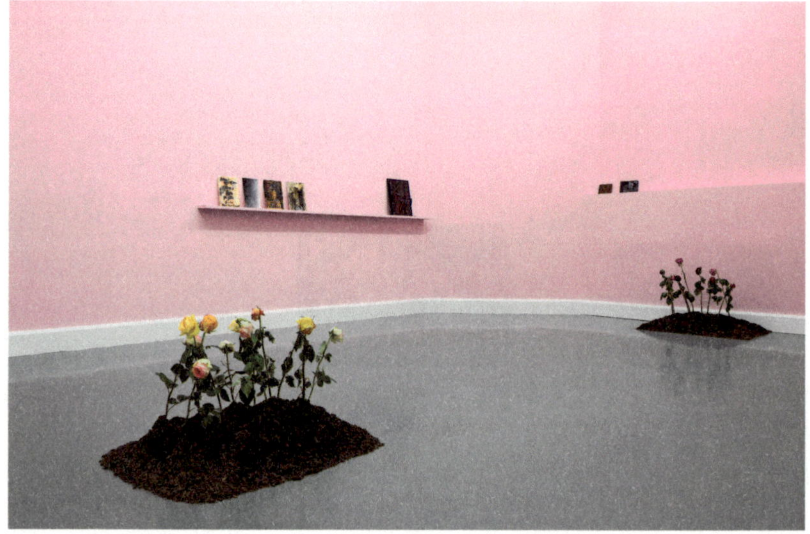

The Demodern Option

Charles Esche
interviewed by Nina Siegal

Charles Esche has been the director of the Van Abbemuseum in Eindhoven, the Netherlands, since 2004.[1] One of the first public contemporary art museums to be established in Europe in 1936, the Van Abbemuseum, with a permanent collection of about 2,700 works, has become known as a venue for "experimental approaches," as Esche puts it. A proponent of a "demodernization" of muscums and art institutions particularly in the Global North, Esche actively looks for ways to disrupt the received canon of art history and recast collections to create new paradigms and narratives that are better fit for the purpose in the twenty-first century.

How do you define "planetary" and how might a museum, especially one based on colonialism and existing within the Eurocentric art system, have a planetary outlook?
I can understand the term better through art theorist Brian Holmes's analysis of the different registers that any museum has to address to be relevant or interesting. He outlines a spectrum from the personal to the planetary through the local, regional, national, and international. Any activity should try to include all of them. The personal interaction with an artwork should have the potential to reach all the way to the planetary in terms of thinking about its significance, it as part

1 Esche also teaches at Central St. Martins University in London and Jan van Eyck Academie in Maastricht, works as Co-editorial Director of *Afterall* Books and *Afterall* Journal, and curated the 2014 Sao Paulo Biennale, the fifth U3 triennial, Ljubljana, 2010; the second and third Riwaq Biennales, Ramallah, Palestine, and many other exhibitions and biennials.

of a connected discussion, and understanding how it affects who you are and what you can do. If we focus on the planetary, it's therefore immediately important not to isolate it from those other levels but to understand their interdependence.

Have you orchestrated exhibitions or events that did this?

We just did an exhibition with The Otolith Group, and one of the works, *Who Does the Earth Think It Is?*, documented people who are sensitive to the earth's movements and believe they can predict earthquakes. What this suggests to me once again is that the earth is not just an inert vessel for human life to exploit, but has its own rhythms and necessities that humans ignore at their peril. If the earth is a living material with an independent logic, it will most likely defeat human rationality and especially the divided forms of knowledge that constitute European-based modernity. How do the global, the worldly, the earthly compare to this thing we are calling the planetary and do they have any place at all in the modern mindset? That for me is a big question because it touches on part of my core learned identity as a White European man working in the Netherlands. What is the value of our traditions and customary beliefs? In terms of exhibitions, that brings me to *The Making of Modern Art* by the Museum of American Art Berlin[2] here in the Van Abbe, which tries to take some distance from the modern art paradigm. This presentation of the museum's collection is crucial to me in terms of how Western Europeans might embrace something like the planetary. It ends with an attempt to

2 From its website: "The Museum of American Art in Berlin is an educational institution dedicated to assembling, preserving and exhibiting memories on the MoMA International Program and its Circulating Exhibitions." See http://museum-of-american-art.org (accessed February 21, 2020).

step outside the west by displaying modern artworks as they might be shown on Thomas More's *Utopia*—the island that a Western writer invented to get away from himself and his world. The promise of the planetary seems to me to suggest a move away from the brutality of economic globalization and free market exploitation. We need terms to refer to other experiences of our place as humans in the universe and not only as masters of the world. Once established, the information at the planetary has to be filtered down to the international in terms of agreements, to the national in terms of policy, and then down through the local to the personal in the way that we make consumer choices about the kinds of food we eat or the kinds of protests we join. Art often initially speaks to that personal or even imaginative level, which then needs to find its way up through those registers again.

What can a museum do to facilitate this process?

I am convinced that we are at a moment just before a major transformation. This is a period of stagnation, intellectually, militarily, politically, and it's one of the less innovative periods of our history. That has been true since 1989 and the effective end of the ideological struggles of the twentieth century. At that point a single sociopolitical dogma, a hyper-modern scientific capitalism and the end of the historical drive toward human emancipation, were all enacted at once. As we reach the end of this period, there comes a real desire for a different kind of planetary settlement, something that we see in the climate protests, in the turn to decoloniality but also in the hardening of religious attitudes or the narrow Anglo-exceptionalism of Johnson or Trump.

Seen in this way, the nature of the transformation to come is not yet clear and is still being disputed. I would like the Van Abbemuseum to be a place where people come to experience those paradoxes and contradictions and to be able to make their own minds up about it. The history of museums demonstrates that they have a crucial role in building modern subjectivity and national consciousness, so there is a reason to think they can be part of changing those definitions and embracing a different sense of the self, the other and the planet. While I am on the side of decoloniality and degrowth, I don't think it's a cost-free option. Personally, I would like to see a transition away from modernity as a horizon of growth, resource extraction, and White supremacy, but that also means reinterpreting or letting go of beloved aspects of modernity like its foundations in the French Revolution; its emancipatory drive; its technological advances; its communist heritage. But as a museum director, I think it's my responsibility to show what's possible and to try to connect people to the discourses that matter for our collective future.

How?

Part of the shift needs to be away from the visual as the primary artistic and cognitive sense toward multisensorial experiences. This challenges the visuality of visual art. I would say it also needs to move away from the universal, modern singularities toward pluri-epistemological and pluriversal understandings of the way the world is put together, the value of human expression and long-form histories. This includes multiplying the subjectives that can speak and the belief systems that are presented as "common sense." This is something I would call the *demodern*, as a subset of decoloniality. The task of the museum is to introduce these ideas without alienating people who have invested so much of themselves in modernity and coloniality. It's not the easiest task, but I sometimes liken it to a bridge where we museum workers do not run over to the other side, but stay on the bridge and try to keep both sides of the river connected and in dialogue with each other. Eventually, it will become obvious which side we need to move toward, but we are not there yet. This in-between state is one of which modernity is rather dismissive. The modern drive is to specialize and focus on difference and clarity rather than sameness and ambivalence. This tendency cuts off the registers of dialogue that support thinking about the planetary, the general, and the inclusive in favor of the particular and the specific. Look how both you and I gesture with our hands to talk about the planetary: we draw circles; we bring things together rather than separating, cutting, and dividing in the modern manner.

This makes me think of the Louvre Abu Dhabi, because it brings together artifacts and art from various cultures and exhibits them together as a single human history. That seems to be an example of a planetary museum, although it is more often described with the word "universal."

There's a discussion in the International Council of Museums about the redefinition of "museum," and the proposal is for museums to encourage the collections to speak with multiple voices; polyphonic and inclusive. One French scholar refused this definition and said the Louvre could never be polyphonic. But why couldn't it? It has access to collections from all over the world and to knowledge from wherever it wants. What was interesting for me in Abu Dhabi was that the Louvre there seemed far more open to non-Western objects and comparative cultural analysis than its mother ship in Paris. It was much less defensive about the assumed superiority of the Western art tradition flowing from Athens. While you can question Abu Dhabi's smooth inclusivity in its divided setting, I think it's a step forward that the native French scholars are still resisting.

Perhaps this is because it was founded as a French museum. The Louvre is weighted with a history of colonization and the collections are presented in connection to the objects' value to the French. In order to change things in the way you're describing you'd have to erase that narrative.

But isn't that erasure precisely the decolonial move? What you've described is one way to decolonize and that's what we need to do. If you say that the Louvre can only tell that story, if it's so stuck in its own narrative that it has to live or die defending it, then the only thing to do with the Louvre is to abandon it. I don't believe that's necessary. I think the Louvre can be relevant again. Look at its origins in revolutionary France, it wrote European history then and it could do so once more.

The other option would be to build a new one in a desert and start over.

That's one answer. Sometimes the process of decolonization is to move the center of attention away from Europe and to share the collections that are locked up in the old imperial heartlands. I do think it would make sense to move part of the Van Abbemuseum's collection to Yogyakarta for instance, though I would never be able to. Still, we work with the collection to try to demodernize without fully knowing what that looks like. The modern is our own tradition, which has also hugely affected the world through colonialism. We need to understand that but also raise it as a question for the present, indeed for the planetary. A friend of mine talks about how we need to humble modernity and to put it in its place. Part of demodernization here is on show in *The Making of Modern Art,* which constructs the origins of the story around Pope Julius II, Alexander Dorner, and Alfred Barr, among others. It puts the modern art museum into its own time, which is no longer "our" time today. That doesn't mean the collections are worthless; on the contrary, they are the perfect tools to allow people to perceive the intellectual and concrete transformations that are happening. They just need to be handled differently whether that's here in Van Abbemuseum, but also, as you say, displaced to Abu Dhabi or Yogyakarta.

How do you demodernize or decolonize your museum?

We look at how the classification of what art is becomes part of the process of establishing modernism and modernity as positive values. We try to at least put a foot outside the modern paradigm and look at it from some kind of outside—the *Utopia* moment, if you like. We can do this because we are "postmodern," in a meaningful sense. We can observe and reassess what was modernity and give it a more modest, appropriate place in our histories. In concrete terms, it means borrowing a lot more from other types of museums, from ethnography museums or history museums; finding works that have not been identified as "art" and showing them alongside a Mondrian or a Picasso; it means bringing in other senses to the exhibition beyond the visual; it means placing the modern into long-form intellectual and aesthetic histories through borrowing a Frans Hals or a death dance mask from Sumatra.

So it's a longer process of questioning how museums have presented art.

It's happening a lot, particularly in ethnographic museums, where I often see more consistent efforts at museum reformation happening now. It's a process of trying to reform our identities and address a changed society that surrounds the museums in European cities in order to see if these public institutions can be reclaimed and repurposed. Some art museums, like Reina Sofia in Madrid, Moderna Galerija in Ljubljana, or MSN in Warsaw, are all busy with this alongside us. Any change is going to mean telling a different story that's less familiar. But I hope we can do it by taking a visitor from the known to the unknown in a way that

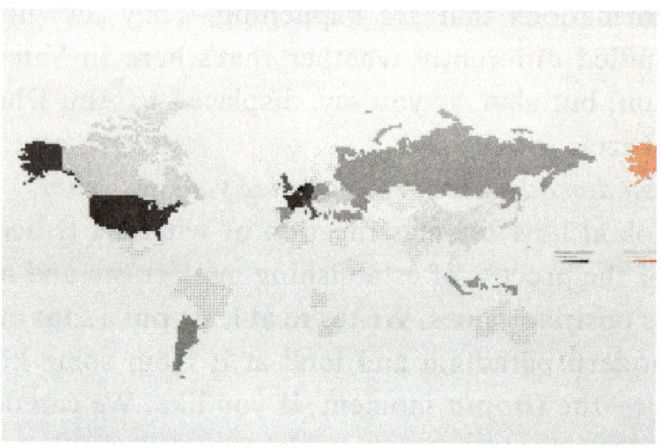

Museumindex, the museum in figures, installation view. The birthplaces of artists in the collection appear in gray; those of people living in Eindhoven in red.

is almost unnoticed, so that you end up in a different place almost without realizing it. The root of your question is one reason why the current collection exhibition is up for three and a half years. We hope people will have the time to come to terms with what it might offer them over a period of time—I always like the German word *Vergangenheitsbewältigung* (coping with the past). We need that again, but such coming to terms needs patience as well.

Are there other examples of how Van Abbemuseum has explored its own relationship to colonialism and global/planetary concerns?

It's in the origins of the museum, which is built from the colonial profits of a cigar factory. This is a story we always want to tell in one from or another in the museum.[3] In another vein, we have two world maps painted onto

3 Henri Jacob van Abbe was a Dutch tobacco industrialist and cigar manufacturer as well as an art collector; his collection was the original cornerstone of the museum. In 2017–18, Van Abbemuseum fellow Michael Karabinos mapped the path of tobacco (van Abbe's "Karel 1" brand) from Sumatra and Java to Eindhoven during the final years of Dutch colonization of Indonesia.

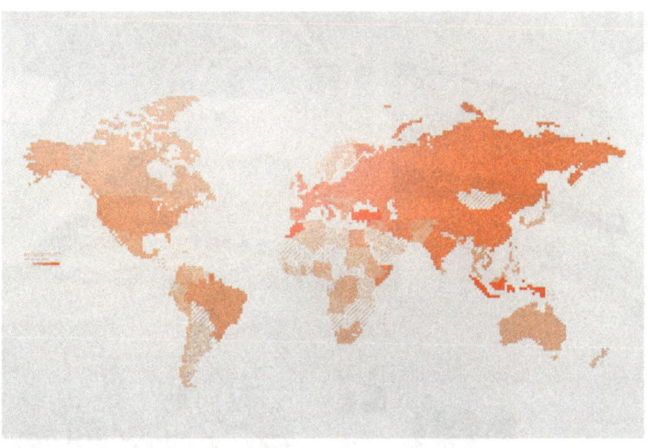

the walls of the entrance to the collection displays. One represents the birthplace of artists in the collection, and another the birthplaces of the people living in Eindhoven. If you look at those maps you see a provincial European collection in an international city, because the diversity is greater in the inhabitants than it is in the collection. But the story of the museum is usually of an international institution in a provincial place. The maps give us a basis for thinking, how do we reflect or mirror better the place we are in? We work more with artists who are linked to Turkey, North Africa, or the Caribbean—people like Ahmet Öğüt, Gülsün Karamustafa, Anna Boghiguian, Quinsy Gario, or Iris Kensmil. We also work much more with artists from Indonesia because of the colonial legacy. So it's a planetary response based on local conditions.

In a way, the maps point to the museum's focus on social experiences.

A while ago I noticed that, almost by accident, we have turned a number of formerly white cube exhibition spaces into places where people can meet each other. If you were to visit our museum, you'd find that it's a place with more tables and chairs and less classical exhibition space, which shifts the nature of the encounters you can have. You make

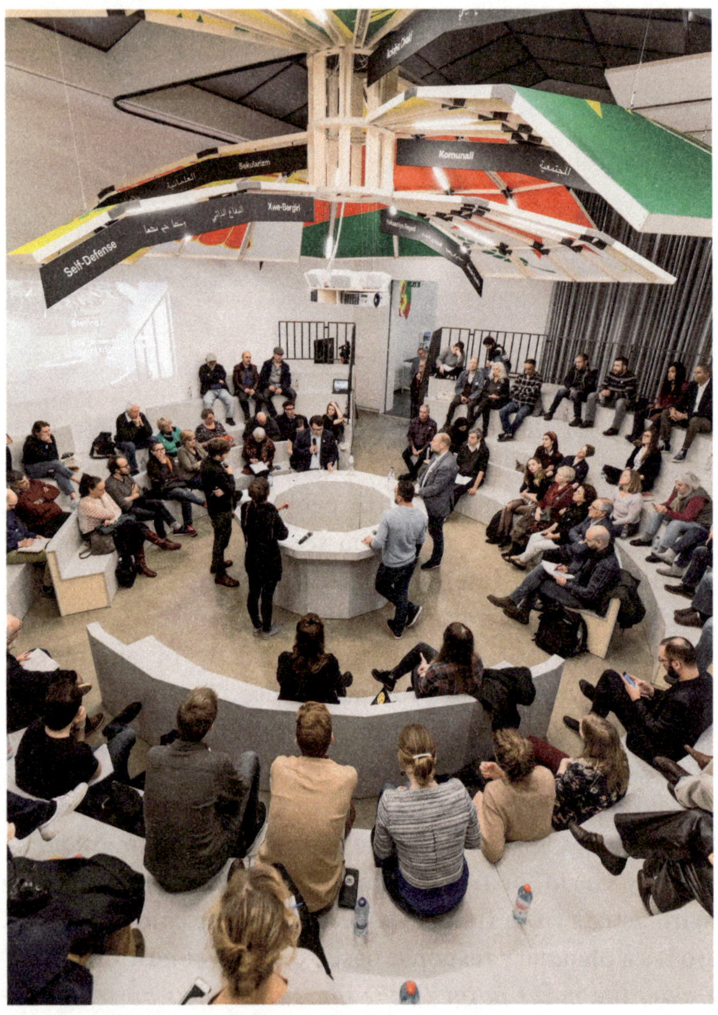

The Netherlands as Stateless Democracy, November 11, 2018, a gathering in the context of the exhibition *Museum as Parliament: The People's Parliament in the Van Abbemuseum, The Democratic Self-administration of Rojava and Studio Jonas Staal*, 2018–2020, Van Abbemuseum, Eindhoven, The Netherlands. Shown here: *Proposition I: The municipality must acquire more power than the state*. With Kenan Testan (Demned); Rutger Groot Wassink (GroenLinks Amsterdam); Murat Memis (SP Eindhoven); Serda Demir (New Democratic Youth, YDG).

more connections when you sit down at a table with someone than when you're shuffling from room to room, looking at art.

Was that a conscious or an organic decision?

It's been evolving. In 2014, for example, we built a parliament in the museum. It was an architectural model of the People's Parliament of Rojava, a project of the Democratic Self-Administration in Rojava, Northern Syria, designed in collaboration with the artist Jonas Staal, who is from Rotterdam, and his New World Summit team. It became another example of a meeting place in the museum. We also organized meetings at this parliament with the Kurdish community or different independence or resistance movements from the Philippines to Chiapas in South America, who are based in the Netherlands. We brought them into a kind of parliament—a form they can appreciate—whereas the white cube was not really a form they can deal with. Now it's one of the most popular rooms in the whole institution.

Is the goal to place the modern museum into a constant state of questioning?

The provisional goal is to humble modernity and demodernize our collection. That's step one. Steps two and three involve what we talked about for the Louvre Abu Dhabi, leaving our stories to be told by other people. Ultimately, it's about listening instead of speaking and most importantly listening to the voices of those who rarely get a chance to speak in our Western world, to voices that are not modern, as Europe and the Anglosphere have defined it. There are systems of knowledge—both human and nonhuman, divine and animal—that are not modern. And I think we need to listen to those systems very attentively if there is to be some kind of livable future.

Case Study: Residência Belojardim,* Brazil

Chloe Stead

Thought to have begun 500 years ago when European noble courts began sending artists abroad to learn new skills, the artist residency as we now recognize it took off in the nineteen-nineties as a result of the increasing ease and affordability of international travel. While the sheer number and heteronomy of these programs makes it difficult, if not impossible, to settle on a definition of a "conventional" residency,[1] artist residencies have clearly come to play a vital role in the careers of young artists in an increasingly precarious and professionalized art world.

As Alexandra Uedl points out in an essay on the history of the International Residency Program of the Austrian Federal Chancellery, the ubiquity of residencies has created a "cycle" where, as visiting an artist residency becomes "'good form' for an artist's CV" that is awarded through more professional opportunities gained by networking, those who do not leave their home base see opportunities reduce at home because "exhibitions tend to show works of

* This artists' residency, in English Belo Jardim, was presented by Cristiana Tejo in the conference Global Academy II 2018 of the Salzburg International Summer Academy in Salzburg in the Pecha Kucha section, https://www.summeracademy.at/wp-content/uploads/2018/08/180724_ISBK_Pecha-Kucha.pdf (accessed March 13, 2020)

1 ResArtists, an online worldwide network of artists residencies, sums it up in its "About Residencies" section: "Artist residencies can be a part of museums, universities, galleries, studio spaces, theaters, artist-run spaces, municipalities, governmental offices, and even festivals. They can be seasonal, ongoing, or tied to a particular event. They exist in urban spaces, rural villages, and deep in nature. Hundreds of such opportunities and organizations exist throughout the world."

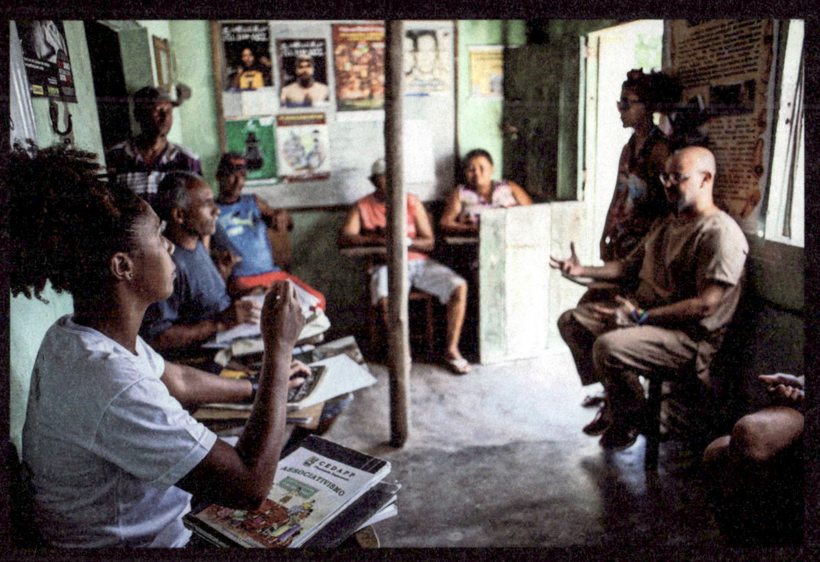

Group discussion at Residency 2018, Belo Jardim, Brazil

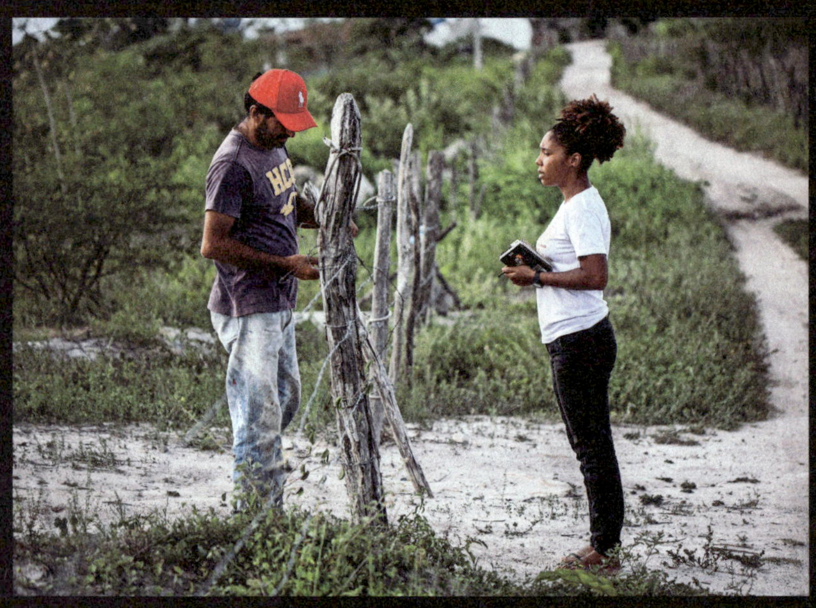

Residency 2018, Belo Jardim, Brazil

artists who already received acclaim abroad."[2] This Catch-22—a trend that also sees artist residencies stand in for, according to the critic Sky Goodden, "the studios we can't afford and the buildings we get evicted from"[3]—has arguably resulted in a situation in which many artists complete back-to-back residencies. As Goodden humorously puts it, some spend half their current residency writing the application for the next.[4]

Beyond the potential negative effects of this forced nomadic existence on artists, a culture of residency-hopping can weaken their ability to engage meaningfully in the location they've been invited to, which at worst can lead to exoticizing the very place and people that the artist is supposed to be engaging with. Rather than addressing this exoticism, many residencies lean into it, advertising locational attributes in a tone that differs only marginally from that of the country's tourism board.[5]

Described by its curators as an "experimental residency and education program," Residência Belojardim is an attempt to create a residency that diverges from these patterns. Each year it invites one artist to stay in Belo Jardim, a Brazilian municipality in the northeastern state of Pernambuco, for one to four months[6] to work on a

2 Alexandra Uedl, "The History of the International Residency Programme of the Austrian Federal Chancellery," in *Away: The Book about Residencies* (Vienna, 2018), p. 28.
3 Quote taken from, "Episode 2: The Artist Residency," in *Momus: The Podcast,* December 2017.
4 Ibid.
5 For more on the connection between contemporary art events and tourism, see *Tourists Like Us: Critical Tourism and Contemporary Art Events*, Frederica Martini and Vytautas Michelkevičius, eds. (PDF, 2013).
6 Although intended as a two-month residency coinciding with *Festas Juninas,* a popular festival celebrating the nativity of John the Baptist, the curators take into account artists' availability and production needs when setting each residency's date and duration.

community-based project. Located 182 kilometers inland from its cosmopolitan state capital Recife, from the outset Belo Jardim is an unusual position for a residency in Brazil. These are normally concentrated in coastal cities, in which most of the country's wealth has historically been located. Belo Jardim is also relatively small city by Brazilian standards—74,000 inhabitants in a country of more than 200 million—and has neither an art center nor a cinema. Unlike the vast majority of contemporary art residencies aimed at professional artists, both in Brazil and abroad, Residência Belojardim isn't attached to a museum, gallery, biennale, or otherwise existing contemporary art project—but was initiated by Moura Batteries, one of the largest battery suppliers in South America. Established in 1957 in Belo Jardim, the birthplace of its three founders, the Moura headquarters continues to be one of the city's primary employers; the company's cultural wing, Instituto Conceição Moura, is its biggest supporter of the arts.

Residência Belojardim is the institute's first foray into contemporary art patronage—in the past it has mainly sponsored music and film events—which came from the wish to increase access to contemporary art in the area. "This is a context where there are no contemporary art institutions at all,"[7] explains Kiki Mazzucchelli, who, along with Cristiana Tejo, has been running the program since its inception in 2016. Instead, music and folk art, known in Brazil as Arte Popular, dominates residents' cultural lives. "Belo Jardim has a very powerful music tradition," adds Tejo. "Bands, orchestras … everything centers around sound in the city." Similarly, there's a long and rich tradition of folk art in Belo Jardim and its neighboring cities,

7 Quotes from Kiki Mazzucchelli and Cristiana Tejo taken from Skype and email conversations, July–September 2019.

with many of the greatest Brazilian Arte Popular masters hailing from Pernambuco.

For the curators, who have a combined total of twenty-five years of national and international curatorial activity with a focus on Latin American artists, the invitation to work in Belo Jardim offered an opportunity to continue the conversation about the intersections between Arte Popular and contemporary art that they'd been interested in throughout their careers, "not from the outside," according to Mazzucchelli, "but from within." Yet the local context threw up a number of questions. What's the value in doing a contemporary art project in a place lacking contemporary art? And, more importantly, how can art be introduced in a way that doesn't promote the colonial attitude that positions artists and art professionals as "saviors" of a supposedly naïve and uneducated populace?

It's an issue that, when thinking about Belo Jardim, goes beyond the contemporary/folk art dichotomy. Northeastern Brazil is still considered economically and culturally less developed than the South, which most readily embraced post-World War II economic and industrial expansion. For a residency or educational program to avoid replicating what Tejo and Mazzucchelli refer to as the "complex cultural construct" of the northeast region developed by their southern compatriots, it would be necessary to develop a program that would take the city's local context as its starting point.

In doing so, they took inspiration from the "museum school" that the Brazilian architect Lina Bo Bardi established in the nineteen-sixties after she moved to Salvador in the northern Brazilian state of Bahia, and became the director of the Bahian Museum of Modern Art. At the time, "Brazil was in the middle of this wave of industrialization,"

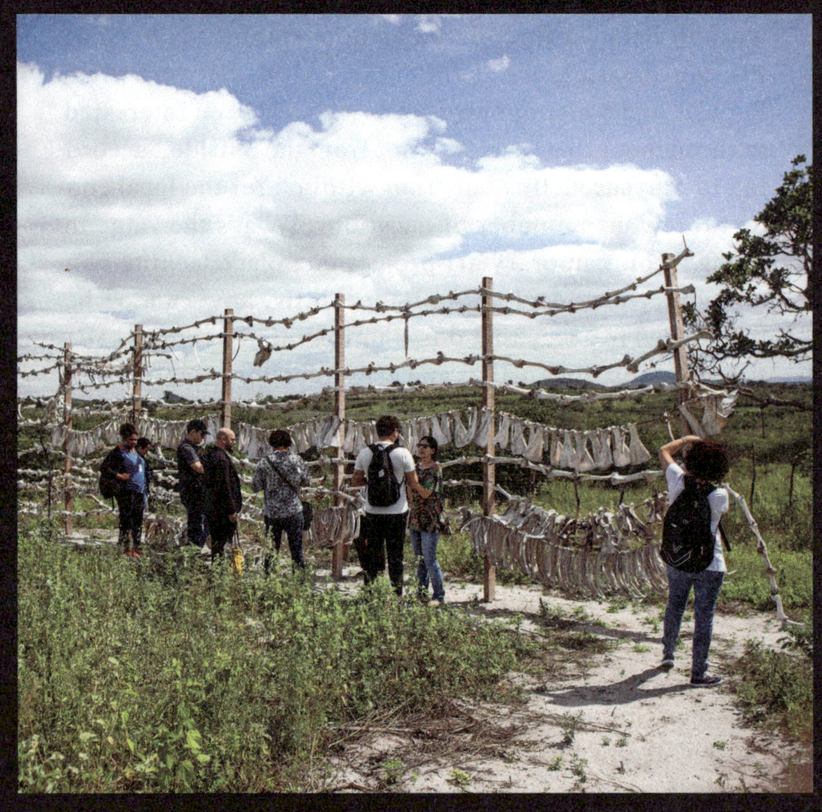

Fence with bones, outdoor installation, Residency 2018, Belo Jardim, Brazil

explains Mazzucchelli. "Bardi's idea was that industrialization should take Arte Popular production as a paradigm. [She realized that] you didn't simply have to copy Western models, but [that it was possible to] create your own model from what's there."

When refurbishing the colonial-era building, Bo Bardi didn't use the accepted industrial methods and processes of the day but instead looked to local knowledge. To create the spiral staircase in one of the museum's central exhibition spaces, for example, she adopted a carpentry method used by regional farmers to build ox carts. This philosophy went beyond the design of the building and into the museum school's programming. By inserting art courses, including a School of Industrial Design, into the museum, Bo Bardi's proposal radically flattened the usual hierarchies between fine art and craft.

Apart from this historical example, the curators struggled to find operational models that they could use as the basis of their residency. If anything, Residência Belojardim's structure came out of what they *didn't* want it to be, to avoid repeating the patterns of existing contemporary art residencies around the world, which often privilege networking above engagement. Having previously run a residency program in Recife, Tejo was particularly sensitive to what can happen when artists and art professionals spend only a short time in a locality before moving on. "I hosted a lot of curators—Documenta curators, biennale curators," she says, "and it was my personal experience that [their engagement with the city] was mostly superficial. They could be in Northeast Brazil or China; it was always this exotic view."

This tendency speaks not only to a colonial viewpoint but also what curator Daniel Baumann termed "a culture of hectic residency hopping."[8] As residencies become as ubiquitous as art fairs and biennales, some, like the Independent Study Program at Whitney Museum of American Art (ISP), have become "certifiable gold stars on an artist's CV,"[9] on the same level as being exhibited at a respected institution or gallery. Attending residencies has become either a status symbol or a novelty—an artist might not get into the prestigious Skowhegan School of Painting and Sculpture for nine summer weeks, but could do a residency in a cargo ship or a tree house in the Scottish Highlands.

Identifying that an important aspect to this lack of meaningful engagement was the limited temporal scale of these projects (usually because of precarious funding models) the curators developed a framework that splits the residency's overall duration, ten years, into yearlong "editions"; a flexible approach that allows each edition to build upon lessons learned during the previous one. Although the project's trajectory is by design not yet fixed, the ultimate goal is for it to become self-sustaining. "The main venue that we use in the city is an old factory," explains Mazzucchelli. While the space is only used during the residencies as studio space and an exhibition venue, the curators are looking for outside funding (current funding can legally only cover events) with the aim of turning the building into a cultural center run by local people.

One criticism of the residency thus far is that there is as yet no formal method for obtaining feedback from locals (the curators, who don't live in the area full time,

---

8　Daniel Baumann, "Taken for Granted: Why bother with art prizes or residencies?" in *Frieze* (October 2016).

9　Casey Lesser, "11 of the World's Most Unusual Residencies," in *Artsy*, May 23, 2016, www.artsy.net/article/artsy-editorial-11-of-the-world-s-most-unusual-artist-residencies (accessed February 1, 2020).

obtain their information through the team of city-based educators and producers), which makes it difficult to measure success, especially in a community-based project where usual measures such as ticket sales and positive press do not apply. It is worth noting, however, that in conversation the institute's director, Mariana Moura, floated the idea of introducing more formalized feedback sessions for the third edition. Tejo likens the approach to skimming stones in a river. Working from the first ring outward, the curators add more possibilities each time, in an attempt to circumnavigate colonial hierarchies. For the first two editions, Residência Belojardim hosted Marcelo Silveira and Carlos Mélo, two Brazilian artists living in Recife. They were invited because of their history of community-focused projects and their prior connections to Belo Jardim, using what the curators have called a "Trojan horse strategy." The artists' knowledge of the area as well as their established links with local artists working within the Arte Popular tradition allowed the curators—who had never been to Belo Jardim before their appointment—to gain deeper access to the city.

The third edition features an artist from outside the region for the first time. As with Silveira and Mélo, artist Camila Sposati has proposed a collaborative project with materials and techniques commonly used in Arte Popular practices, in this case ceramics. She will work with local artists in groups to make instruments. It's not the only change Tejo and Mazzucchelli have instigated. Responding to informal feedback from locals who sometimes felt sidelined during the production process, the duo decided to formalize the residency's educational aims by creating an events-based program, featuring discussions, seminars, screenings, and workshops. These deemphasize the notion of a centralized project and create a more collaborative atmosphere.

As a residency that takes place in the Global South, Residência Belojardim is an intriguing case study for others interested in developing a program that is collaborative without replicating existing colonial models. While its admirably long duration and lack of formal evaluation makes it difficult at this stage to measure long-term effects, it is an attempt to refocus the residency away from an artist's career and back onto a relation to place.

By not celebrating international exchange as an end, the choice to invite Brazilian artists who are already sensitive to the context and history of northeast Brazil and a readiness to continue to tweak the selection process and residency through criticism and feedback, could result in a more meaningful relationship with local people and their needs. Time is a factor here, but so is the dedication of the funder, Instituto Conceição Moura, who rather than expecting a return on their investment in the form of international exposure is content to watch the program slowly take root in the city in which it was founded.

Imperial Hangover

A conversation between
Roger M. Buergel and Peter Osborne

Roger M. Buergel is the founding director of the Johann Jacobs Museum in Zurich, an institution that explores "the cultural residue of global trade routes." He was the artistic director of Documenta 12 (2007). Peter Osborne is Professor of Modern European Philosophy and Director of the Centre for Research in Modern European Philosophy at Kingston University London, and is widely known for his research and writing on conceptual art and its intersections with philosophy. In this conversation, they discuss disjunctive temporality, historicism, and the contradictions of transculturality.

Roger M. Buergel: *You have remarked that, for all its emphasis on the novelties of globalization (or perhaps rather precisely because of it), the historical consciousness of the current art world is still largely an extension of that of the nineteenth century. This is a good starting point for our conversation about planetary matters. Historical collections in both encyclopaedic and ethnographic museums pose grave challenges today, but they also offer more clues to a proper understanding of "the now" than a contemporary art that gets shown solely on its own terms. With respect to Documenta, for example, it is no accident that the exhibition format—which calls itself a "museum of 100 days"—adopted a strategic historicism from Documenta X (1997) onwards. Although the biennale-type exhibition has received some critical appraisal, there is a certain amount of amnesia when it comes to the empty shell it inhabits: the nineteenth-century world exhibition and its representational regimes.*

Peter Osborne: For me, it is the effect of globalization, or "planetarization," on our understanding of history that is the crux here. Today's planetary condition (post-"1989") is the result of a geopolitical extension ("globalization") of the core social processes of capitalist modernity. But once a certain systematicity took hold at the level of the whole—what we might call the "social planet"—this quantitative expansion produced a *qualitative* difference in the spatio-temporal dynamics of the social and economic relations involved. First and foremost it introduced a new historical temporality of "con-temporaneity"—an articulated set of disjunctive synchronizations of multiple differential social times—complicating the internal structure of the classically modern (Euro–North American) "developmental" time of the new. This rhythm of the "the new," from which "the now" still derives its frisson, is the distilled abstraction of the temporality of capital accumulation, the cultural generalization of which we know as "modernity" (*Neuzeit*); and the affirmation of which we know as "modernism"—Adorno's "aesthetic seal of expanded reproduction" (Marx's technical term for the process of accumulation). Contemporary art, we might say, is *the aesthetic seal of disjunctive synchronization,* the disjunctive synchronization of multiple differential social times.

As you say, the way the art world deals with this new complexity is to compartmentalize these two temporalities, the modern and the contemporary—the tense and deeply contradictory unity of which makes up our present—into two different institutional spaces, governed by two different sets of ideas. These are, first, the temporal continuity of a naturalized "progressive" conception of history (institutionalized in the nineteenth-century museum) and, second, the conjunctural punctuality of a debased understanding of the contemporary as the "now-ness" of the latest things ("contemporary art" as an exhibitionary and sales category). You and I both want to break down the walls of these institutional and ideological compartments, the separation of which prohibits a proper understanding of both history and the present, but we approach them from opposite sides. You, by introducing new, contemporizing curatorial strategies into historically museological spaces; myself, by rethinking "contemporaneity" as a *historical* form of time, which weaves together a multiplicity of different sociohistorical times, exploding the nineteenth-century myth of history as a single developmental path. This allows us, once again, to comprehend the present as history, but in new, more constructed ways, which require a new, as yet unformulated concept of politics.

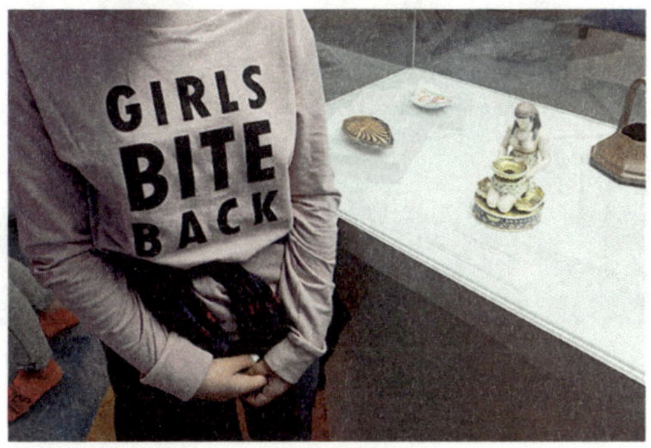

Hamburg student visiting *Mobile Worlds* at Museum für Kunst und Gewerbe, Hamburg

You're right in thinking that for me, the way forward lies in tackling historical collections and reassembling them, interspersed with contemporary works, into exhibitions meant for wider and more diverse audiences. This curatorial practice fits with what you call the "postconceptual condition" of contemporary art. If successful, it would create public institutions that are not indifferent to society (churning out

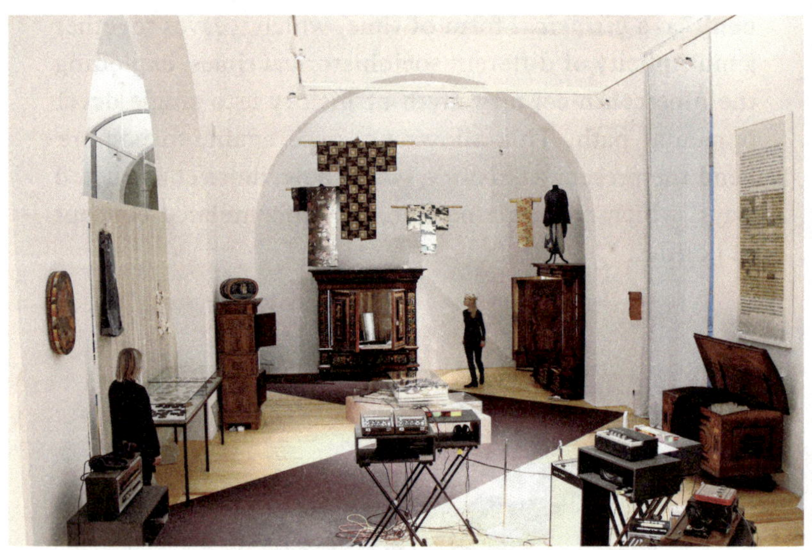

An installation of drum machines (by ARK) and kimonos (1880–1940), whose patterns and motifs dramatize Japan's engagement with the West, *Mobile Worlds* exhibition, Hamburg

feel-good exhibitions that ignore contemporary realities) but rather act at eye level with today's political challenges of right wing-identity politics and its mystifications.

The problem of populism and right-wing identity politics gets to the core of matters of historical consciousness here. For me, right-wing identity politics is a reactive life-support system for dying social and cultural forms, all the more dangerous for its acute sense of the existential threat to those forms posed by the global political economy of the present, on the one hand (in relation to which purely defensive measures take the general form of self-harm: Brexit) and various politics of internationalism, on the other. These are forms of societal self-harm that are opportunistically manipulated by political actors representing factional interests within the very (globalized) forms of finance capital that they purport to be resisting in the name of a phantasmatically unitary, nationally defined "people." As always within this system, the profits are private but their considerable costs are socialized, on a national basis, further fueling the reaction against the supposedly hostile, cultural "Other" that was allegedly making people poorer in the first place.

These are fairly obvious political dynamics. My deeper worry is that the way that the contemporary art world and cultural-philosophical discourses alike are coming to terms with the breakdown of the old, single, Eurocentric narrative of history actually feeds into the right wing-identity politics to which you refer, at a structural level. They do this by virtue of their revival of a nineteenth-century anthropological concept of cultures as socially self-sufficient forms, but with the normative coding of the relations between particular cultures either equalized or simply reversed. In the process, phantasmatically

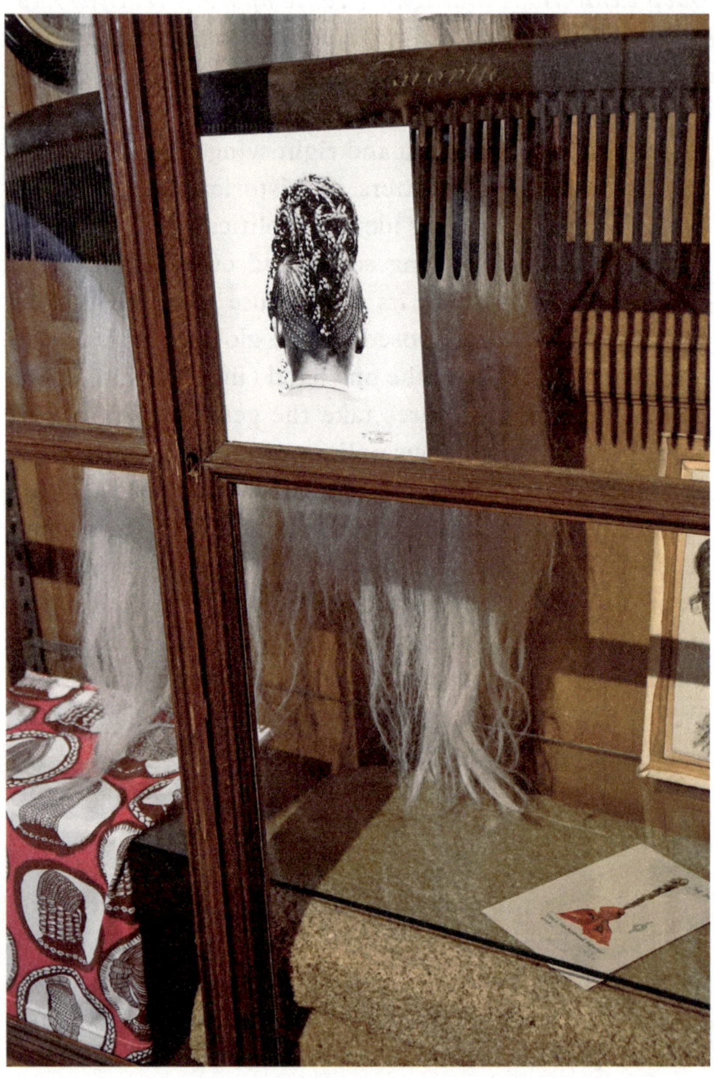

An advertising comb (made from rubber), manufactured around 1900 by Hercules Sägemann, Hamburg's first industrial company, shares the display cabinet with a J. D. 'Okhai Ojeikere photo of a Nigerian hairstyle, a T-shirt by Comme des Garçons (with African hairstyles), a hair dress by Sarah Ama Duah, and a block made of natural rubber. *Mobile Worlds* exhibition, Hamburg

identitarian cultural rights become the general currency of political demands, obliterating any sense of the actual relations of dependency, mutual and otherwise, that make up the fabric of social practices. The biennial-type exhibition to which you referred is often a laboratory for the commodification of such cultural identities staged as acts of political self-determination. This is a profoundly contradictory structure. And as you say, one way to counter it is to introduce a more concrete sense of history, by presenting new relations between geopolitically and historically differential objects. But these relations need to be politically constructed relations

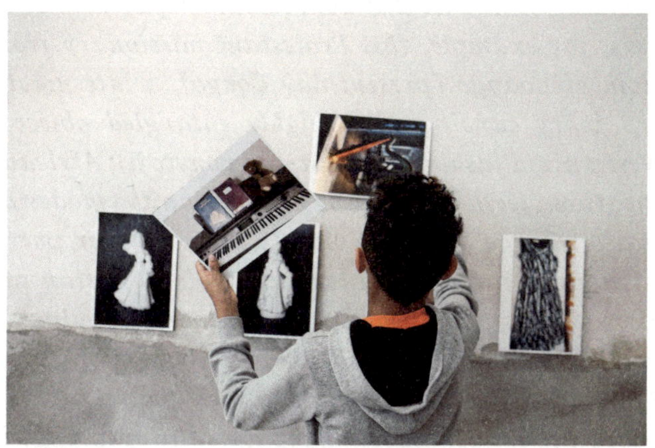

A young visitor interacts with the *Mobile Worlds* exhibition, Hamburg

that challenge, rather than restore, historical continuities, which for me always become falsely naturalistic. At least, that is the Benjaminian stance I would adopt, and the way I understand your practice, in the 2018 *Mobile Worlds* exhibition, for example.

Mobile Worlds, *an exhibition I conceived with Sophia Prinz, a cultural sociologist, was held at the Museum für Kunst und Gewerbe (Museum of Arts and Crafts) in Hamburg. The museum is an offshoot of the nineteenth-century world exhibition in terms of both the range of its collection and in its categorizations, like the distinction it draws between applied and fine art, for example.* Mobile Worlds *summed up five years of experimental exhibition making at the Johann Jacobs Museum in Zurich and addressed topics as diverse as Japan's encounter with the West, Chinese-African trade relations, the Baghdad Railway, and Maya Deren in Haiti.[1] All of these topics were shown to be interrelated using a curatorial method that both emphasized the ability of certain objects or constellations of objects to speak different languages and tell different stories and allowed the objects to serve as go-betweens across thresholds dividing otherwise distinct museum departments.*

Take, for example, this Protestant missionary from the Kingdom of Loango (present-day Congo), a late nineteenth-century ivory carving. This highly entangled object gives you Westernized fashion (the hat and ponytail); African body modification (teeth sharpening); Christianity; modes of representation in the spiritual world (as the carver portrayed the missionary rather than less accessible Christian saints); the ivory trade; King Leopold II's murderous regime in the Congo; the Berlin Conference of 1884–85, and so on.

It would be naïve to relegate this figure to the past. Viewed in the proper light, metaphorically speaking, it can be shown to inhabit the present and perhaps the future as well; futures already indicated in current debates surrounding the restitution of artifacts from Western collections.

---

1 Between 1947 and 1955, avant-garde filmmaker Maya Deren made several trips to Haiti to study dance and trance in the context of Voudoun rituals. The artist died in 1961, leaving the six hours of film stock from Haiti unedited. The material (currently restored by Johann Jacobs Museum in cooperation with Anthology Film Archives in New York, and filmmaker Martina Kudláček) is evidence of the rare balancing act Deren attained with her camera: the film neither ossifies in the aloofness of anthropological observation, nor collapses in romantic overidentification.

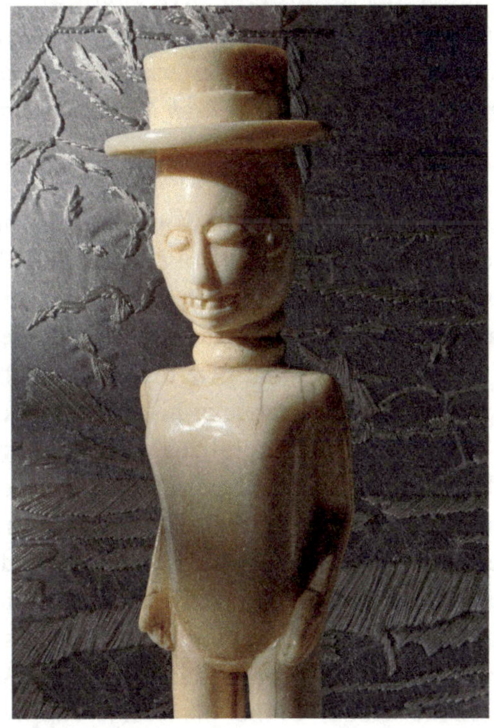

Protestant missionary with filed teeth, top hat, European style braid, and embroidered shoes, Loango coast (now the Democratic Republic of the Congo), late nineteenth century

Western museology is clearly at a loss when it comes to displaying contradictory temporalities. It also lacks the narrative or transdisciplinary grid that would offer glimpses of the whole or "planetary" story. In my own experience, this incapacity is seldom due to curators' active refusal to embrace the challenges, contradictions, and emancipatory needs of today's society. It rather seems that Western museums cannot let go of their dreams of Empire, as though these very dreams are part of their institutional DNA.

Yes, so we must now look at both the dreams of empire that are encapsulated in those collections and the Indigenous cosmologies which are their counterversions in a new way. We need to view them not as evidence of "past cultures" embalmed in some geographical and historical self-sufficiency, but as evidence of historical aspects of the present. This at once denaturalizes and politicizes these historical relations. In this regard, with respect to the abiding naturalism of the historical consciousness of nineteenth-century historicism—which remains the dominant academic and popular form of historical consciousness—I am suspicious of the terminological shift that some propose (in the wake of the popularization of the "Anthropocene") from the "global" to the "planetary." I appreciate the problems associated with the ideality of both the term "globe," and the naturalized historicism of most social scientific understandings of globalization as a process; the combination of which leads to a simplified and reductive homogenization of the process. But the terms "planetary" and "planetarization" invoke a deeper and perhaps more pernicious naturalism. The apparently harsher literality of *planet*—as the object of ecological scientific discourses— quickly becomes cosmological, in a metaphysical sense that is then used to encompass the social, renaturalizing history as a whole to the point of its abolition. This is an ironic reversal of the polemical point of the concept of the Anthropocene, which is to highlight the susceptibility of even the most long-term natural processes to human intervention. Most of the fashionable tendencies in European philosophy at the moment are variants of this naturalism: from actor network theory to various so-called "new materialisms," such as object-orientated ontology or the "flat" monistic ontologies of the post-Deleuzeans.

But what is the antidote? It has been convincingly argued that Europeans do not know their history. This brings us back to the notion of Empire and to "planetary" museum collections that are basically illegible to most visitors because the museum's mode of intelligibility (with its dubious chronologies and departments like "Islam," "Modernity," "Musical Instruments," and "China") makes it impossible to read the past in terms of entanglements and power relations, and blocks the way for a proper understanding of the "now," e.g. of today's conflict zones in the Middle East or on the African continent, which are holdovers from these same imperial structures. Consequently, contemporary audiences are denied an understanding of modern power dynamics, including the deployment of forms of violence that keep circulating within the social body. There are, of course, contemporary artists who address social and cultural trauma. But those lacking the aesthetic means of a Goya or Claude Lanzmann can easily lapse into producing kitsch. As a curator it seems more worthwhile to address historical collections and their repressed, if materially present, memories than simply to indulge contemporaneity as a mode of art making.

Well, it depends on how one conceives contemporaneity, of course. If it is made up of disjunctive combinations of different social times—rather than being the nowness of a flat temporal space—it is itself a series of articulations of the present forms of different pasts; precisely what you seek, in fact.

The big nineteenth-century institutions with all their accumulated stuff—objects, programs, shops—do not function as brokers of civil society. They are mainly fed by tourism and feel no need to stage meaningful, eye-level encounters with local (for example, migrant or post-migrant) audiences. They fail to address the political debates that matter. Their incapacity to link the present with the past denies people the platforms necessary to stage genuine political debates. There are spontaneous movements, of course—the Sardines in Italy[2] come to mind. But such movements remain all too fragile without a proper base and coherent theoretical grounding.

This is partly connected to the reduction of radical critical discourses to university discourses. There is an increasing separation of the standpoint of the production of critical discourses from that of the social practices and productions they want to theorize. They have themselves become industrial, as universities bow before the so-called "knowledge economy." Academic writing has become industrial and career-oriented. Meanwhile, institutions are gearing toward new forms of allegedly instrumental connectivity to society via terms like "impact" and "social relevance." There is a peculiar double movement, within which critical discourses got marooned. They used to be the moment of critical practicality that connected university discourses to social practices. But they're now marooned in discourse

2 A grassroots movement founded as a flash mob in November 2019 to counteract the rise of the right wing in Italy.

itself, while connections to society are all about academics appearing in the media, or being able to turn their research into a patent, or being able to produce an exhibition as part of a research grant. Do you still have a sense that curatorial practice can produce things that escape a lot of these problems bedeviling general theory, because it is a more direct staging of relations between materials and processes and histories?

Curatorial practice differs from exhibition making to a degree. The processes that truly matter are collaborative in character and involve people from outside the museum and exhibition structure. You cannot break the institutional spell as a mere individual; you need to form a movement, so to speak. Like the ivory missionary, you have to become a go-between yourself and operate both from within the institution and against it at the same time. I believe, however, that this form of curatorial practice has also consequences for the artistic set-up of the exhibition proper. You were using the term "distributive unity" in your characterization of the post-conceptual condition. I always find that notion extremely helpful because it points to a form of exhibition that oscillates between a heterogeneity of voices and the prospect of a common ground.

That said, the processes that matter—the staging of relations—have assumed a more and more private character in my experience. It is as though the eighteenth century were back! These processes of collaboration building, artistic research, and interwoven displays require a lot of patience as well as confidence; building them takes an enormous, even excessive amount of time and energy that is hardly compatible with the logic of public institutions. They require a shielding away—limited visibility, for instance—when you're working with Kurdish activist women or kids from Syria. They also require the suspension of performance indicators. There is nothing grandiose about such an approach and it carries no big political promise. Empire's grand theoretical schemes don't apply here. Perhaps genuine transcultural exchange was always either subtle or nonexistent. It calls for a psychic embrace of contradictory forces.

If you can keep the contradictory character of the institutional spaces going, that is in some sense itself an achievement. Only some things are possible in certain institutions at certain times. One has to try to make space for them.

And for the standpoint of new generations. Because if we stay among ourselves we won't find the angle ...

... or the anger.

Case Study: RAW Material Company, Senegal

Olamiju Fajemisin

Movement—lateral across borders, forward in one's practice, temporal, or ideological—has become a primary concern for the contemporary art practitioner. Koyo Kouoh, the Founding Artistic Director of RAW Material Company based in Dakar, Senegal, considers her decolonial, curatorial practice to be "digestive." Digestive of colonialism and its effects; digestive of past realities. "How can we digest an experience of such an important impact on the psyche, landscape, economy, politics, which are still effective today?" she asked during her lecture at the Global Academy conference at the Summer Academy of Fine Arts in Salzburg in 2016.[1] "How do we work from that experience, toward a reappropriation of a reality, of an identity that is ours?"

It is a question of space and access. RAW Material Company is a center for contemporary art, pedagogy, and critical reflection on social contexts. It was founded as a modest mobile art initiative in 2008 and has grown to work across two sites within walking distance of each other in residential neighborhoods in the Senegalese capital: the residency known as Kër Issa; and a multipurpose space for exhibitions, a library, and programming. The present variant of RAW Material Company is deeply entrenched in collaboration, audience involvement, and

1 All quotes attributed to Koyo Kouoh are taken from *Koyo Kouoh@Global Academy '16*, YouTube video, 25:35 min., uploaded by "summeracademy.at," November 4, 2016, https://www.youtube.com/watch?v=g6IIiHnv47w (accessed February 20, 2020).

programmatic insight as well as decolonial and transcultural exchange, and has come to exemplify new modes of postcolonial pedagogy.

RAW Material Company's programs, many of which have existed since the center's early days, naturally feed into one another, a testament to Kouoh's description of RAW as an "organic imposition." As of 2020, RAW Material Company operates a publishing imprint and an exhibition program. It organizes a residency that has welcomed more than forty artists, writers, researchers, and curators from a multitude of nationalities in its nine years, and a weekly public programming series including lectures and film screenings. It invites students and faculty to participate in RAW Académie. It also organizes the "Condition Report" symposia. RAW Material Company also initiated RAW Base, a library, archive, and resource center residents and visitors are encouraged to investigate. RAW Base plays host to <B/Look Club>, a bimonthly meeting that fosters discussion following an "activation of the archive."[2]

In addition to these activities, which take place in their combined 400 square-meter space, RAW operates off-site as well. The symposia, for example, take place beyond the walls of the center, be that elsewhere in Dakar or abroad. The inaugural two-day "Condition Report" symposium, held at Maison de la Culture Douta Seck in Dakar, was organized in 2012 in cooperation with the Goethe-Institut and German Cultural Foundation. It sought to address the changing role of art institutions in the face of cultural urgencies within the African context. The second, held in 2014 and co-hosted by the Ecole Nationale des Arts de Dakar and subtitled "Symposium on Artistic Education

2 All facts and quotes on RAW Material Company from its website: http://www.rawmaterialcompany.org/_2515.

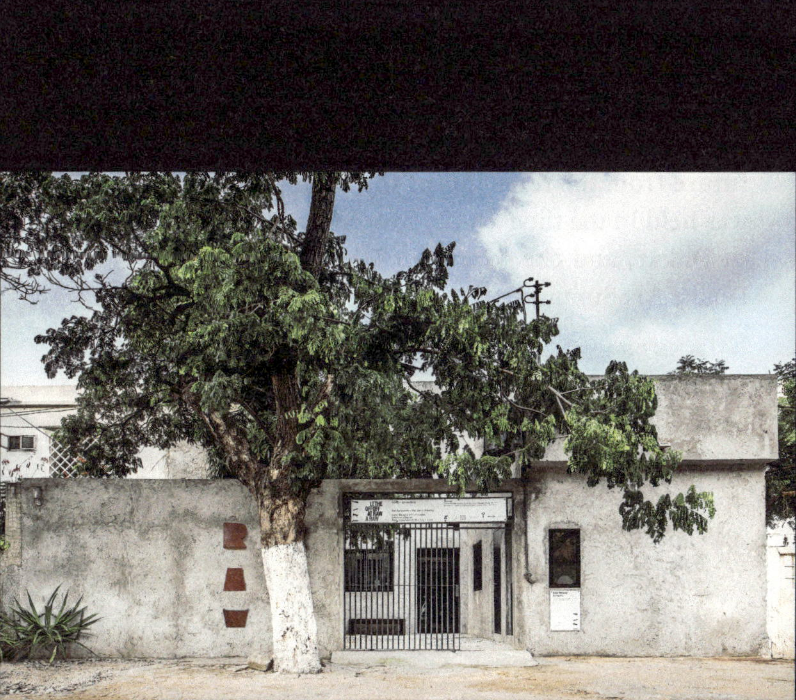

in Africa" looked at how art schools in Africa might be "reinvented and retooled to become sites of new transdisciplinary pedagogical approaches and ambitions," and how these new proposals can contribute to the transmission of artistic knowledge in African art-educational institutions. RAW has organized two symposia since—in 2018 and 2020—and continue to champion discursive tools before the backdrop of a continent still entangled in divorcing its future from the remnants of the colonial epoch. The third was held in the then-empty Musée des Civilisations Noires in Dakar, and the fourth in Dhaka, Bangladesh, at the Dhaka Art Summit 2020.

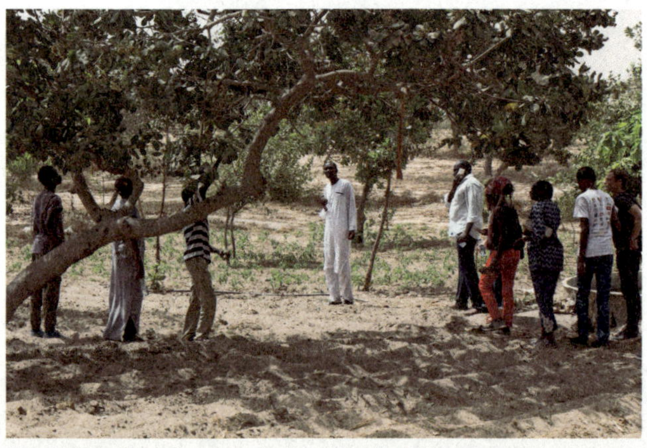

Site visit to Gad Gomene during interdisciplinary workshop on environmental activism

RAW Material Company's latest venture, RAW Académie, exists as a sum of the center's values. The Académie—which has run sessions every spring and autumn since 2016—investigates novel modes of teacher-student interaction, as it is, at its heart, an experimental pedagogical program for the research and study of artistic practice, mediation, and production. With RAW Residency, the resources available at RAW Base, and now the research-based emphasis of RAW Académie, RAW Material Company urgently configures the notion of an institution in the Global South according to the needs of current realities and future art histories.

"The broader context of the contemporary art landscape in Africa has grown rapidly in the last twenty years, particularly in the last ten," explained Kouoh. As true as this is, institutions such as RAW Material Company came to exist out of necessity. The lack (or inability) of national organizational structures to host projects and conduct convincing debates surrounding the contemporary postcolonial experience is often cited as the catalyst for initiating these private spaces and institutions, though it would be irresponsible to attribute full responsibility to this negligence, as it "reduce[s] the courage it takes to run independent spaces in a context like our African societies to a near mechanical reaction that didn't follow independent or original thought, which is more often than not the case." Kouoh asks again: how can we digest such a matter? Working free from the expectations and constraints of the postcolonial North/South–East/West binary and its repercussions is, after all, a privilege.

The New York Times described Cameroon-born Kouoh as "one of Africa's pre-eminent curators and managers."[3] Although she has spent most of her career in Senegal, her curatorial practice extends globally, and has seen her serve as curatorial advisor for both Documenta 12 (2007) and 13 (2012); curate the Educational and Artistic Program at the 1–54 Contemporary African Art Fair in London

3 Ginanne Brownell Mitic, "Curator Puts Contemporary Art on the Map," in *The New York Times*, October 1, 2015, https://www.nytimes.com/2015/10/01/arts/international/curator-puts-contemporary-african-art-on-the-map.html (accessed February 20, 2020).

and New York eight consecutive times; co-curate Rencontres Africaines de la Photographie in Bamako, Mali, in 2001 and again in 2003; and begin her tenure as Executive Director and Chief Curator of the Zeitz Museum of Contemporary Art Africa in Cape Town, South Africa, in Spring 2019. Kouoh is committed to providing the space and access needed to nourish African contemporary art's future. Nevertheless her initial questions persist: can a residential academy function as a decolonial tool?

"It wasn't a Western institution, so I had nobody to convince. I didn't have to write things in a specific language. It was a great, simple freedom,"[4] said assistant curator Eva Barois De Caevel, of the time spent in Dakar on Kouoh's invitation a few years before the Académie began. She was there to take part in an "unofficial and informal" six-month young curator residency. Barois De Caevel has since spent periods living in Dakar and works for RAW Material Company at large: her independent curatorial, editorial, and written practice applies decolonial and feminist theories to a "critique of Western centered art history and thus the renewal of writing and critical speech," and she co-runs the international curatorial collective Cartel de Kunst.

RAW Académie is an experimental residential program for the research and study of artistic practice, curatorial practice, and thought. The individual chosen to lead the faculty of each session is always personally connected to RAW. Contemporaries of the lead faculty whose work complements or challenges the session's theme are invited to teach alongside them. None of the faculties hosted by RAW have comprised scholars of exclusively African background,

4 All quotes attributed to Eva Barois de Caevel from an interview conducted in July 2019.

nor have they constituted of those solely educated in Western institutions. A small group of eight to eleven students, or "fellows," attend the biannual Académie, the majority of whom are recent graduates of curatorial programs, art schools, or humanities degrees. The fellowship's open-call application model seems as if it would favor those with access to financial resources predominantly privy to students of Western institutions (something Kouoh and her team are actively working to combat) but the attendee's demographic make-up is similar to that of the faculty. For seven sessions now, fellows and faculty have traveled to Dakar from within Senegal as well as countries such as Nigeria, Turkey, Brazil, Iceland, South Africa, Costa Rica, and Sri Lanka to engage with the curriculum.

The fellows share their projects with the faculty and rethink artistic pedagogy, asking: what can an art education be today? Franco-American artist and filmmaker Eric Baudelaire led the Fall 2019 session. Naturally, emphasis was placed on film. As outlined in the curriculum published on the RAW Material Company's website, the seven-week period was an opportunity to attempt to question "the urgency of the present," and reflect on how film related to actuality, images to events, and art to the real. Titled *Images For Our Times*, the sessions were based on routine. Each morning began with a screening of a film either authored or selected by Baudelaire's faculty, and was followed by a "perambulation," through the city "towards a new location" where fellows and faculty would sit and discuss the morning's film. Baudelaire's faculty—which included seminal filmmakers Mati Diop and John Akomfrah—formulated a program that allowed their fellows to consider film as a critical tool and means of resistance. "New ways to see, to hear, and to share, to help us questions the urgencies of the present, not so much to

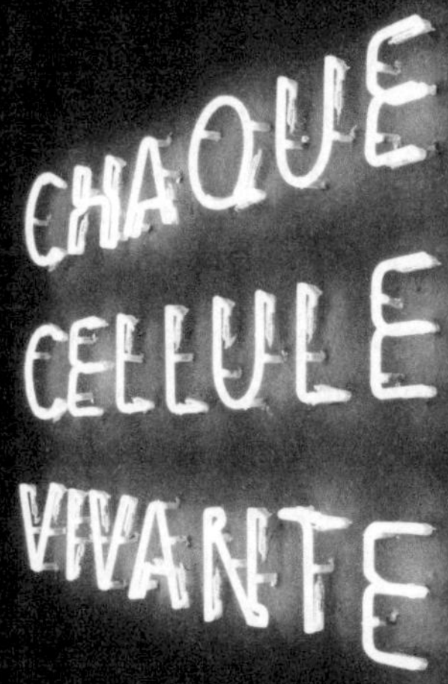

Detail from the exhibition *PO4 (Blackout)* 2019, by RAW Material Company
resident Christian Danielewitz. The artist's work focuses on the extraction of
phosphate, essential for life and extensively mined in Senegal.

explain them but to question ourselves in the face of them. Today the word 'mess' as a synonym for the word 'real' seems as prescient as ever," reads the curriculum. When asked whether this temporal relevance was coincidental or intentional, Barois De Caevel said, "We want them to bring whatever is important to them. And the period is short, which creates the sense of urgency."

RAW Material Company's present focus on the Académie is certainly educational, but it would be incorrect to describe it as a school. "You will not learn how to paint, or write a curatorial statement, but you will definitely learn how to think, and structure your thinking, and apply that thinking in your immediate environment," says Kouoh. The pedagogical stance is not only digestive but perhaps also investigative and experimental: "We see our work as a process-based practice that questions, thematizes, critiques, and celebrates art and culture as a means to build an informed audience," she continues. In removing themselves from the practice-exhibition cycle, RAW Material Company has succeeded in nurturing a space that simultaneously considers art history and future within the context of an African art world that doesn't exist as a case to be compared to its European and American counterparts.

But problems ill the prospect of Dakar's art future, as they did its past. "When it comes to Africa, arts, and culture, everyone talks about Dakar," Kouoh, a twenty-year resident of the city admits. "We hardly live up to that reputation." Kouoh reports that the city's art school, which had been active since the first post-independence years of the nineteen-sixties, "is of no real value today"; nor is the University of Dakar, arguably *the* Francophone flagship institution in Africa. She sees it as a "shell," holding on only to those who simply cannot afford to leave.

And RAW Material Company does not find itself exempt from criticism on both sides of the binary. The circumstances under which RAW could exist as an African hub for contemporary creativity seemed antithetical. They must be representative of a continent, but avoid tokenism. They mustn't rely on the Euro-American centric pedagogical and financial framework that has historically dominated the industry; instead they should fabricate their own microsystem in less than ideal conditions. Despite the impossible critiques, Kouoh and her team have always explored ways of consolidating the issues with special programs for meeting with local artists, studio visits, informal rendezvous, and VOX-ARTIS, a series of public artist presentations based at RAW in Dakar.

In 1991 (as some of the first to do so in postcolonial Africa) Marilyn Douala Bell and her late husband, Didier Schaub, founded doual'art, a non-profit center for contemporary art in Douala, Cameroon. The center still operates today, "functioning as a laboratory for artistic experiments in urban areas."[5] To Kouoh, it is the "exemplary" model for independent art spaces in Africa, having flourished as a meeting place for local and international artists during a socially and fiscally trying period. One year prior to the RAW Material Company's founding in 2008, doual'art launched a triennial festival of art in public space—Salon Urbain de Douala. One could argue that the history and subsequent activity of doual'art set a perfect example for Kouoh as to how a new location for site-specific artistic intervention should be nurtured.

The continual reconsideration of what to program, how to approach postcolonial artistic and curatorial

5 Entry on doual'art, *Contemporary&* website, https://www. contemporaryand.com/place/doualart/(accessed March 3, 2020).

practices, and the eventual shift to a focus on pedagogy is what sets RAW Material Company apart from other contemporary African institutions. Formal artistic training in Africa has a history of more than a century, Kouoh has stated, "either as a part of nationalist programs of cultural development, or as an ancillary component of colonial education." Since its founding, RAW has come to exist as an entity separate from the many other autonomous national programs that manifested during the initial period of African post-independence. It is the devastating educational and cultural impact of this postcolonial structural adjustment between the eighties and nineties that Kouoh would like to focus upon, instead of simply pressing forward, trying to work with a systemically fragile infrastructure. "It's not a school where you come and learn how to make art, it's a place where you come to be exposed to ideas you wouldn't usually be exposed to in your traditional education," she explains.

Kouoh reflected on a visit she and participants of the second symposium took to the studio of the late Senegalese painter, Issa Samb. In one exchange, it was said there should be a "dedicated place, or recognizable place" to discuss art the way she and Samb thought it ought to be discussed. The idea for RAW Académie emerged from this and other conversations. She also clarified RAW's position as rooted in Senegal but eschewing nationalist promotion, continuing: "We are a 'Center for Art, Knowledge, and Society,' which has a very clear intra-African focus, and a very clear international scope." It is precisely this international, or rather, planetary, gaze which renders RAW Material Company, and more specifically, the RAW Académie exemplary as a residential artistic program seeking to recast postcolonial narratives in the artistic context.

The future of the RAW Material Company can only be defined by its present. The center's ability to transfigure its format and processes according to the cultural and social needs of the moment is not only appropriate, but will ensure its survival as a hub for critical cultural thought on a continent still digesting its art histories and planning its futures.

Ethics and Aesthetics: Renegotiating Power in the Planetary

Tania Bruguera
interviewed by Hildegund Amanshauser

Tania Bruguera is one of her generation's leading performance artists. Her work often explores the manifold ways in which art can be applied to everyday politics, creating a public forum to debate ideas and focusing on the transformation of the condition of viewer to one of citizen. Bruguera uses the terms *arte de conducta* (conduct/behavior art) and *arte útil* (useful art) to define her practice and works on appropriating the resources of power to create power. In short, she creates political situations through art. In 2018, Bruguera assembled a group of twenty-one people who live or work in the Tate Modern's postal code in London for her commissioned project in the museum's Turbine Hall called *10,148,45* or *Tate Neighbours*. They explored how the museum could learn from and adapt to its local community. During this process they decided to rename Tate Modern's Boiler House in honor of local activist Natalie Bell, to underscore that naming art-world spaces doesn't always have to be connected to financial patronage.[1]

1 Bruguera asked: "How can we bring the neighbors into the institution, not as witnesses of what happens here, but as peers, who have also something to challenge the institution with?" See https://counterpointsarts.org.uk/video-tania-bruguera-and-tate-neighbours-the-art-of-social-change (accessed January 13, 2020).

Your work deals with "global" issues like imbalanced power structures, migration, and censorship, showing their effects on individuals and specific communities. What is "global" to you?

What was once referenced as universal has been replaced by globalism, as if they were the same thing. Also, the global is "sold" as a new phenomenon, but in fact it has existed for centuries: Asian cultures influenced Europeans, Arab language took on a permanent presence in Spanish, and vice versa. Knowledge has always traveled and taken root in different places. What is truly new today is that Black and queer people from the margins and from the so-called Global Southern philosophy are slowly being incorporated into a common culture. This is not out of an understanding of the Other but because of the exhaustion with the traditional "universal" culture coming from the old metropolis. The old regime of truth, of a universal truth, however, has become eroded and is lacking some sort of renewal. This is why it was easier to proliferate the fake news culture now.

What are the aims of recent projects like Tate Neighbours *in London or* Atlas of Transitions[2] *in Bologna?*

2 *Atlas of Transitions—New Geographies for a Cross-Cultural Europe* is a Bologna-based European cooperation project that promotes cross-cultural dialogue by bringing local communities closer through culture and performing arts. In March 2019, Bruguera realized two projects within the festival *Referendum* and *School of Integration.* See http://www.atlasoftransitions.eu/indepth/school-of-integration-by-tania-bruguera/ (accessed January 13, 2020). *Referendum* was a ten-day urban performance that activated a referendum campaign that addressed Bologna citizens. *School of Integration* worked as a temporary educational institution and offered daily lessons conducted by the communities of foreigners residing in Bologna, dedicated to the different cultures they come from. See Ginevra Ludovici, "Conversation with Tania Bruguera," in *Made in Mind Magazine,* https://www.madeinmindmagazine.com/conversation-with-tania-bruguera (accessed March 6, 2020).

My artwork is always positioned clearly on the side of the not-winners, on the side of people who historically have not been approved, just because they belong to a tradition that has not been considered the predominant tradition. In my work I aspire to use principles, ethics, ideas, desires, and even topic goals aligned with what is seen as the "marginalized." A few years ago, I did an interview for a book on socially engaged art,[3] in which one question was about generosity. There was a small misunderstanding because generosity was presented as an exchange process in which I give you something because you will give me something back. Where I come from, that's not how we see it. Those cultural and ethical differences are what I try to highlight in my work. I attempt to infiltrate the "Western canon" and talk to these people from the perspective and values of where I come from, with the hope that other knowledges and other parameters are not automatically discarded. At this moment, when you have a lot of autocratic political figures in the world, it would be nice if people paid attention to those who already have been in the same situation, and learn from them. This is why I started new concepts like *arte de conducta* and *arte útil*, because I felt that my artwork was forced into concepts that were alien to me. I had to learn the vocabulary because there is a kind of common language in the international world of art, but I have always wanted them to learn my historical and referential vocabulary as well. We quickly identify injustice and colonization around us, but there is much of it happening right now in the so-called art world that needs to be addressed as well.

3 Tom Finkerpearl, *What We Made: Conversations on Art and Social Cooperation* (Chapel Hill, 2013).

How would you describe where you come from?

I come from a place where ethics are a measurement of things. What I want to test is the belief that ethics are an aesthetic concept, an element of beauty. Hopefully my work presents some ethical construct or dilemma you are part of. This is a key element in understanding the work I and other people do. We don't start seeing our projects based on how they look, but what they make you do; what they transform. This is where I come from. There is a tradition in such practice, and part of what I have done is to show it in New York and in Europe, where people think their way is universal. But now I ask myself why I need to prove anything to them by bringing my concepts to the mainstream. Maybe I should just go somewhere else, live somewhere else in the middle of nowhere and do whatever.

I also come from a place where altruism was a goal. This is something I would like to recuperate. My aesthetic spectrum is not defined by how well the brush was applied or how realistic the feeling is, but by social feelings. I think art criticism is in crisis and maybe it should start talking about terms like enthusiasm, cooperation, empathy, energy, and satisfaction—and seeing how artists today are developing such concepts through their work instead of asking whether the documentation is a good image or not. Instead of discussing aesthetic shock we should be talking about ethical development. Most of the problems we have in the world at the moment are due to a lack of ethics, a lack of understanding of how to be with each other.

That's why for the Turbine Hall commission at the Tate, the Tate neighbors and I named one of its two buildings after a local social worker who has focused on youth at risk for the past twenty-five years. It was a gesture that brought up a discussion about what values we operate with, also within the cultural institutions. What do we value today?

It's a moment of crisis of value, in culture, but also in politics. To address and challenge this ethical void, we can't use the same elements that generated it. We need to propose different values in the artwork itself; an ecosystem that stands as a clear alternative.

It's fascinating how you describe where you are now and what interests you, because I have the feeling that what we imagine with our Planetary Academy has to do with something like this as well. But exactly what it is—goodwill, caring, a more inclusive future—is difficult for us to describe.

One of art's powers is that with it you can imagine something with an extraordinary amount of detail and focus. You can imagine something entirely different. It's not escapism or alienation; it's just projection. Some political systems work in a similar way. Another crisis we are living is the way we organize our political systems. Socialism didn't work because individual rights were sacrificed for collective ones, and in capitalism collective rights are sacrificed for individual and corporate rights. Neither of those systems solved injustice of inequality; now we have to start imagining other ways in which we can live together. This is why ethics must be on the forefront of any potential solution. Ethics are simultaneously an individual and a collective construction; it's not something already assumed without question, like morals.

One important subject in ethics is the question of negotiation. How do you negotiate what is ethical or unethical, and with whom do you negotiate?

It is about consensus and balance; about leaving your own power at the door so everyone has the same rights during negotiations, so you can focus on the issue and the best solutions without thinking how much power you have to sacrifice for it. It is about empathy instead of sympathy, about not speaking for others and recognizing your mistakes. It is about transparency and equality.

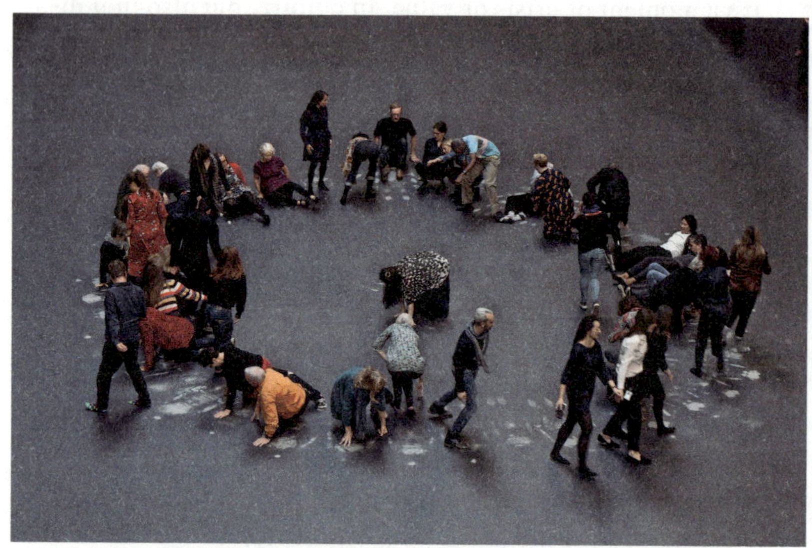

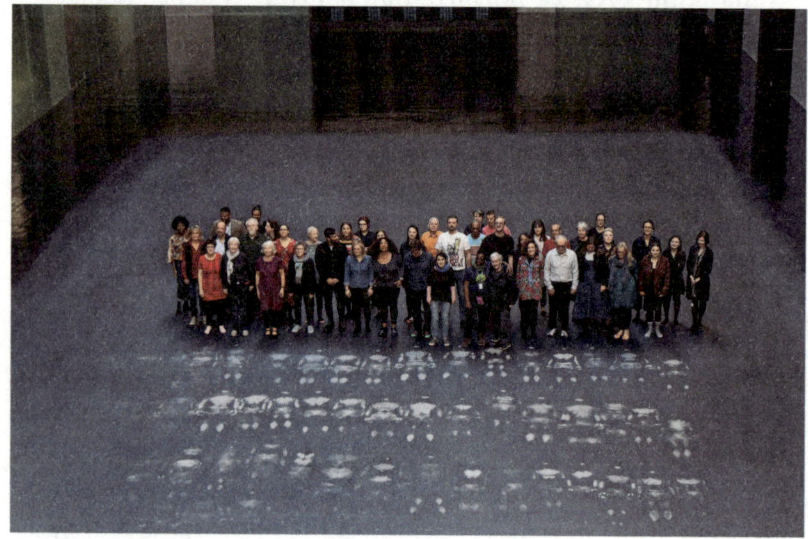

Tania Bruguera, *10,142,926*, Hyundai Commission 2018, installation and performance views of the artist and participants. Turbine Hall, Tate Modern, London

The problem is that negotiations are often used to exercise power on people instead of solving problems, and they are often directed by fear, embarrassment, and resolutions that are often decided before negotiations. In good negotiations you arrive at a consensus and everyone feels the best possible outcome was achieved but, sometimes, those who play power games think they have "lost" and because failure is so feared in our society, that is quite a danger. The most important thing in negotiations is to forget your ego and to be able to use your privilege until you lose all your privilege. Privilege is something to be used.

Can you give an example?

Yes. When I did critical work in Cuba, I lost my privilege. I used it like the cultural currency that I had, and I risked it, like on a table in a casino.[4] You put it there and you give it up for other things. But a more recent example is *Tate Neighbours*. The goal was to apply what I call constructive criticism to the institution, and in the process, give the group of neighbors a certain power within the institution,

4 Bruguera regularly travels to Cuba from the United States and elsewhere. Several of her projects and performances there, however, have landed her in jail, including her piece *Tatlin's Whispers #6 (Havana Version)*, which was performed in March 2009, at the Havana Biennial. Viewers were invited to take the stage and speak uncensored for one minute, after which time they were escorted away by two actors in military uniforms. A white dove was placed on each speaker's shoulder, an allusion to the one that landed on Fidel Castro during his first speech in Havana after the 1959 revolution. Bruguera wanted to perform *Tatlin's Whispers* again in 2009, this time on Havana's Revolution Square, where Castro held mayor speeches, but it was prohibited and she was arrested several times. Her passport was confiscated and held on the condition she leave Cuba and never return. Bruguera insisted on her rights as a Cuban and firmly refused the offer; she was then put under "city arrest." (See Luis Camnitzer, "Tania Bruguera's *Tatlin's Whisper #6* and the Hannah Arendt International Institute for Artivism," in *Art-Agenda*, May 28, 2015.) During this time the artist developed the Hannah Arendt International Institute for Artivism.

so that they had to be heard. I was in the room in which the group negotiated ideas, but I didn't often speak. It's important to understand each other's role. Sometimes your role is just to be present to support and not intervene, to direct the attention to those to whom the people in power or the institution should be accountable to. Sometimes it is to provide a safe environment. In this case privilege was used not for personal gain but to have a room where people sat for an intense and honest conversation with the director of the institution, something that otherwise would be harder to happen. Privilege is closely related to trust.

Does that mean that because it's art, institutional people or people in power take it more seriously, which they would probably not do under other circumstances?

Most people relax around art projects, because they think they have no consequences and nothing will happen. It's just a reflection, a temporary thing. Maybe the first step is to make sure people understand that there will be consequences to an art project, therefore they take it politically seriously. When I negotiate with institutions, it is not to destroy them, because their disappearance or weakening would open a path to authoritarianism, totalitarianism, and dictatorship. Institutions should protect us from political capriciousness.

The idea is to put the institution in crisis with art. Meaning, to make the institution look at itself and be put in a position where it cannot do anything other than its job. The Tate neighbors who developed and negotiated the idea of renaming the building consisted of twenty-one neighbors, including activists, an eighty-seven-year-old neighbor who visited the museum for the first time, and two people who have been coming to the Tate since the beginning; some people who were critical of the institution and some who adored it. It was a good collaboration.

This was also because the director, Francis Morris, was amazing; she understood our project accurately and was willing to play with us. At the end she even made the re-naming permanent, which was beyond the group's wildest dreams. But it is also important in negotiations to not be complacent, or satisfied only with representational or symbolic gestures. This is why it was so important that Natalie Bell, the person after whom we named the building, became part of the Tate's advisory board. So now, somebody from the community is sitting in a place in which decisions are made.

The next question has to do with education. Many of your projects are schools or educational projects. What do you think about our idea of the Planetary Academy, which asks, "How could one teach and learn art on a planetary scale?" Does it make any sense to you?

In these times of immediate reaction—in which the emotional spectrum has been reduced to "like" or "not like" and when telling the truth has become a difficult act and values are underestimated—education and knowledge are extremely important. Today, understanding complexity as well as our own ignorance is indispensable. We need emotional education.

And do you think this is possible in an art school? Do art schools still make sense? The Salzburg Summer Academy's Planetary Academy project makes interaction possible between students and teachers who come from all over the world to try to understand each other's contexts and to produce something new together.

Using the word "planetary" makes more sense than "global." It makes you think in ecological terms and reminds us that the planet has been through many periods and this is just one of them. It makes it a little easier to imagine that what we are now living in maybe just one period, so the "universal" and "eternal" are a way of thinking in an era, and not the only way to measure things.

Do you consider yourself a planetary artist?

I would like to think that I am.

Yes, but the challenge is always to be connected to a local situation.

Exactly.

And this is what you always do.

It is about connecting through understanding and being open to something completely different.

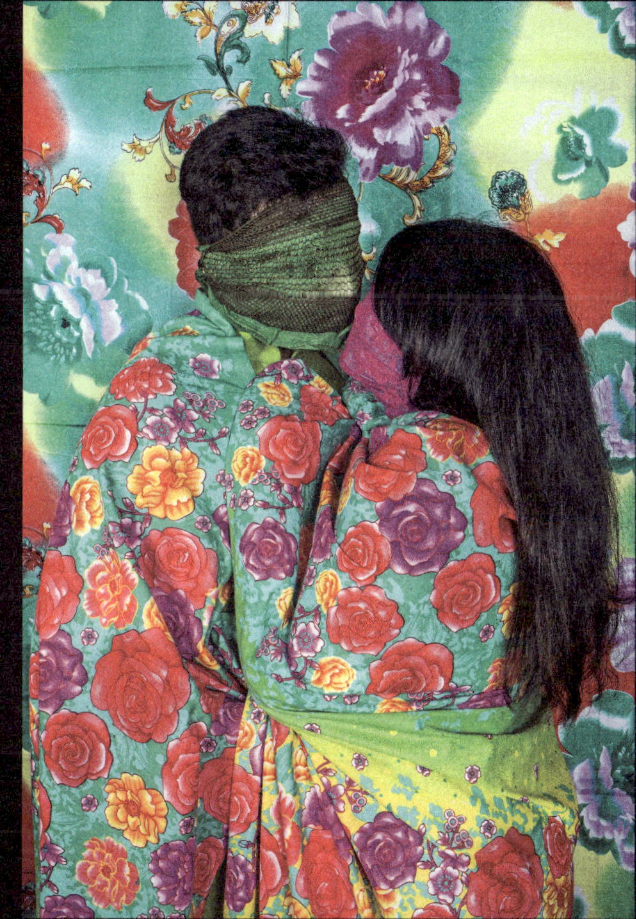

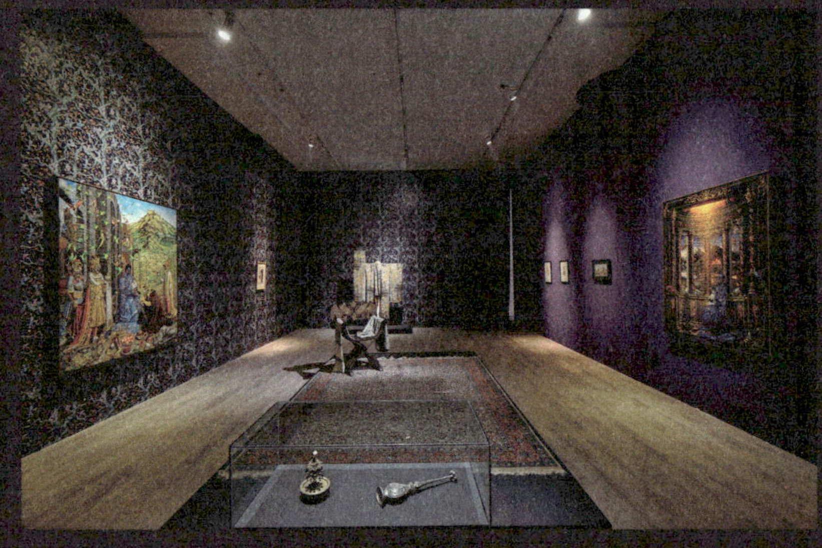

Installation view of Raqib Shaw's solo presentation at the Dhaka Art Summit 2018

Case Study: Dhaka Art Summit, Bangladesh

Rosalyn D'Mello

When the Dhaka Art Summit (DAS) held its inaugural edition in April 2012 at the state-sponsored cultural center Shilpakala Academy, it was consciously postured as a not-for-profit version of the model that inspired its conception—the India Art Fair, which in its 2008 debut also strategically used the word "summit" as part of its nomenclature. Nadia and Rajeeb Samdani, the Bangladeshi couple who own Golden Harvest,[1] launched the Samdani Art Foundation in 2011 as part of a corporate social responsibility initiative and to extend the scope of their collecting practice. They sought to create a similar catalytic meeting point in South Asia, but divorced from commercial agendas. Over three days, the Academy became a platform for 200 contemporary Bangladeshi artists alongside their peers from the subcontinent and beyond. Perhaps motivated by its reception among the local art community—they registered 20,000 visitors—the Samdanis continued the event, but decided to maintain it as a biannual affair.

The second edition consciously focused on South Asia. The couple invited curators from Bangladesh and elsewhere to mount five exhibitions, while also offering free booth space to regional galleries. The American curator Diana Campbell Betancourt was among the guest curators. At the time, she was living in Mumbai and had established a reputation for promoting and engaging with South Asian

---

1 A Bangladeshi conglomerate with diversified interests in frozen foods, dairy, commodity, information technology, logistics, real estate, aviation, infrastructure development, and insurance.

artists. She had been asked to commission solo projects for the Summit and was already artistic director of the Samdani Art Foundation, but her counsel was soon sought for other logistical issues. "Some of the curators didn't understand the complexities of making a show here," she explained. "Through that process, the Samdanis realized they needed someone to manage the whole thing."[2] For three days in February 2014, the second edition of DAS took place at the same venue to great acclaim. It was unprecedented for South Asian art audiences to see thoughtfully mounted installations and performances by local and international artists within a format that was presumably not dictated by market demands, and with a display that rivaled the setup of the Asian Art Biennale taking place in Dhaka since 1981. Yet the general structure still resembled an art fair, with solo projects, talks, booths, and small thematic exhibitions.

Perhaps the singular move the Samdani Foundation made that has yielded rich, yet-to-be quantified dividends was in retaining Campbell's participation and instituting her in a dual role as Artistic Director of the Summit and the Foundation, allowing her free rein to envision the biannual event that came into its own by the third edition, held February 2016. "The Samdanis were responsible for deciding to have someone responsible for whoever might want to engage with Bangladesh and for figuring out who that person might be," Campbell Betancourt said. "I'm here till 2022. They see things in a long-term way."

For its third edition in 2016 under Campbell Betancourt's lead, DAS did away with the galleries section entirely. In shedding the most visible trace of the art fair

2 Conversations between the author at Diana Campbell Betancourt conducted in late 2019.

structure, the DAS set a new standard for what a large-scale art event in the Global South can encompass, even if, as a result, its identity became more amorphous. In 2018, it claimed the scale of a biennial with 300 artists from thirty-five countries and speakers from some of the world's most prestigious art institutions. Its duration was extended from three days to nine; entry remained free and ticketless. The fourth edition saw 317,000 visitors, 189,000 more than in 2016, and an overwhelming majority comprising local Bangladeshis. In 2020, it expanded to 477,153 visitors.

While it had initially positioned itself to evolve into a leading platform for South Asian art, DAS had now wildly surpassed its regional gaze. Attending the fourth edition were directors of Tate, MoMA, Castello di Rivoli, and the National Gallery of Singapore; attending the fifth were directors and senior curators of institutions including the Tensta konsthall, Stockholm, and the San Jose Museum of Art as well as curatorial delegations from Australia and other biennials like the Bangkok Biennial, Liverpool Biennial, Asia Pacific Triennial, and Kathmandu Triennial. What was previously a section featuring solo projects commissioned by the Samdani Art Foundation, the core of previous summits, had transformed over the years into a set of five large-scale sub-exhibitions, in 2018 collectively titled *Bearing Points*, seeking to reorient viewers toward lesser explored transcultural histories, like Bangladesh's relationship with Southeast Asia and its location within the Global South, while weaving together strands of conceptual thought from the nine other guest-curated exhibitions and public programs.

The scale was extravagant and effects wide reaching: Many works from DAS 2018 later toured internationally. Cosmin Costinas's show *A beast, a god and a line* traveled

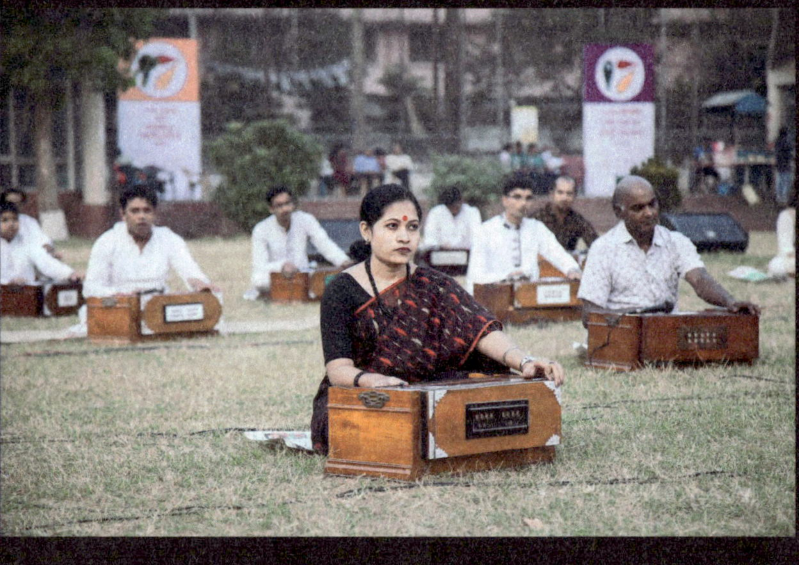

Reetu Sattar, *Lost Tune* 2016. This work was later performed at the Dhaka Art Summit 2018

to Hong Kong, Myanmar, and Warsaw, while Reetu Sattar's *Harano Sur (Lost Tune)* was part of the Liverpool Biennial, was performed in Dubai during the 2019 edition of Art Dubai at Campbell Betancourt's show *Fabric(ated) Fractures* at Alserkal Avenue, and was scheduled to open at the MoMA in New York in June 2020.[3] The Samdani Art Foundation had been invited by Alserkal Avenue founder Abdelmonem Bin Eisa Alserkal to retrospectively consider Dhaka Art Summit's journey since 2012. The show brought together commissions from various editions and encouraged an enhanced dialogue between compelling works by South Asian artists. The 2020 edition expanded the transcultural focus, expounding, over nine chapters, on its titular curatorial thesis of *Seismic Movements* as a series of conceptual shifts that are registered on a transregional, tectonic scale. Core movements from the last two centuries, such as anti-colonialist struggles and the fight for gender equality were revisited through various exhibitions and the responses of artists from different parts of the world were meaningfully contextualized.

Considering Bangladesh's "developing" status in world politics; the fact that it still relies heavily on foreign aid and philanthropy; its struggles with local terrorism; its import restrictions (a motivating factor for the Samdani's decision to commission artists to create work in Bangladesh); the distress on resources due to the Rohingya crisis; and the pervasive grunt of traffic snarls and the ensuing time loss, the magnitude of both DAS 2018 and 2020 was extraordinary. Unlike the Kochi-Muziris Biennale in Kerala, India, DAS is not financially supported by the government

3 Alserkal Avenue is a warehouse district in Dubai that has been transformed into an art hub with galleries, studios, and residencies for artists.

and doesn't enjoy funding from the tourism wing. The culture ministry offers the use of the Shilpakala Academy (and the government visa support for visiting artists), but since the Summit doesn't charge entry, visitor participation generates no income. Campbell Betancourt theorizes that their impact owes much to the Foundation's policy of prioritizing artists. "Artists are at the center of what we do," she says. It is of note that the Summit does not serve to expand the Samdani's collection—the works commissioned belong to the artists.

The Summit lives from its rapidly connecting network and multipronged activity; by now the event has commissioned a vast stable of international artists, and the local arts community has infinitely benefited, evident in the quality of the art included in the 2018 exhibition of the eleven Bangladeshi artists shortlisted for the Samdani Art Award, guest curated by Simon Castets, director of the Swiss Institute in New York. The award is as old as the Summit, and was instituted to "support, promote and highlight Bangladeshi contemporary art" as well as encourage talent between the ages of twenty-two and forty.[4] Many shortlisted artists have been invited to participate in international exhibitions and biennales. The Tate recently acquired a work by 2014 winner, Ayesha Sultana. The award has enjoyed wide exposure by partnering since 2013 with the Delfina Foundation in London, offering a residency whose 2020 selection jury included Adrián Villar Rojas, Carolyn Christov-Bakargiev, Julie Mehretu, and Eunjee Joo.

4 Winners have included Khaled Hasan, Musarrat Reazi, Ayesha Sultana in 2014; in 2016, the prize went to a young photographer, Rasel Chowdhury, while the 2018 winner was Mizanur Rahman Chowdhury. The 2020 edition saw two winners, Soma Surovi Jannat and Promiti Hossain. The latter artist was awarded a special mention prize with cash donated by the jury using their fees because they couldn't choose only one winner.

Campbell Betancourt's curatorial strategy for the Dhaka Art Summit has been invested in building and nurturing a cross-border community of stakeholders, from international institutions and collectors to curators, installers, art educators, critics, and academics.[5] The local game has thus been upped: the Shilpakala Academy and the Bangladesh National Art Exhibition, which is also on view in the Academy, profit from adapting elements of DAS's technical and exhibition design infrastructure. "It is great to see that just hanging art on walls is no longer seen as an acceptable way to show art here," says Campbell Betancourt. "And the bar gets raised every time with each show." Local curators from the photography festival Chobi Mela, for example, focus more on exhibition design than in the past.

There's also been a focal shift away from the Indian art scene under whose shadow Bangladeshi artists had long languished. "We in Bangladesh, and also the region, and the rest of the world, saw India as the center of South Asia," she said. "The more time I spent here, and the two years in the Philippines,[6] I realized that Bangladesh is the crossroads of South and Southeast Asia, and India's presence in DAS has therefore decreased dramatically as we try to reorient a regional and planetary view with different coordinates than those implied by geopolitics."

During Campbell Betancourt's travels to Manila, she often had to stop in Singapore or other parts of Malaysia,

5 Near the award exhibition in 2018, was a show titled *The Asian Art Biennale in Context*, which sought to refocus attention on Dhaka's historical locus as a site for arts innovation through hosting the Asian Art Biennale, the continent's oldest surviving biennale. It included works from the Shilpakala Academy's collection and the archive of the Fukuoka Asian Art Museum, and in doing so, located DAS's future within the continuing present of the Asian Art Biennale.

6 For a time Campbell Betancourt simultaneously functioned as artistic director of Bellas Artes in Manila.

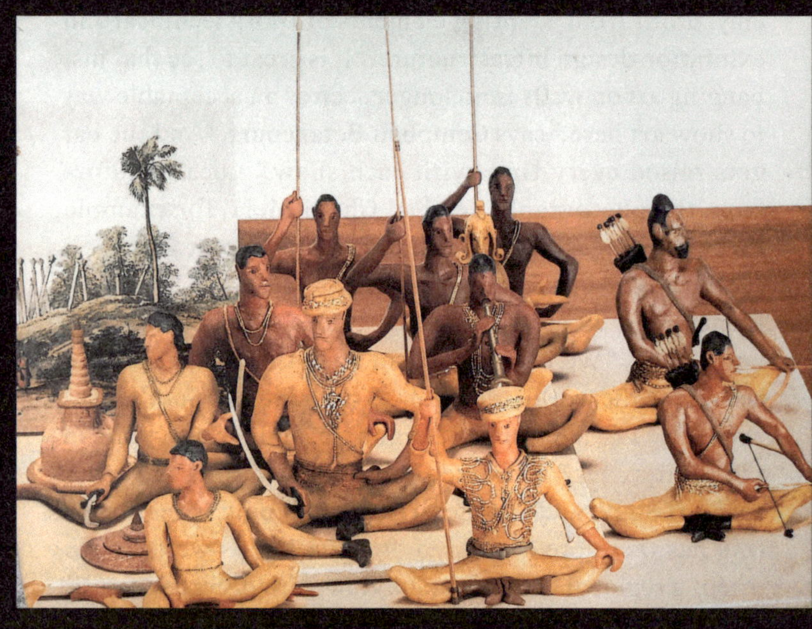

Tissa De Alwis, *Yellow Set*, 1999, installation view, *One Hundred Small Tales*, Dhaka Art Summit 2018

and she'd often encounter many Bangladeshis, especially laborers, who were based there or transiting. "Southeast Asia is a Cold War term, while South Asia a British colonialist term. I saw an opportunity to recharge Bangladesh by looking at its parallels with Southeast Asia." The Bangladeshi art scene, after all, shares more affinities with Indonesia than India, because of the strong role of artist-led initiatives that drive the local scene. This is why the Summit began increasing its annual support of artist-led projects.

Such curatorial nimbleness is viable not only because the Samdanis are not risk-averse, but also because Campbell Betancourt remains relentlessly critical of her own and the Summit's accomplishments. A less self-aware artistic director might rest on laurels. One poignant criticism that she has made is that the Summit has thus far modeled its display on Western white-cube models. The fifth edition worked to correct this internalized tendency. "We realized we are transforming the Shilpakala to look like a Western art space rather than curating for the space that we have, which is primarily an open plaza," says the curator. "This means we can't show museum-condition work here, but artists here don't work in museum conditions and building museum conditions as we did [in part] in DAS 2018 doesn't make sense in terms of being climatically responsible."

For Campbell Betancourt, the 2020 edition was a conscious pushback against the hegemony of Western/ Northern arts funding. "We are trying to be a meeting point for these Souths without Europe or North America as the mediating point," she says, referring to where the most powerful funding bodies are located. Organizations in the Global South are often forced to adhere to conditions set by the North. Within the paradigmatic shift in her

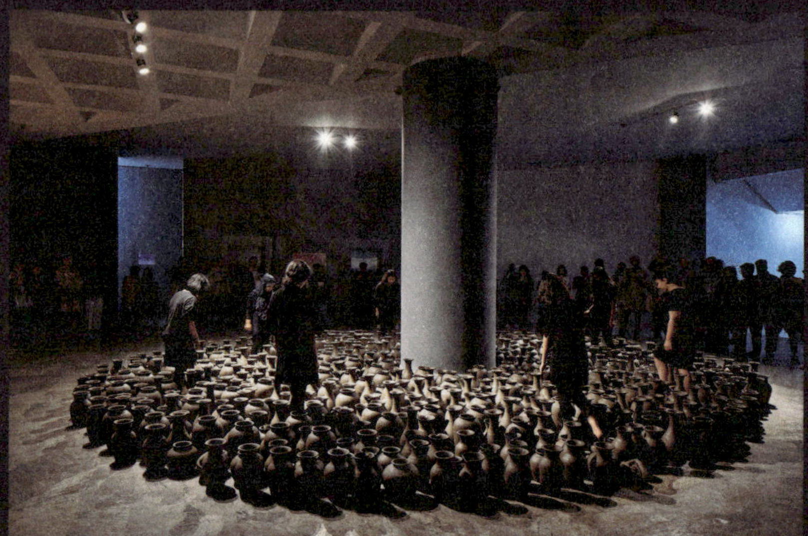

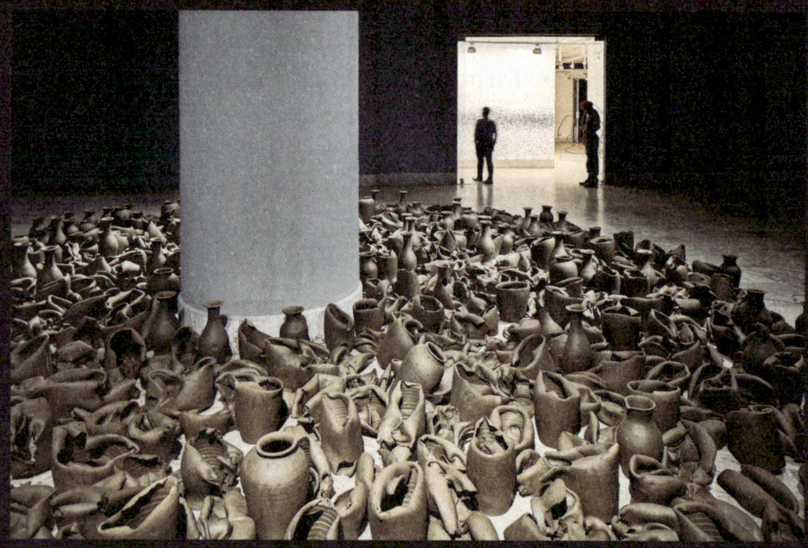

Héctor Zamora, *Movimientos Emisores de Existencia* 2019, performance view from Dhaka Art Summit 2020

proposed modified axis—the attempt is for foundations in places like South Asia to exert more agency over how funding can be used in a manner that impacts sustainability.

Long-term perspectives are possible because one person has been at the helm over a sustained duration. Other large-scale art events in South Asia, including the Lahore Biennale, the Karachi Biennale, the Colombo Biennale, and the Kochi-Muziris Biennale select a different curator for each edition. They are also frequently funded by multiple collectors and philanthropists and cannot claim single stakeholders. While functioning as artistic director of DAS, Campbell Betancourt follows a decentralizing approach wherein she invites curators not to form a core curatorial team, as in the case of a biennial, but to each conceive their own exhibition. Instead of one thematic exhibition that expounds a chosen curatorial premise, DAS favors a more variegated approach accommodated within an overarching ideological framework. *Seismic Movements* in 2020 posed a basic question: what is a movement and how do we ignite one beyond the confines of an art exhibition? The theme was meant to provoke us to reconsider (art) histories, movement, borders, and fault lines.

The Samdani Art Foundation's mission is building something in Bangladesh that cannot be found anywhere else.[7] What has evolved is the culmination of Campbell Betancourt and team negotiating the many infrastructural

---

7 Beyond DAS, the Samdani Art Foundation has also laid the groundwork for a permanent institution in Sylhet—the Srihatta Samdani Art Center and Sculpture Park. The inaugural phase includes several commissions for a 40-hectare sculpture park, 930 square meters of artist residency spaces, 930 square meters of plazas, and a 464 square-meter gallery, designed by Dhaka-based Bangladeshi architect and 2016 Aga Khan Award-winner, Kashef Mahboob Chowdhury. Construction is underway, but is currently delayed due to the impact of climate change and ensuing budget issues.

challenges and converting limitations into strengths. They have networked among the international art community to secure funds in various formats: loans, insurance coverage, supporting residencies, and collaborating with local artists. The Summit has located itself within the gaps between several institutionalized modes of art exhibition. Its short duration enables a fertile intimacy between visitors, facilitating exchanges between international artists, members of the art cognoscenti, and their local counterparts. Its noncommercial aspect makes it more amenable to experimentation. The seminars and talks provide a discursive dimension; while film, music, and performance programs add a multidisciplinary element.

The scale is akin to a biennial, except the Summit unfolds within the confines of the Academy, making for easier viewing. There is, inarguably, a passionate engagement to building a legacy. The Serendipity Arts Festival in Goa and Colomboscope in Colombo most closely resemble the Summit, but the scale of the former's multiple venues differentiates it, while Colomboscope doesn't have the Summit's funding, which goes beyond the Foundation to include corporate and private donors. The Samdanis' rise to power in the international art world (the couple and Campbell Betancourt were ranked 47 in the 2019 *ArtReview* Power 100 List) certainly positions them as influential role models for South Asian art collectors looking to support and build a local non-Western focal point for contemporary art.[8]

8 Whether this is necessarily an enviable development is subject
to discussion, considering how many collectors in South Asia,
especially in India, are complicit in using art as a way of laundering money and to further the perception of their indispensability as "philanthropists." The means and methods behind much that is disguised as foundation-run grant-giving within South Asia haven't been sufficiently studied, and were it to be, it could emerge

For Campbell Betancourt, the commitment has acquired a personal dimension: "I realize that my allegiance or interest in giving Bangladesh a voice when it was previously drowned out by bigger powers in the region comes from the personal place of my background in Guam, which is ignored, stereotyped, and is still technically a colony," she said. "Guam has less than one-third the population of our visitor numbers, but when I think of transfers of Indigenous knowledges outside of formal Western education structures, the importance of language and the pain of its loss, the transfer of the same lands across different imperial borders across history (Japan, Spain, and the United States)—all of this comes from my lived family experience of being Chamorro diaspora. These stories are also found in Bangladesh, and elsewhere in the world with displaced Indigenous communities." As an example of such knowledge transfer, she questions her mother's decision not to maintain a collection of Oceanic objects. Her mother told her the object was merely a carrier of knowledge, especially considering typhoons, common in Guam, can wipe out everything. Artist Taloi Havini, from the Autonomous Region of Bougainville, once told Campbell Betancourt that where she comes from, they periodically burn the village huts not because there's anything wrong with them, but so the community remembers how to make them.

Campbell Betancourt considers these elsewheres in DAS's future. She is interested in exploring other meridians of South-South dialogue by opening lines between South Asia and South America. Hacking into the Samdani

that most collectors are not keen on building a sustainable arts ecosystem that actually puts artists at the center and imagines their own redundancy. Most collectors thrive on deriving cultural capital from their association with the art world, which makes it more complex and enabling of hierarchies.

budget, she has built allies in South America who support reciprocal exchange. Her next curatorial milestone involves decoupling DAS from the English language. "When DAS is envisioned in Bengali is when it will have matured," she says. For the 2020 edition, Campbell Betancourt rewrote curatorial texts to suit local audiences, restricting International Art English, and more Bangladeshi curators were on the team than ever before. The long-term goal is for her own role to become less visible. "I hope to see DAS envisioned in Bengali by a Bangladeshi curatorial team that I support in a more logistical capacity, like a coach. I want to leave eventually. I've said this publicly. It's not an institution if it can't be curated by someone other than me."

It's perhaps a welcome stance for a curator of privilege to somehow intuit her own redundancy. Had Campbell Betancourt not used her position to encourage and empower curators and artists from the South Asian region there would certainly have been backlash and resentment. If anything, DAS's success—in the eyes of not only the planetary art world but also the Bangladeshi art scene—has shown how collaborations between those with the advantages of a Global North/West educational background and network, operating with a relative consciousness of Indigenous and postcolonial realities, methodologies, histories, and politics and those from postcolonial contexts with access to resources and will, can be nurtured in transnational ways.

Dynamic Evolution

Sammy Baloji
interviewed by Kimberly Bradley

From Lubumbashi in the Democratic Republic of the Congo, artist Sammy Baloji's work in photography, collage, video, sculpture, and installation exposes hidden and forgotten narratives, many of them connected to the industrial extractive mining activities that built the foundations of his home city a century ago under Belgian economic and colonial control, but also the region, Katanga, in the centuries prior to this. Trained in social sciences and communications and first working as a cartoonist, he turned to photography after discovering the medium's potentials. His work is often a dance between eras, meldings of memories lost and then found, and novel translations of old information.

Baloji's visual language sensitively explores the colonial era's causes, effects, and misconceptions, but it also imagines a more interconnected future in which notions of separation or the Other are no longer relevant. His work has been on view at major exhibitions including the 2015 Venice Biennale and Documenta 14 in 2017, and has shown in museums around the world such as the Louisiana Museum of Modern Art in Humlebæk, Denmark, the Tate Modern in London, the Smithsonian in Washington, D.C., and many others. He has taught courses at the Salzburg Summer Academy and is a cofounder of the Picha Encounters / Biennale de Lubumbashi, which launched in 2008.

You've stated in the past that Africa is a European notion and construct. But what was the notion of Africa ... in Africa?

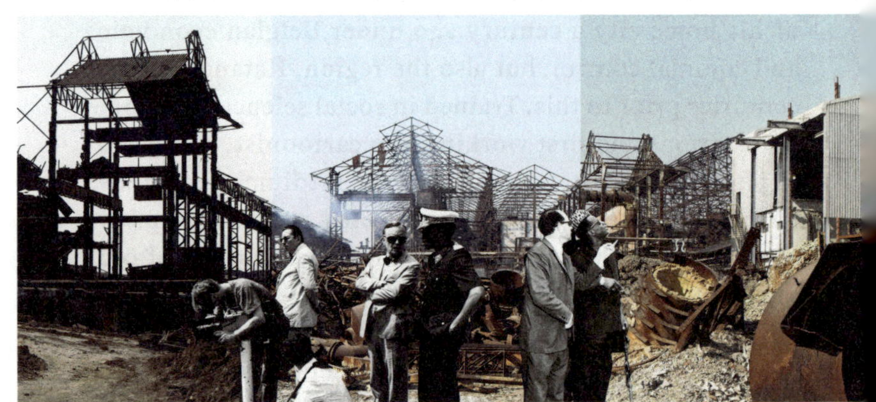

Sammy Baloji, *Memoire* series, *Untitled 25*, 2006

Africa as a European invention happened in the late nineteenth century with the Berlin Conference.[1] Precolonial Africa was under the rule of kingdoms and local organizations that identified themselves with administrative and political rules other than those imposed within the arbitrary colonial boundaries established from 1885 onwards. In the case of Zanzibar (a region quite close to the current province of Katanga, where I was born), archaeological excavations bring to light the long-distance trade undertaken with the Gulf between the fifth and eighth centuries. Later on, one will note intensified exchanges between Bantu, Arabs, Persians, and Indians in the middle of the eighth century. The Timbuktu manuscripts are among many others of traces of precolonial civilizations such as the Great Zimbabwe.

Contact with European kingdoms came late. One reason I'm here in Rome[2] is that I'm interested in the first encounter between the Portuguese and the Congo Kingdom in the fifteenth century, for example. And when you go through the writings of the sixteenth century, you find the King of Congo writing to the King of Portugal, sending ambassadors to Portugal. People from both sides were well educated and treated equally.

Things started to progressively degrade with the massive slave trade undertaken by Portuguese, Spanish, Dutch, British, French, and so forth. The relationship changed in the next centuries. The African kingdoms started to collapse, because people were leaving enslaved. In art, during the Renaissance period, objects collected from Africa and

1 The Berlin Conference of 1884–85, also known as the Congo Conference, regulated European colonization and trade in Africa.
2 Sammy Baloji was a fellow in 2019–20 at the Académie de France in Rome–Villa Médicis; this interview was conducted in January 2020 during Baloji's residency.

other discovered continents were at first seen as objects of curiosity. Jesuit missionaries were in the Congo in the sixteenth century and started to collect those objects. It was a way of learning through other knowledges. Later on, Europeans started to categorize things in all fields; creating the idea of the Other, which also came through this colonial reality based on the slave trade. When you go through all those elements, you can more easily understand how art, art history, ethnography, and anthropology are intimately connected with the evolution of politics and economy.

You grew up in the Congo but are now at least in part based in Brussels as well. Why is that?

I was invited to a residency program at the ethnographic museum when they realized I was interested in the colonial archives. I decided to stay in Brussels for personal reasons and to continue my research. It was the first time that I worked with institutional archives; the experience was different than the one I had in Congo when I discovered images in an abandoned mining area.[3] But working with institutional archives leads me to better understand how the colonial propaganda played a role in terms of creating ideas of the Other through ethnography and anthropology, or how photography and films were key instruments in the colonial enterprise. Even though ethnographic museums are interested in other cultures, they have a certain agenda.

Other essays and interviews in this book discuss these concerns at length, and they also talk about current efforts to

---

3 In the mid-2000s, Baloji uncovered a trove of archival images in an abandoned mining area in his native Katanga, the mineral-rich region surrounding Lubumbashi. The images shown here, from the series *Mémoire* (2006), are portraits of past colonial mining activity superimposed upon Baloji's own contemporary photography, representing the landscapes and infrastructure of the now largely depleted resources.

demodernize and decolonize. The word "decolonize" is currently everywhere in the art world. How do you decode it and what do you think it means?

When you talk about decolonization, the global network, or transcultural exchange, one thing that we could also look at today is what is going on around the topic of Anthropocene.[4] The fact that human activity impacts the climate and the environment is strongly linked to industrialization; human transmutation of ecosystem elements, pollution, and so on is a major concern. These aforementioned activities are mostly carried out or even initiated by so-called developed countries that had colonies. The current consumerist and capitalist economy leads to such exploitation of human and natural resources with the result of an inequitable distribution of wealth.

These natural affects show us that we are all linked, and we are all responsible for what is going on in the world. So it's not so much about decolonization; it's really through physical effects on the earth that we can start to learn from each other and stop relying only on dominant and imposed knowledge. All those notions of the Other, color, or racism don't make sense if the effects are about the earth that we all share. Our planet has undergone damage because of our actions.

Everywhere, really.

I was observing all those events that led to the kind of categorization I mentioned before. And later in the industrial revolution, there's also all those International World Exhibitions. Think of British architect Joseph Paxton, who created the Crystal Palace in London[5]—you can see in

4 Our present geological age, during which human activity has been
the dominant influence on the environment, and a point of discourse
and production in contemporary art.

5 The Crystal Palace was erected in Hyde Park in 1851 to host
the "Great Exhibition of the Works of Industry of All Nations," a bid

the architecture that he was inspired by plants from the Amazon. Colonial gardeners brought plants to other places in the world, and therefore changed ecosystems. Since the colonial period in Congo, we eat foods made with corn flour, but this isn't from the Congo! It's from Mexico and America. It's the same with potatoes. So things have been moved through this knowledge of controlling nature and controlling the differences between people.

Speaking of the Crystal Palace and its historical exposition, you cofounded Picha Encounters, which later became Biennale de Lubumbashi. The biennial format of course hearkens back to these World Expos, but what might make this one different?

The Biennale takes place in the interstices of an urban space with a colonial heritage. But it is intended to interrogate and reveal the local and national identities built up over the different policies that these territories will have known. This investigation is done in echoes and dialogue with what takes place in art and discursive thoughts at the international level. How I came to create the event with other artists and art producers is all linked with what I told you before in terms of the archival material that I discovered in the mining area; it clarified my view of the city by understanding how and why it was created. I was born in a city and raised in the "modern" culture, but by being Black from a Black family, the relation with tradition was all directed through the knowledge imposed during the colonial period. When I discovered the images in the abandoned mine, I was then intrigued by the colonial system, its violence and agenda. Cities in Africa are colonial, not local, inventions. And you can see it in how those cities were planned.

at asserting British industrial power (France had hosted several World Expos prior to this). Six million people attended.

Can you provide an example?

In Lubumbashi we had a sanitary corridor separating the White city from the Indigenous city. The space between them existed because the colonialists wanted to avoid malaria. The second reason was also to not permit a certain connection between those cultures. Not even mixed-race children were exempt from this; hybrid children were taken away. The economic system was absolutely Belgium and not Congo at all. Even access to knowledge was colonial. When I went to school, I wasn't allowed to speak Swahili because it was a local language. If you wanted access to knowledge, you needed to learn French. There was hierarchy between White and Black in this segregated system.

So this biennial is a way to question these structures.

In my country's thirty-seven years under a dictatorial regime,[6] nothing was happening in terms of free thinking or redefining those local models. As an artist, it's interesting to question those elements, right? And that's why I worked on a biennial. The first edition was linked to the notion of urbanism and the architecture of Lubumbashi itself. It connected to those spaces and places—what is the meaning of space? And what discussions can emerge? I'm quite aware that I will never change the city, because it must be part of political, economical, and architectural agendas. But what's interesting on the artistic level is that it can raise and propose ways of thinking or opening discussions. The cities are there; you will never erase them and start new ones.

6 Congo gained independence from Belgium in 1960. From the early 1960s to 1997, Mobutu Sese Seko ruled Congo under a military regime; his early rise was the result of series of civil wars between local factions and were also Cold War proxy conflict between the Soviet Union and the United States, the latter of which had interests in the region's uranium to support its nuclear weapons program.

Are you connecting in any way to the African biennial circuit that evolved with Dakar, or Bamako, in the past thirty years or so?

Dakar's biennial and Bamako are governmental initiatives. Lubumbashi was founded by artists without any support from the cultural ministry. After fifty years of colonization and thirty to forty years of dictatorial regime and worse after that, there was a hole that we needed to fill. But it's a kind of utopian thinking. We decided how to respond to the things we were seeing. It started from local needs.

And is it for local viewers?

My participation in the Bamako Biennale in 2007 was certainly more decisive in the choice to organize a similar event in the city of Lubumbashi. Bamako offered a platform around which not only artists and cultural actors from Africa and its diaspora could gather and interact, but also people and audiences interested in the artistic dynamics of and from the continent. The Lubumbashi Biennale aims to be a platform that takes Lubumbashi and the Congo as a critical starting point for analyzing the political, economic, and artistic dynamics. It aims to bridge the local, the national, and the international. In this sense the Biennale does not claim to have a target audience. But local realities in terms of infrastructure, mobility, and comfort don't favor accessibility. This challenge of access and organization also makes it a singular event, as many difficulties have to be overcome.

Are you reasserting an African viewpoint of art?

Whenever we want to start to speak about African art, we have references like *Primitivism in 20th Century Art* at the Museum of Modern Art in New York in 1984 or *Magiciens de la Terre* in Paris in 1989. These two references are at the same time the trigger of polemical debates around a "Western egoism still as unbridled as in the

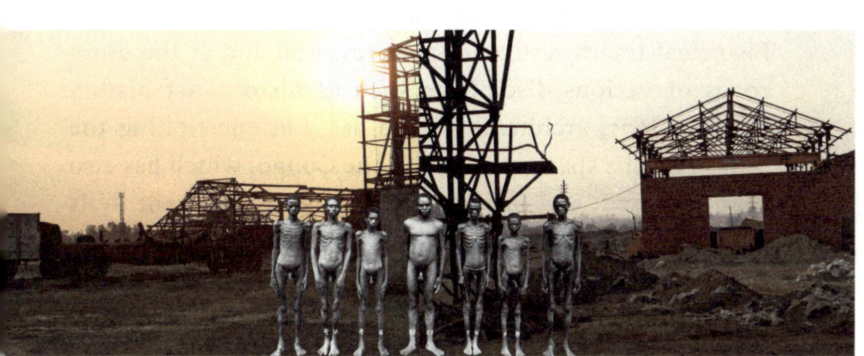

Sammy Baloji, *Memoire* series, *Untitled 4*, 2006

centuries of colonialism and remembrance,"[7] and a will to identify, name these artists, and contextualize artistic creation long excluded from Western channels. These empty pages of an art history of exclusion constitute a vast field of exploration, creative speculation, and even artistic re-appropriation, by revisiting these past centuries and collections of natural history, ethnography, curiosity cabinets, and existing gifts. Not with a view to returning to the past, but to creating a critical and inclusive discourse more inclined to the contemporary.

My artistic approach is indeed impregnated with data; historical traces resulting from research and at the crossroads of various disciplines such as history, art history, anthropology, architecture, and art. I'm questioning the notion of this space we share in the Congo, which has also been imposed, and bringing to life all the different tools or strategies or tactics linked to space. But at the same time those elements connect spaces such as the Congo to the rest of the world. These spaces have been created from outside, but that means they are also *linked* to the outside. Whenever you say that Africa is somewhere else, it's not —it's connected. This is why I also decided to work with photography and installation. Photography is based on the fact that things can be interpreted from a different perspective. It's polysemic and directed. And so to work with photography and how it's been used in anthropology and creating the image of the city has become the kind of material for me that shows ambiguity. The direction that I'm taking now is this: how can I express and incorporate local knowledge? Not coming back to what is authentic; I don't believe in this kind of notion. I'm more interested in dynamic evolution.

7 Thomas McEvill, "Doctor Lawyer Indian Chief," in *Artforum* (November 1984), a review of the *Primitivism* exhibition.

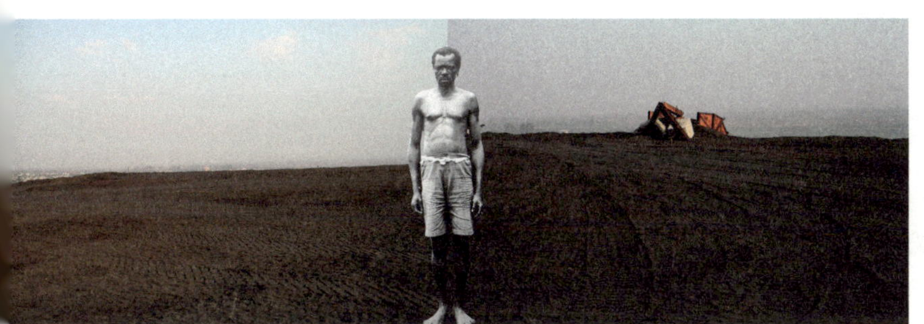

Sammy Baloji, *Memoire* series, *Untitled 15*, 2006

Perhaps the planetary *is mostly about expressing the knowl-edges of many localities, and if those knowledges are perceived, validated, and connected.*

Yes.

FUTURE

FUTURE

Notes on the Necropolitics of Ethnographic Collections

Clémentine Deliss

In the context of practices that combine historical residuals held in museums with contemporary searches and acquisitions and therefore new retention strategies, ethnographic collections offer the most violent, urgent, and ethical cases in point, for these so-called ethnographic collections continue to evoke symptoms of exploitation in the "afterlife of property."[1] That the incarceration of chattels should persist even today is due to the large-scale excoriation of the original authorship of these artifacts and their ontological reinscription within the colonialist discipline of anthropology. Such that one particularly sinister crime from the past now remains the eradication by museum anthropologists, missionaries, and collectors of the names of the original makers; those artists, designers, engineers, and architects who devised complex representations of survival and belief. To remediate this erasure today is to steer against the dominant current of reductionist strategies, including exhibition display, that confirm the logos of ethnos and the questionable custody of these collections.

As such the ethno-colonial museum, with its recoil of goods and chattels, remains the milieu of the dead.[2]

1 Christina Sharpe, *In the Wake. On Blackness and Being* (Durham, 2016), p. 15.
2 I developed this notion of the hold in relation to the writings of Christina Sharpe, presented during the event "The Milieu of the Dead," curated by Hannah Hurtzig and Marian Kaiser of the Mobile Academy in Berlin, December 2017.

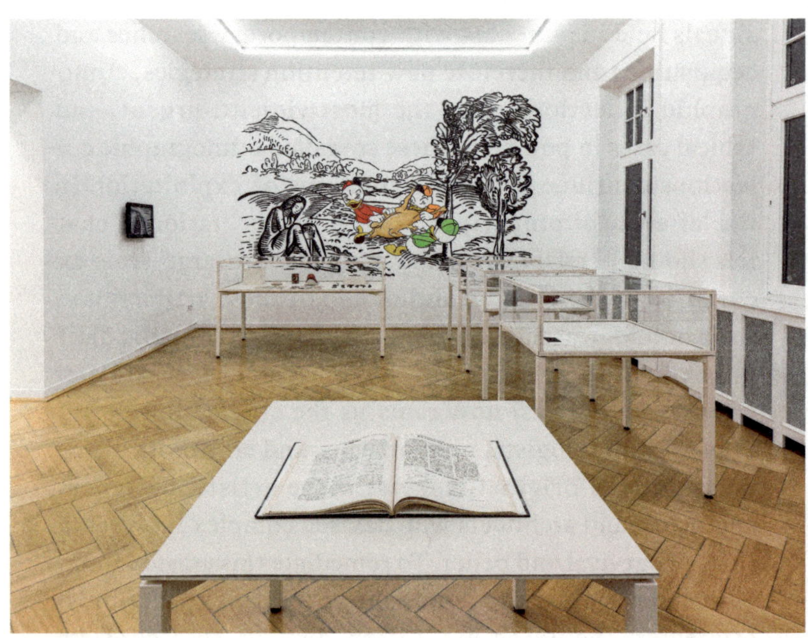

Installation view of work by Minerva Cuevas (wall drawing) with artifacts from the collection of Weltkulturen Museum Frankfurt. From the exhibition *Foreign Exchange (or the stories you wouldn't tell a stranger)*, 2014, curated by Clémentine Deliss and Yvette Mutumba

In this publicly inaccessible crypt, belongings acquired, looted, even wrenched away in the name of science and cultural exchange are safeguarded and inscribed within the annals of an Other's institution. Narratives in museum ethnography continue to retain master-slave terminologies that concur with the language of seclusion and control, such as the keeper, the custodian, and the conservator.[3] Indeed, this sealed reservoir of cultural heritage is maintained on the implicit understanding that therein lies an ambivalent energy yet to be converted and exploited by its current owners. Arguments surrounding toxicity help to legitimize the safeguarding of these artifacts within the impenetrable confines of the repository, which can even be placed below a river, as is the case with the Seine, where the 300,000 artifacts "belonging" to the Musée du quai Branly are incarcerated like a muted population in the holdings of a slave ship. It is claimed that toxic residues remain as traces of poisons formerly sprayed onto foreign objects upon arrival in the museum. But toxicity also lies latent as a potentially contagious microbiome, identified on fragments of human remains. More than ever before, the former ethnological museum has become a paranoid site of retention with increased stockpiling and extensive lab testing.

How might one forge an internationally binding legal resolution, which obliges state museums to provide access

3 "In the wake, the semiotics of the slave ship continue: from the forced movements of the enslaved to the forced movements of the migrant and the refugee, to the regulation of Black people in North American streets and neighborhoods, to those ongoing crossings of and drownings in the Mediterranean Sea, to the brutal colonial reimaginings of the slave ship and the ark; to the reappearances of the slave ship in everyday life in the form of the prison, the camp, and the school." Sharpe (see note 1), p. 21.

to their collections for several months each year, during which different forms of unconditional research could be undertaken? When will architects be commissioned to consider the challenge of transforming repositories from nothing short of object-prisons to new spatial environments for experimental inquiry? How can one impress upon museums that the issue of gaining entry to the storage units of these museums is more than a sporadic requirement by a specialist in the field, than a systemic necessity in the twenty-first century? For these museums, it is actually about going beyond the ethno-logical question and deconstructing the diverse conceptualizations of collecting, ownership, and possession today. Nevertheless, why do these so-called ethnographic collections remain shrouded in non-visibility when they are increasingly discussed in the press? Should legal leverage for rights of access be left to the underrepresented efforts of indigeneity claims and the unwieldy politics of restitution? Notwithstanding the proliferation of postcolonial studies today, ethnology's scientific inferences continue to frame these collections and discern which objects are to be exhibited on the world stage and how they should be named and presented. Where is the collective voice of artists, curators, and students on this matter?

At a conference held at the British Museum in London in May 2017 and aptly entitled "The Museum as Battleground," Hartwig Fischer, the German director of the British Museum, claimed: "The British Museum is a world. It's about enticing visitors to be inspired to address contemporary issues. We have to make the British Museum work in terms of display."[4] If Fischer is currently fashioning a museum of the world for the world in London, then one

4 Quotation recorded by the author at the conference.

might ask, post-Brexit, how will it be possible for certain nationalities to acquire the visa necessary to visit their heritage? Further, the current capital investment in systems of display not only bolsters a museum's standing, but also implicitly works toward defining the desirable visitor, determining their country, income strata, class, and education. Here the economic and the political combine with the ergonomic to prescribe how much time a person should spend in the museum, how they should behave and how they may respond to what they see, a process which is ideally animated by interactive and commercialized cultural consumerism. The museum as an institutional organ expulses not just histories, but people.

In Berlin, the German state seeks to reinstate its cultural magnanimity through the Humboldt Forum, a museum and entertainment complex in a reconstructed Prussian palace the size of three football pitches built over the course of more than ten years and at an estimated cost of 650 million euros. By exhibiting works of non-European origin sequestered in German holdings, this new cultural mouthpiece of the nation constructs a series of self-entitlements. These work to recognize the complexity of provenance while maintaining the authority of ownership and interpretation. Efforts are made in museum ethnology to compensate for the insufficient probes into the colonial history of these sequestered artifacts. Tracing provenance—the newly revived industry of ethnological research—is long overdue as Bénédicte Savoy, a former member of the Humboldt Forum's council of experts, rightly pointed out in the summer of 2017.[5] Her outcry led

5 Bénédicte Savoy, "Das Humboldt-Forum ist wie Tschernobyl," in *Süddeutsche Zeitung,* July 20, 2017, www.sueddeutsche.de/ kultur/benedicte-savoy-ueber-das-humboldt-forum-das-humboldt-forum-ist-wie-tschernobyl-1.3596423 (accessed February 3, 2020).

to a veritable flurry of activity within the inordinate number of German ethnographic museums now seeking to make public the origins of their collections. However, provenance studies, if uncritically deployed, actually succeed in embalming the actions of the colonizer by producing a new, necropolitical formulation of the ethnological point of departure. Dusting off cardboard boxes, revealing discarded paperwork—if it exists at all and has not been lost in the bombing actions of World War II[6]—draws the scholar back to the moment of contact and subsequently to their fascination with origins, a desirous inquisition that underpins the discourse of museum anthropology. As a branch of neo-ethnological historiography, provenance studies constitute the minimum action to be taken within the wider and urgent politics of restitution.

In the market context, however, provenance partners in crime with pedigree—which resonates uncomfortably with the reformulation of a racial concept. Insurance and thereby monetary value is calculated on the basis of a lineage of acquisition, established beyond the objects' original ownership or site of production. By circulating in the salons of well-known European or North American socialites and industrialists, such masterpiece objects acquire an additional layer of toxicity: the patina of investment capital. And this connects the issue of access to cover all future impounded artworks beyond the specificity of the

6 "There are no documents. Everything was lost in the war." This comment is one that I heard repeatedly while directing the Weltkulturen Museum in Frankfurt between 2010 and 2015. In effect, the Allies had bombed this museum and destroyed not only artifacts but paperwork too. Nevertheless, the spoils of war do not dispense one of critical circumspection, as the revelation of damning material discovered in the museum cellar in Frankfurt soon proved leading us to curate the exhibition *Foreign Exchange (or the stories you would not tell a stranger)*, 2014 in Berlin.

ethnographic collection. Can one imagine a moment when researchers no longer have access to museum banks regardless of whether their collections originate from the wealthy nations of the world, or not?

Finally, as elsewhere in Western Europe, Germany restricts public access to colonial collections for reasons of conservation and "pre-emptive angst,"[7] proposing digital databanks as an alternative to direct engagement with the physical objects themselves. However, this begs the question of who selects the artifacts to be documented: are these internal experts or external researchers, with all the cultural and disciplinary multiplicity they may bring with them? Currently, it is the museum custodians and tribal art experts, charged with defining the pedigree of selected artifacts, who continue to distinguish what should or should not be photographed for posterity. The situation is nothing less than circular and endemic. What is to be done? What might generate a process of critical remediation?

Occupy? Lie demonstratively on the floor of the ethnographic museum's repository and wait until one is physically dragged off by the police? This tactic is likely to draw in the press and make people aware of the condition of sequestration and inaccessibility affecting these collections that, uniquely and generically, represent the world's art histories. But what can it bring in the long term?

Strike? To strike presupposes that the employees of ethnographic museums in Europe are sufficiently discontent with their conditions to wish to change them. Yet to date no incentives can be identified that demonstrate that staff are ready to change the ways of operating with these collections. Museum anthropology, like colonial

7 Ann L. Stoler, *Duress: Imperial Durabilities in Our Times* (Durham, 2016), p. 31.

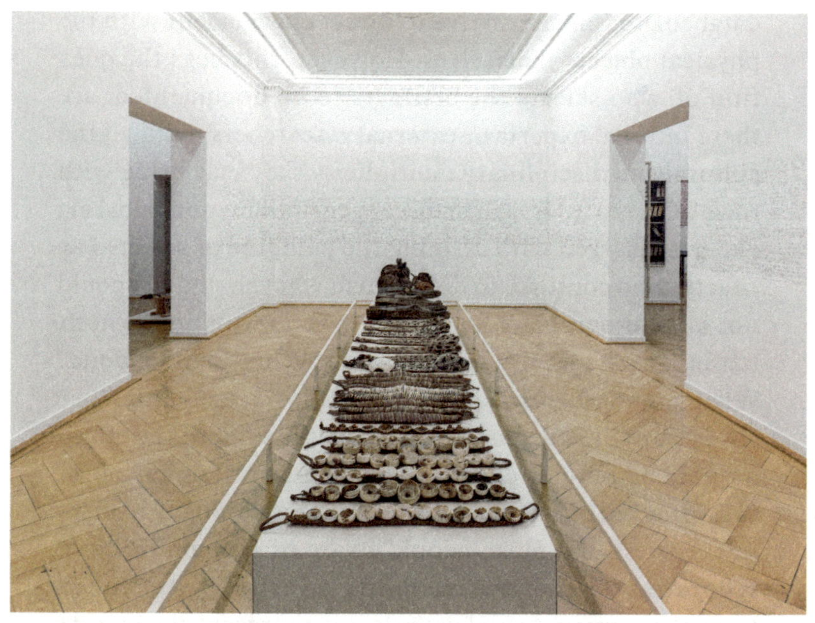

Wall drawing by David Weber-Krebs with artifacts from the Weltkulturen Museum Frankfurt collection. From the exhibition *Foreign Exchange (or the stories you wouldn't tell a stranger)*, 2014

plantations in Southeast Asia or the African continent, remains a monocultural field. To cultivate expertise and hold onto one's select object of desire requires preventing other disciplines from staking a semantic claim or practicing alternative forms of remediation.

Petition or Manifesto? Is today's militancy reduced to that of petition signing? Can this chainmail of virtual democracy, published in one of the ubiquitous online art journals, activate rights of access? The format of the manifesto may be more to the point; it speaks faster and more efficiently than longer academic treatics. This particular manifesto on the rights of access to sequestered collections states that the world cultures museum has no longer any power in and of itself, and that as a result it effectively no longer exists. It cannot continue to usurp other peoples' histories and thereby control the meta and necropolitics of the world's art and design histories, not to mention belief systems.

Adulterate market forces? Perhaps one could act against the sentimentality of national institutional heritage and lift the embargo on deaccessioning, effectively letting these artifacts from colonial collections circulate once again perhaps with heightened speed, slipping from the stronghold of state museums, risking the ravages of the black market, being traded beyond the logic of value attributed by tribal art auctions and private dealers in New York, Paris, London, or Doha? A naïve option? Perhaps. But if stasis is the order of the day, how otherwise can the dynamics of desire and evaluation be regenerated, fought for, and shared?

Restitute no matter where or how? What should one think about the unwillingness to send the ship back to base, together with its booty? What prevents making real the returns of these goods and chattels, however unwieldy?

The argument that museums in this or that country have insufficient air conditioning; an absence of professional conservators; an untethered urge to resell to private dealers; or even the propensity to destroy artworks, does not suffice. What permits the former colonizer to determine criteria and conditions for museums other than their own? No argument concerning the inadequacy of museums in the countries of origin is a plausible argument for nonrestitution. Museums should not be classified hierarchically according to conservation. Conservation and perdurance are culturally specific and highly malleable concepts. So, too, is the notion of a universal museum that can house everything. Today, the worst scenario facing these museums would be for their universalizing displays to be instrumentalized for sinister, xenophobic intentions.

The Model of a Museum University: Today there is a palpable tension between the sheer overflow of materiality, the occluded histories and biographies of things, their necessary movement across worlds, and the current condition of global exchange. Against these contradictions, it should be possible to radically rethink the museum, thereby enabling it to transition from the "orgone accumulator" (Wilhelm Reich) of cultural consumerism that it has become into a "museum university": a backstage venue for students and researchers to engage in transdisciplinary inquiry and develop new interpretations based directly on the collections. A museum university resembles the conflation of an autonomous art school, a university "without condition,"[8] and an advanced production space. It articulates an extended family of ethical, ideational, imagistic, and technical operations that center on a reworking of

8 See Jacques Derrida, "The Future of the Profession or the University without Condition," in *Without Alibi* (Palo Alto, 2002).

collections and archives. Paul Rabinow's notion of "remediation" provides a valuable conceptual tool kit with which to rethink the object of study in a post-ethnographic context.[9] In the first, perhaps more contemporary sense of the term, to remediate means to bring about a shift in medium, to experiment with alternative ways of describing, interpreting, and connecting objects in a collection to one another. Here one recognizes the value of reintroducing a laboratory or workshop space into the museum as a physical site for collection-centric, post-ethnographic inquiry. To remediate also implies to heal, for example, the ambivalent and persistent resonance of the "political grammar of colonialism's durable presence," as Ann L. Stoler has written.[10]

The earlier assumption of epistemological authority in ethnology does not extend comfortably within the post-colonial situation. One can critically integrate earlier narratives and hypotheses drafted by anthropologists and experts from area studies, but the imperative is surely to respect testimonials that originate from the producers and users of these artifacts. The museum university enables one to expand on these multiple, non-exclusive meanings by taking these artifacts as the starting point and stimulus for contemporary interpretations that respond to a multitude of sociopolitical developments, aesthetic practices, and modes of translation. By emphasizing, for example, the formulation of new patents based on innovations derived from historical artifacts, one may advance juridical arguments for proprietary rights. If an engineer develops a matrix for a type of filter, or an architectural element,

9 Paul Rabinow, *Marking Time, On the Anthropology of the Contemporary* (Princeton, 2008).
10 Stoler (see note 7), p. 9.

from the weaving systems of certain fish traps from Papua New Guinea, this design can be legally defined as an innovation if it demonstrates proof of technicity. The designer is qualified to patent the model they have developed in the context of this object's previously undocumented authorship and inexistent copyright. Similarly, with new educational formats of polymathic research, it may be possible to develop further strategies of reappropriation. Only through the results generated by rights of access to the collections can the ethnocolonial museum transition into a museum of the commons and produce an equitable reassessment of former ethnographic collections in Europe and North America.

For many, this post-ethnographic model represents the symptom of a restive institution that seeks to dissolve the authority of museum studies. Yet, what is proposed here is closer to an agonistic relationship between different fields of know-how. The expertise of the museum ethnographer lies in their contextual, bibliographic knowledge of the broader history of the object in question. The information they provide inserts the artifact within a given landscape of erudition. In contrast, an artist cannot be expected to conform to the same disciplinary boundaries or styles of elucidation. They are likely to identify other aspects of an object's making, touch on alternative meridians within the stores, walk through shelving units using a different route, stretch up to the top shelf of a sealed cupboard, or ask for a ladder to inspect something that has been placed out of reach for decennia. In this manner, the assemblages that external artists and researchers produce from the ethnographic collection are necessarily unorthodox and experimental, reflecting a series of criteria whose identification is not always clearly defined from the start.

In his work on agency, Bruno Latour introduces the distinction between "ostensive" and "performative definitions." He writes: "the object of an ostensive definition remains there, whatever happens to the index of the onlooker. But the object of a performative definition vanishes when it is no longer performed—or if it stays, then it means that other actors have taken over the relay. And this relay, by definition, cannot be 'the social world,' since it is that very world which is in dire need of a fresh relay."[11] Applied onto the condition of ethnological artifacts, Latour's proposition infers that the ostensive definition actually presupposes and precedes the ethnographic, and thereby the process through which ethnographic exhibitions are developed. An object that is searched for in order to illustrate or represent a sociocultural context, or any other ethnological category, will not be altered by its display. Contextualization is predetermined by the selection of the item and presentation, which is intended to be read in a specific manner. In contrast, a performative definition suggests that the artifact can actually generate new, unexpected interpretations that are mutable, possibly incommensurable with one another, but by no means set in stone. This impermanency enables the artist to act as the "mediator" rather than the "intermediary" of meanings or definitions.[12] Remediation, in the sense of Paul Rabinow's

11 Bruno Latour, *Reassembling the Social: An Introduction to Actor-Network-Theory* (Oxford, 2005), pp. 37–38.
12 "An intermediary, in my vocabulary, is what transports meaning or force without transformation: defining its inputs is enough to define its outputs. (...) Mediators, on the other hand, cannot be counted as just one; they might count for one, for nothing, for several, or for infinity. Their input is never a good predictor of their output; their specificity has to be taken into account every time. Mediators transform, translate, distort, and modify the meaning or the elements they are supposed to carry. (...) it is this constant uncertainty over the intimate nature of entities—are they behaving as intermediaries or as mediators?— that is the source of all the other uncertainties we have decided to follow." Latour, ibid. p. 39.

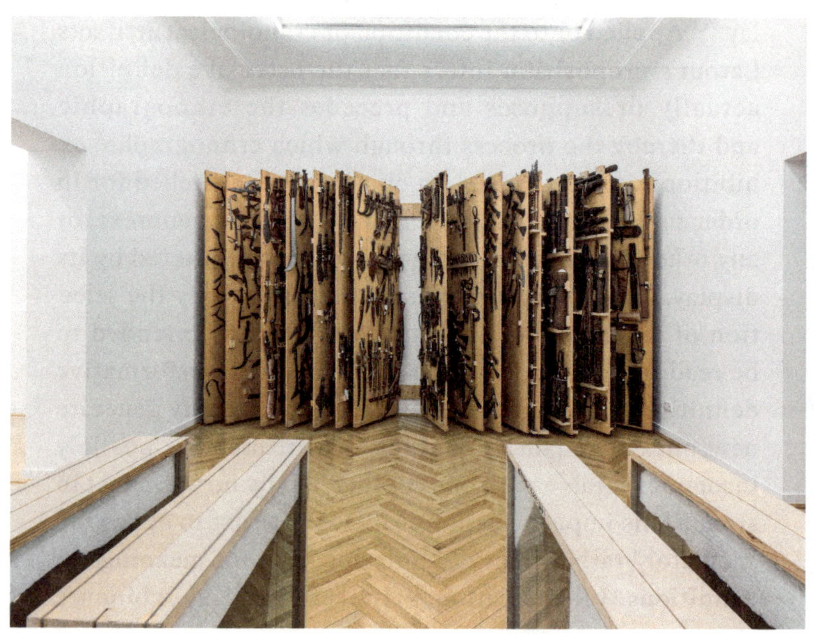

Installation view, panels of weaponry usually in museum storage, Weltkulturen Museum Frankfurt. From the exhibition *Foreign Exchange (or the stories you wouldn't tell a stranger)*, 2014

dialogical methodology of healing and transferring, is predicated on this "mediatory" role.

"The challenge," he writes, "is to turn a collection of separate entities, however distinctive, into a dynamic site for experiencing and reflecting on our history, our future, and our uneasy and unsure mutual connectedness. We need to move from a vision of a world of separateness and hierarchy to one of multiplicity, creativity, and worth beyond the exotic. Said another way, the 'our' in our history, future, and potential connectedness is what needs to be thought through, reinvented, and presented in such a way that it matters for those who come to a museum of world cultures. Placing too much emphasis on diversity and discreteness leads to a pale relativism with a complex if at times sordid history; placing too much emphasis on their commonality leads to a pale humanism with its own thinned out legacy. One way to navigate this slalom between the too particular and the too general is to turn the parceled collections into an assemblage, carefully wrought, and to produce a vision, open, detailed, and precious of World Cultures. If that vision or presentation is open to change, conflicts of interpretation, creative reinvention then vitality, or at least its possibility, can be restored to these artefacts of lives once lived and collections collected."[13] The guest artist becomes both the intermediary (Latour) and the remediator of the collection.

The distinction between intermediary and (re)mediator identifies the implicit friction between the anthropologist internal to the museum and the external guest. The common assumption is that the museum anthropologist's status of "scientist" can be pitted against the uninformed extrapolation of the artist whose lab work is aligned, at

13 Paul Rabinow, *Object Atlas, Fieldwork in the Museum* (Bielefeld, 2011), preface.

best, with inspiration or new formulations of "artistic research." The expertise of museum ethnographers relies on owning the keys to context and thus, the authoritative frame of the "object" in question. In this sense, their input is isomorphic with their output, like some self-fulfilling and self-perpetuating prophecy of ethnological eschatology. The knowledge they trade in finds its currency in the construction of authenticity projected onto the unauthored exhibit. The artist however dislodges the authority of ownership and expertise that the custodian holds onto. Penetrating the confinement of the storage space, the outside eye transgresses. It selects and releases a response from the object, bringing it out of the dark by reappropriating, recollecting, and reclassifying it through a heterodox dialogue of elucidation. In so doing, the exogamous interlocutor, who collects the collection anew, breathes presence back into the artifacts, restores a consciousness of their unfinished status, and helps to heal the institution. "We need to help objects to move," philosopher and artist Issa Samb once said, "for neither wind nor fire can."[14] In turn, the objects become agents, animating a new indexical relation to the phenomena in question, revealing another side to their optics, forms, grammar, and genealogy. Agency goes viral in the museum university—it multiplies perspectives and propagates new recursive researches, encouraging conflicting as well as complimentary interpretations that extend beyond ethnic, cultural, or sociological explanations.[15]

14 Issa Samb, in *La Coquille,* a film by Antje Majewski, 2009. Samb says, *"il faut aider les objets à se déplacer. Ni le vent, ni le feu peuvent les déplacer."*
15 Latour writes: "Controversies about agencies have to be deployed to the full, no matter how difficult it is so as not to simplify in advance the task of assembling the collective," (see note 11), p. 50.

If the model of the museum university stimulates, it also faces hindrances. It assumes that in-house workshopping has to be rendered, a process which runs the danger of reifying rather than expanding emergent meanings. Yet research has to be slow, seeking to prolong the adjacent, tentative, uncut, and unedited phases of inquiry. As Christina Sharpe states, "We must become undisciplined. The work we do requires new modes and methods of research and teaching; new ways of entering and leaving the archives of slavery."[16] Transitioning into a plurality of new identifications and alternative methodologies is a necessary part of the ethnographic collection's transformation in the twenty-first century but, as James Clifford reminds us, such "cultural translation is always uneven, always betrayed."[17] This "betrayal" reflects the tense relationship between the normativity of institutions and those unruly, experimental practices that seek freedom of expression.[18] Today, colonial collections are nothing short of a combat zone, tugging at the discipline that grew out of their expropriation. And yet even today, the dog won't let go of its bone.

16 Sharpe (see note 1), p. 13.

17 James Clifford, *Returns. Becoming Indigenous in the Twenty-First Century* (Cambridge, MA, 2016), pp. 48–49.

18 German philosopher Christoph Menke defines the experiment as "a mode of action" which produces "constellations, situations, arrangements in which something then takes place. The experimenter creates something and exposes him or herself to an event. The experiment shows that in order to know something, one must do something. The experiment connects receptivity with activity; indeed, it binds receptivity to activity." See Christoph Menke, "The Experiment between Art and Life," paper given in Montreal, 2015, p. 2.

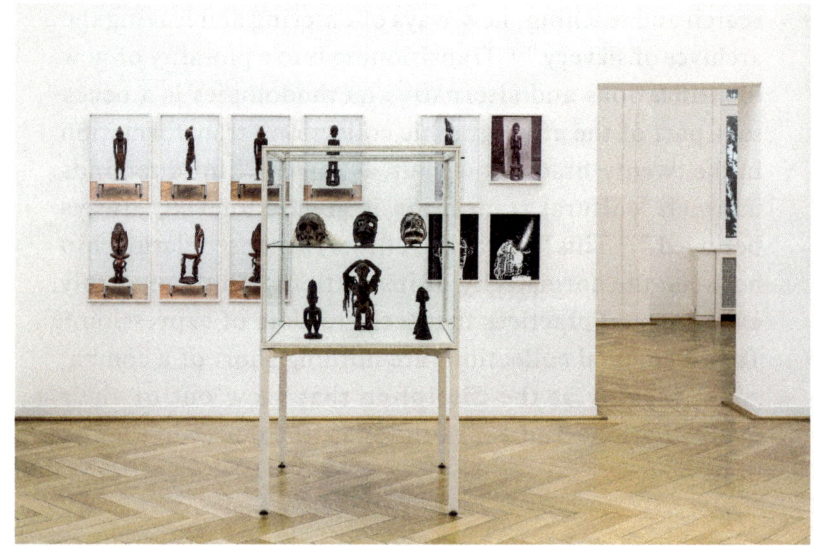

Installation view, photo series by Wolfgang Günzel and artifacts from the collection of Weltkulturen Museum Frankfurt. From the exhibition *Foreign Exchange (or the stories you wouldn't tell a stranger)*, 2014

Manifesto for the Rights of Access to Colonial Collections Sequestered in Western Europe

Clémentine Deliss

Where are we in 2019?

Twenty-seven years since the first edition of Dak'Art,
the Biennial of Visual Arts in Senegal.
Twenty-seven years since Alpha Oumar Konaré,
former president of Mali and of ICOM, stated,
"It's about time that we questioned the fundamental
basis of the situation and *killed*—I repeat *killed*—
the Western model of the museum in Africa
in order for new methods for the conservation and
promotion of our heritage to flourish."[1]

Let's think back to these colonial museums

1863: Saint-Louis in Senegal, and the museum of "Tropical
Africa" created by Louis Faidherbe in the service of the
French Republic;
1907: Windhoek, Namibia, and the museological structure
set up by colonial Germany;
1910: Nairobi, Kenya and Lagos, Nigeria, and the museums
founded by British imperialism.

And one century later,
in the throes of post-independence

In 1966, the Musée Dynamique of Léopold Sédar Senghor
—that *dynamythical* museum—opens in Dakar, Senegal.
(Rest in peace!)

---

1 From ICOM's (International Council of Museums) 1992 message
from the president.

And with it all the desire for internationalism,
for festivals, gatherings, and workshops,
those manifestations at the Village des Arts in Dakar,
the artists' collectives of Tenq and Huit Facettes,
and the infamous Laboratoire Agit'Art!
(Rest in peace.)

And slowly, but far too slowly,
the issue is raised of collections in Europe,
engendered by imperialism and the market,
by noxious colonialism with its sinister discourse
and serial kleptomania.
These collections locked up still today in
the vaults of the ethno-colonial museums of Western
Europe.

Intellectual and governmental plantations!
Notions of imperialist progress!
The monoculture of ethnology!
Disciplinary and discursive closure!
Taxonomies and scientific racism!
Metabolisms covered in blood!
"Colomentalities!"
(Rest in peace.)

What to do today
with the mass of what are called "objects"?
Objects in collections that are named "ethnographic,"
"object-witnesses," in the words of anthropologist
Marcel Griaule, "objects" from the market in so-called
"tribal art"?
These millions of objects, an inordinate quantity in
Germany alone ...

All!
without name,
without author,
without intellectual rights,
incarcerated by ethnology and its genealogies,
which originate, more often than not,
outside the countries of origin,
identified by collecting, resales,
and swapping between museums.
A provenance at home in the salons
and "secret gardens" of "patrons,"
from Nelson Rockefeller to Marc Ladreit de Lacharrière.

All these objects in inaccessible depots!
Under the river Seine in Paris,
where sleep, in the holdings
of ships built for slavery,
these muted bodies,
these human remains.
Or otherwise, secreted in the urban periphery,
in the "prison house of radical difference and negativity"
(Simon Gikandi),
confined in that fridge-freezer of the soul,
because of their double or triple toxicity,
as carriers of a microbiome, capable of
unleashing unexpected pandemics,
or so they tell us ...

Necropolitics of sequestered objects!
Hyper-restrictive access!
Discursive claustrophobia!
Exerting control!
Control!
Control!

Control over future interpretations!
Because anything is possible if you omit
the artist,
the author,
the producer,
the name of the non-documented,
to replace it with ethnos.

Where are we now?
Restitution?
Yes, please!
Provenance research?
Yes, please!
Retrace the biographies of objects acquired or stolen?
Yes, please!
Find out what those object hunters and organ poachers
of the Other excluded?
Yes, please!
But where? With whom? With what?
Ah okay!
So, reify omission instead?
Return to the source,
bring back the handmaidens of colonialism,
the priests of ethnological phantasmagoria,
encourage their hermeneutic labor once more,
restore the legitimacy of their discipline,
just as they were about to go into retirement ...
Not sure? No thanks!

That's when the State magnanimously walks in,
hand in hand with the universal museum
of the twenty-first century!
Now, go get a visa to visit your heritage
in Paris, Berlin, London, Amsterdam, or Vienna!

Fashioned by interior design, exclusive and expulsive.
An exhibition that only adds a sentence or two ...
Because that's the point!
They didn't document much
on those colonial collecting expeditions, did they?
Instead, it was collect!
Collect! Collect!

Ah, the excoriation of the name of the engineer, the artist, the architect!
And the bombs of World War II
that destroyed the archives.
The fires in the reserves ...
We know them all too well.
Yet, what a relief for biographical analysis!
What comfort for the status of the "masterpiece"
but then, how to heal the colonial wound?
Kill the museum! declared Alpha Oumar Konaré.

Hold on! We insist upon restitution!
But not blindly, at the pace of a snail.
We won't wait for ethnological resuscitation
and the organ trade to restore the ghosts of the past.
We won't wait for the discourse of provenance,
with its polite politics,
step by step,
piece by piece.

We have to act now, while restitution is underway
and push for legislation between museums,
for the rights of access to the art histories of the worlds,
held in the British Museum in London
the Museé du Quai Branly in Paris,
the Humboldt Forum in Berlin,

the Tropenmuseum in Amsterdam,
the Tervuren Museum in Brussels,
the Weltmuseum in Vienna.

Open up those bunkers!
And revise these collections,
while they are still in Europe.
Dare to radically rethink the condition of the museum,
and begin with the deepest of injuries,
where no redemption exists for the intermediary:
the curator.

Let's build museum-universities!
Physical and conceptual spaces for remediation,
with an architecture made for healing
and reinterpreting these agent-objects.
Let's face their stubborn materiality,
which has been so terribly neglected.
Build incongruous and problematic assemblages,
and yes, integrate digitalization.
But wait a minute!
Who will select what is to be digitalized?
Who will access these material worlds
knowingly hidden and forgotten,
if not the priests of ethnology and the market?
And, let's not forget the parameters of conservation!
That ideology of material survival,
which is remarkably impenetrable,
with its *longue durée* of a thousand years or more.

No more monocultures!
No more intellectual plantations!
No more museum mimicries!
No more aesthetic hegemonies!

No more object hierarchies!
No more museological pyramids!
That "absent air conditioning,"
those "inadequate conservators," et cetera et cetera …

Let's take control
of these reservoirs of ingenuity!
And change the ergonomy of museums,
those "orgone accumulators" of consumerism.
Open museum-universities!
Build spaces for inquiry
with rooms for conceptual intimacy,
sites for transborder art production
and disciplinary transgression
centered on these anxious and contested collections.
Museum-universities to welcome the new
generation of students and researchers
more diasporic than ever before.
With their politics of communication
and future transitional methodologies.
So that, with patented prototypes,
based on these occluded historical collections,
they can rename the excluded authors,
and return both respect and copyright
to their ancestors!

All of you!
Artists!
Writers!
Curators! Filmmakers! Lawyers!
Architects! Ecologists!
Brothers and Sisters!
Organs and Alliances!
There is no time to lose!

Clémentine Deliss presented this manifesto, previously published in French in the journal *Multitudes* (Volume 4, No. 73, 2018), at the Global Academy II conference, Salzburg Summer Academy of Fine Arts, Salzburg 2018. See https://youtu.be/7k7nC6G_D7E (accessed March 13, 2020).

Do You Want a Future?
A Protocol for
New Cultural Commons

Alexander Koch

FEBRUARY 14, 2020 BERLIN

Today we all know that we are in urgent need of viable and strong solutions for planetary problems. But then it always sounds a bit dubious when someone claims to have a truly good solution to a planetary problem. You're quickly suspected of being pretentious or, more likely, of being a populist. So this morning I was delighted to read an interview with Judith Butler in *The New Yorker* in which she said, "Sometimes you have to imagine in a radical way that makes you seem a little crazy, that puts you in an embarrassing light, in order to open up a possibility that others have already closed down with their knowing realism. I'm prepared to be mocked and dismissed."[1]

So here we go—I'm certainly going to look a bit ridiculous when I say that I can think of at least *one* good idea for planetary problems. It isn't my idea, but it's a good one.

LES NOUVEAUX COMMANDITAIRES

I first heard about Les Nouveaux Commanditaires, or New Patrons,[2] in 2007. In a Berlin street café I met François Hers, a Belgian artist from Paris. He told me that in 1989 a major private foundation, the Fondation de

1 Masha Gessen, "Judith Butler Wants us to Reshape our Rage," in *The New Yorker,* February 9, 2020.
2 *Nouveaux Commanditaires* can be translated into English only rather inadequately as *New Patrons*. According to country and language area, these groups are called *Nuovi Committenti, Concomitentes, Nieuwe Opdrachtgevers, Nya uppdragsgivare,* etc.

France—which promotes innovative projects ranging from medicine to education—had been looking for a new initiative for sustainable and social cultural funding, and he was asked if he had any ideas. He did, suggesting setting up a program to enable citizens to commission new works from contemporary artists. Cultural mediators and public producers would assist them, contributing the necessary know-how. He explained:

Ever since Dada and the Russian avant-garde, it has been clear that art can find its forms and take its place in society anywhere, at any time, in any shape, and on any subject. Nevertheless we could see that almost everything we did as artists after that ultimately landed in galleries and museums; that in the end there was no other place for us than the usual institutions and a market whose requirements were uncertain and that most people have nothing to do with. The autonomy of art and artists had at some point reached a dead end. Since the Romantic Age, the principle had become established in Western cultures that artists were committed to nothing and no one apart from their own inner need to create new works. Their independence from commissions and external rules governing what they did and how they did it was synonymous with the independence of free citizens who had shaken off authoritarian régimes and gradually built up democracies in which they could manage their own interests.

This historical sense of the autonomy of art, however, had at some point exhausted itself. With the globalization of the art world, concepts of the middle-class modern movement and its discourses on autonomy became the international standard—but in the nineteen-eighties it was clear to us that the individual's inner need for the democratic project could not longer occupy a central place. The question now was how people around the world, in their new-found relative freedom, could find ways of living a self-determined life together. This question could have only collective answers. It was no longer compatible with the idea that artists should rack their brains alone as to what art society might require, what forms would be appropriate, what critics, and what representation would be needed.

So as an artist, I wanted to turn the tables: Let society itself tell us what it needs. We needed to ask every single citizen, what do you need art—and us artists—for? What are your demands? What do you expect from painting, architecture, literature, music, film? My personal need is not important. I want to know what your need is. What do you want to achieve? What can we as artists do about it? And so the protocol of the New Patrons emerged. The crucial point is that with the mediator, a new protagonist appears on the stage of the art world to help citizens to commission artists with projects they consider important. We need a mediating entity, so that citizens and artists can come together with a purpose and cooperate.

That was the idea: a new kind of art commissioned by citizens, as an operative model for democratic cultural production. True, history shows sundry instances of artworks commissioned by citizens who are not part of the cultural, economic, or political elite. But there had never been a systemic approach, a general policy allowing people with no particular privileges an active, decisive role in the art scene. The Fondation de France adopted Hers's suggestion. In 1990, New Patrons was established as a decentralized network of mediators and nonprofit organizations, which

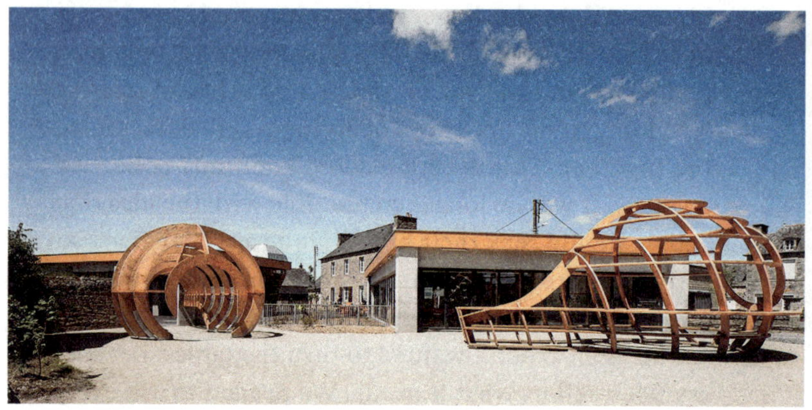

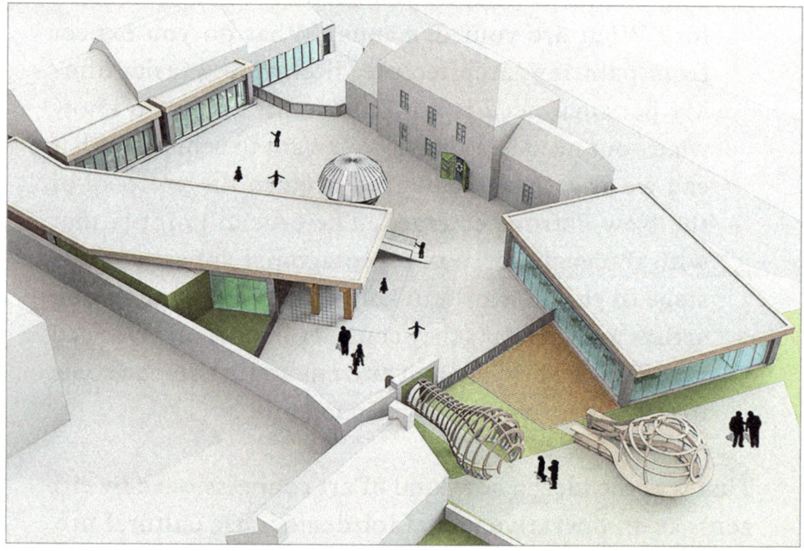

In the French village of Trébédan, a group of mayors, school board members, and friends worked with artist Matali Crasset and mediator Anastassia Makridou-Bretonneau from 2007 to 2015 to add facilities to a school called Le Blé en Herbe. The project linked the school to the village and created a lively community center.

enter independently into dialogue with citizens in their regions, asking them what they expected from art. Soon people from villages, small towns, and metropolitan areas across France were commissioning artists to develop local projects that would provide innovative answers to local challenges.

COMMENTS ON THE PROTOCOL OF NEW PATRONS[3]

In both the analogue and the digital worlds, protocols regulate many things. They ensure the Internet works; they determine what billions of people can see, and when. The protocols of diplomatic services stipulate how political hierarchies are included in formal processes and their representation effected for the public. There are the written protocols for church weddings; unwritten ones for Tinder dates; protocols organize large parts of communal life, of (re-)production, consumption, and representation. They are designed to ensure functional rules, to avoid errors, to establish trust and reliability. Thus every new protocol recognized as such is a major intervention in the social world, and a tool for regulating future processes.

The New Patrons protocol is exactly this kind of intervention and tool—not, however, in the form of a norm or specification, but as a proposal for a shared practice by people who desire this practice, who organize it together and, should they come into conflict, have to resolve the conflict themselves. This means that there is no external authority that can intervene—whether to help or to regulate. The New Patrons protocol knows no authority apart from the protagonists involved in the process. At the same

---

3 Protocol available online at https://neueauftraggeber.de/en/ about-the-new-patrons (accessed April 30, 2020).

time, it is universal insofar as it can be put into practice in any community, in any place, and at any time. Legally, it is drawn up as an artwork which anyone may adopt, comparable with the model of the Creative Commons License. This is exactly what is being sedulously implemented today.

THE HISTORY OF SELF-DETERMINATION HAS NO BEGINNING AND NO END

When in 1992 the first mediators went door-to-door trying to motivate residents to commission artworks, it was no more than an experiment often greeted with a patronizing smile. Weren't citizens interested in more important concerns than contemporary art, of all things? Why should artists engage with citizens' concerns? However, the history of cultural self-determination goes as far back as human cultures themselves. Skepticism proved unfounded. Soon people were approaching the mediators, seeking to exchange ideas, and one project after another emerged: sculptural memorials to previously uncommemorated people and events, architectural interventions to change the shapes and spirits of rural environments, new spaces and venues for communities that had none, works that made unresolved conflicts tangible, or that gave bold expression to previously shy visions. After eighteen years, at the turn of the millennium, there were already several dozen projects, and from a bird's eye view, all of them stood in a long tradition of self-empowerment that runs throughout history. In 2002 the first projects in the Nieuwe Opdrachtgevers in Belgium began, soon followed by the Nuovi Committenti in Italy, then the Concomitentes in Spain. Word spread. In more and more regions of Europe, the protocol inspired art experts, cultural practitioners, and activists to become active as mediators and to support citizens' commissions, and it motivated citizens to visit artists' studios to discuss their wishes, aims, and problems.

In Germany, the Neue Auftraggeber e.V. was founded in a back room in Berlin in 2007. The first members were a few curators and people interested in culture—including myself. Some initial funding came from France, then from Bonn, Lübeck, Hamburg, and Potsdam—but hardly enough to keep body and soul together. As mediators with tiny budgets, we started pioneering projects and learned through experience, along with citizens' groups, patrons, and the artists themselves. Lots of things went wrong; quite a lot worked well. A protocol may be brief, clear, and simple; the corresponding practice is not necessarily so. Today, in 2020, we've made some progress. A poster of the protocol hangs on the wall in our Berlin office. We work as a team in roundtable discussions to coordinate the program in Germany. With support from the Federal Culture Foundation and many other partners, we currently support nine mediators, and more than a hundred citizens have joined forces in throughout Germany to commission new works and projects in their towns and villages. Many of them express the need for more community and less social isolation, or trigger silent local issues in order to become conscious. It's about getting voices and bodies into the public sphere to draw new distinctions there. The artists come from the worlds of theater, performance, sculpture, architecture, painting, and comic books.

We have contacts with new colleagues in Switzerland, Spain, Cameroon, Sweden, and Lebanon. Fifty-two mediators are currently active in eleven countries. Worldwide, more than 500 projects have been implemented, each one autonomous in form and content. Tens of thousands of citizens are behind these projects—mayors and municipal

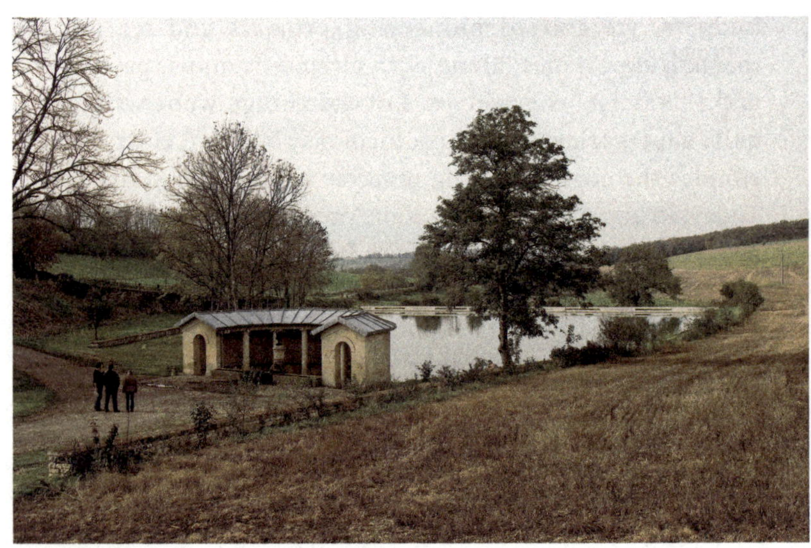

After restoring a 1836 washhouse, the twenty-odd residents of Blessey, a village
in Burgundy, France, decided to erect a sculpture. Through mediator Xavier Douroux
they commissioned artist Rémy Zaugg, who recognized the issues of the shrinking
village and convinced the residents of a more ambitious plan. Old paths and walls
were rerouted to a new pond dug behind the washhouse. It became a focal point for
the village. Executed from 1997 to 2007, the project was a turning point for Blessey,
which began to grow in population again.

authorities, sponsors and foundations, societies, and associations have provided both moral and financial support. Many of the artists commissioned are well known. Some of the projects have become famous; others have failed. More than 100 million euros have been spent on encouraging people to speak to one another so that their conversations give rise to new cultural common goods that are not ordained from above, not ordered by any committee, not decided by any parliament, and all of which are community property and nonprofit.

The protocol for new art commissioned by citizens is working well, and there have long since been commissions going beyond the field of culture. For some years now, besides artistic projects, unprecedented scientific research programs have taken shape, commissioned by citizens. In architecture and urban planning, in development and conflict resolution, in the educational sector and music production: the New Patrons model is being discussed as one of the more recent methodologies—one might call it a cultural technology—for democratic production of meaning in the twenty-first century.

Precisely because the form of the protocol is universal (ultimately, it is no more than a proposal for a specific relational model which may or may not find appeal), and because the New Patrons are not an organization, but a loose network of independent protagonists who share a common idea, interest is increasing in regions of the world that are tired of colonial encroachment and foreign aid, though not tired of meaningful forms of collaboration and collective action.

It is a loosely associated community of practitioners, within which each individual is in turn involved in further local, regional, national, and international networks of

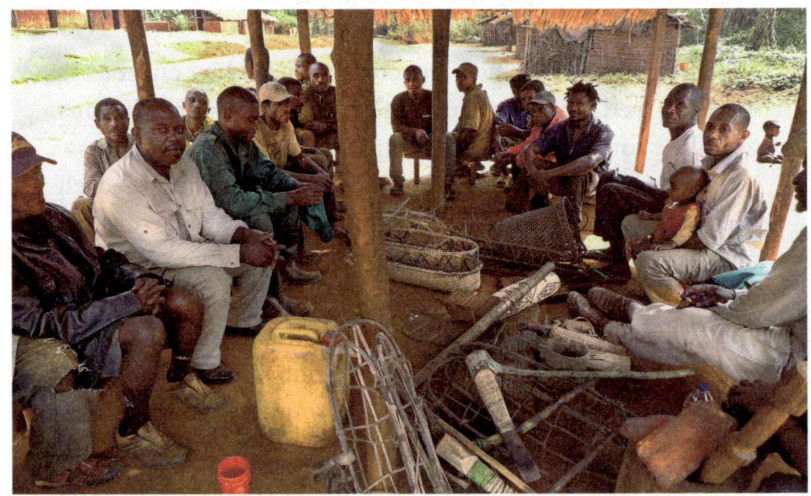

The Baka, an Indigenous community in southern Cameroon, were forced to create a permanent settlement in a place called Bifolone after centuries of nomadic existence. The villagers want to preserve their knowledge of the forest and their traditional artifacts while living a more modern life. Since 2014, with New Patrons mediator Germain Loumpet, they have begun to create new spaces, such as a living museum and botanical garden.

citizens' initiatives, social movements, politics, funding programs, economics, media, artists, and colleagues. Thus the international program of the New Patrons is now a wide-ranging network of complex individual, collective, and institutional relations that cannot be represented in its totality. Nevertheless, there are constant points of intersection in the exchanges between protagonists, and the debates and discussions linking them, as well as common public platforms. This may sound complicated, but it isn't really. It is in the nature of decentral and particularly planetary networks that their complexity cannot be reduced— and why should it be? This may not always please politicians and funding bodies—but it is perfectly fine for democratic initiatives in civil society.

BOTTOM-UP—TO THE PLANETARY?

When I give talks about New Patrons, I am regularly asked whether its protocol would also work in Nigeria, Venezuela, Russia, China, Liechtenstein, or in Germany's eastern states. I always answer yes, because all initiatives that follow the protocol are local. They are formed locally, organize their own content, and all decisions as to what should be done, and how, with whom and with what resources, are taken locally. Such initiatives can of course fail, and occasionally do so—usually if they are politically impeded, which is one problem, or cannot be funded, which is another problem. Both problems are serious and systemic, though not a question of principle.

There are people everywhere who desire a future that is different from the present. I therefore see no reason why the New Patrons protocol should not work in principle anywhere on the planet[4]—especially since for many

---

4 To date, initial plans have been formally or informally drawn up in Cameroon, Tunisia, Nigeria, South Africa, and Lebanon.

societies it ultimately means not much more than adding a new variation to the countless forms of collaborative activity, one that is neither particularly complicated nor costly, but that is well suited to the twenty-first century. For other societies that have little cultural infrastructure, the New Patrons offer all the more a model for creating structures that point the way to a future—to a more democratic future.

What comes next? It doesn't take much imagination to picture how, over the next ten years, New Patrons' existing network will produce several hundred projects commissioned by citizens and thus be further consolidated as a cultural technology. It takes only a little more imagination to picture how, given funding and the necessary political will, further mediators will start more New Patrons initiatives in more regions of the world. Somewhat more imagination is necessary to visualize a possible situation in 2050: if over the past thirty years 500 projects have taken shape with a moderately exponential growth,[5] then over the next thirty years, even with a stagnating growth of the network, 1,000 projects could be added, or with a continuation of the past growth of annual new initiatives, perhaps 2,000 projects. Looking at the long list of countries already involved, this number could be quite different again, which brings us back to Judith Butler.

Protagonists from Holland, Austria, Poland, Croatia, Greece, Iceland, the United States, Argentina, India, China, Australia, Namibia, Sudan, Senegal, and Iraq have connected with the New Patrons network to talk about adapting the protocol to their own regions. Various pioneering projects have been or are being planned. The crucial hurdle is generally a lack of funding.

5 Approximately twenty-five completed projects in the 1990s, 150 in the 2000s, 325 in the 2010s. There are no precise numbers, since a systematic registration of all projects and relevant data will not be completed until the end of 2020.

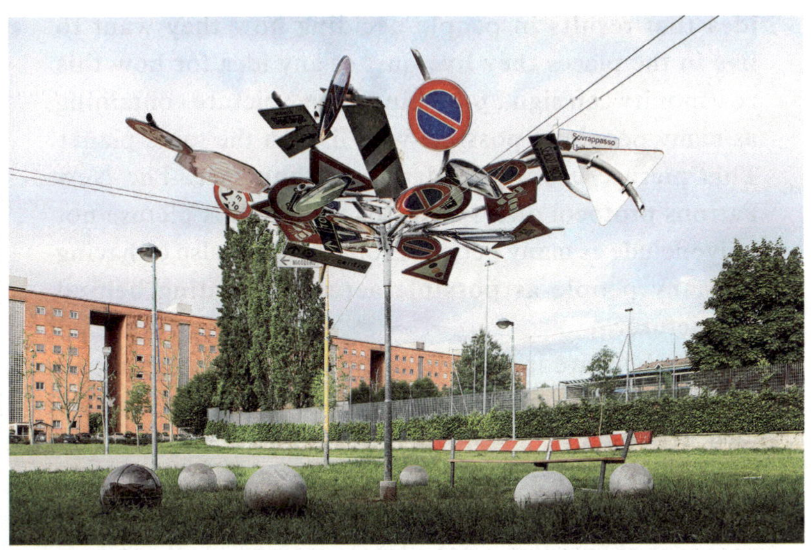

Between 2010 and 2013, in Nichelino near Turin, Italy, twenty young residents worked with artist and designer Martino Gamper to create public seating and this tree sculpture made from discarded road signs. Local artisans and the poet Chiuto also collaborated. The project was developed from an idea by Elena Greco.

Of course, it is not a question of numbers and growth. It is a question of opening up *a possibility that others have already closed down with their knowing realism.* The quest for planetary, and particularly planetary democratic, approaches is difficult. The planetary suggests proximity to the universal, and the universal has long been corrupted by colonialism. Despite this, we need universal—planetary—concepts if we are to make progress. I welcome any idea that results in people deciding how they want to live in the places they live, just as any idea for how this community can sign up within a larger picture containing as many people as possible who live on the same planet. This picture cannot be drawn without art. The New Patrons protocol offers a way of making this picture not only include as many people as possible, but also of having as many people as possible actually standing behind the picture.

Numbers are important to explain to politicians and funding bodies on the planet that something is feasible, what it will cost, and what the possible result could be. There's no point in being diffident. If a bottom-up movement—and the New Patrons is one of many of these—has a prospect of integrating the local, regional, and national into a larger common perspective and narrative, then there is a chance, beyond any major global institutions, or parallel to them, of making progress with the great themes of diversity, of cultural identities, of the counter perspective to national-populist attacks. I would not have helped to build the program of the New Patrons in Germany and presented it in other countries if I hadn't hoped that there was a real possibility of this joint prospect.

Even if it's only this perspective: to share the idea that anyone can and should be a protagonist in the story,

in the community; to share the idea that in our own practice as people, citizens, artists, scientists, and so on we
can achieve the paradigm shift, as far as possible to distance ourselves from unwanted authorities, as well as from
our singular necessities. It's a question of understanding
the interests of our complex communities and thus succeeding in creating new alliances acting in the collective
interest and not solely the personal. Does that sound
pompous? As I said at the beginning, I'm prepared to be
mocked and dismissed.

DO YOU WANT A FUTURE?

Lionel Manga and I sit facing each other. Between us are
microphones on stands, a bottle of wine, and two glasses.
We are in the studio of Radio Nostalgie Cameroun in
Douala, doing a live broadcast. I went to Africa with the
help of the Goethe-Institut, to discuss and explain the experiences of New Patrons in Europe. I have just said into
the microphone that in my opinion, the New Patrons idea
can work anywhere in the world, because everywhere
there are people who want to do something, artists who
also want to create something. Potential commissions by
citizens, and money to implement them are everywhere—
except that generally the money is deplorably distributed.

"That may well be," says Lionel. "But if we now leave
the studio and ask people on the street what they expect
from their future, they'll answer: 'Nothing. We have no
future.' Here in Cameroon, a mediator of the Nouveaux
Commanditaires wouldn't find it easy to meet patrons who
want to do something, because they don't believe they
can do anything." I answer, "In Germany, the same thing
would happen to us in many places. Perhaps we should ask
people not what they expect from the future—but whether

they want a future. I can't imagine that anyone, when asked whether they want a future, would answer no. And if someone said yes, the next question could be ... what future do you want?" That might get us further. Lionel finds the idea pretty good, and we drink a glass of wine during the commercials.

This scene has stayed in my memory because this tiny shift in the question made a difference for Lionel and me through the rest of the conversation; not only the difference between having and wanting, a sense of reality and a sense of possibility. The question "Do you want a future?" implies more. When you say it quietly to yourself, a feeling of empowerment resonates; asking the question is almost a performative act. Do I want a future? Yes, I do. Here a decision has almost been made; something has almost been done. The next question, exactly what future you would want if you could wish for it, almost presses for an answer. It suddenly becomes urgent. Something needs to be done and could be done tomorrow. Thus the future may become—perhaps again—a project for us, the many around the globe.

Translated from German by Gail Schamberger

On Future Possibilities for Transcultural Education

Mohammad Salemy
interviewed by Hildegund Amanshauser

Mohammad Salemy is a Berlin-based artist, critic, and curator from Canada—and cofounder and organizer at The New Centre for Research & Practice, a nonprofit art institution that primarily exists online. Founded in 2014 after a conference Salemy organized in Vancouver, The New Centre, which considers itself a "parallel academia," is licensed to provide graduate-level seminars and certificates of competency in the arts, transdisciplinary studies, critical philosophy, and social and political thought, among other topics. Yet it is not a degree-granting institution, and doesn't want to be one. Instead, it offers online seminars and certificate programs—as well as research groups, a writing center, a virtual library, and other resources that continue to grow and evolve.

Hildegund Amanshauser: I'd like to discuss the future of art education in the planetary *framework of this book, based on your ideas and practice with The New Centre for Research & Practice. What are The New Centre's objectives? Where did The New Centre come from? Where will it go?*

Mohammad Salemy: The objective of The New Centre has been manifold. First and foremost, we thought of The New Centre as a place where conversations about the role of technology in examining politics and aesthetics will be discussed, particularly what we've come to know as the computational paradigm.[1] We question the role of the

---

1 The computational paradigm is a state in which computers are not only used to solve problems or accelerate work processes in all aspects of life, but also when their operational logic is employed to explain natural and social processes.

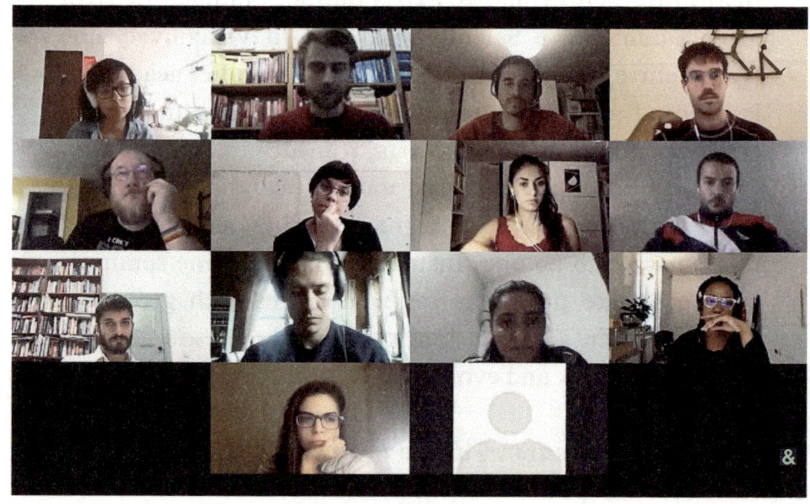

Screen shot from The New Centre course *Introduction to Narratology, Narratives & the Question of Subjectivities* (1 of 4), accessed April 4, 2020.

computers and automation on different aspects of human experience, from the philosophical questions of subjectivity and its future, down to how these technologies impact production of art and knowledge.

As these conversations were and are still not being picked up in a systematic manner by regular academia, we thought it was necessary to create an ongoing venue in which we could conduct them. Not simply like a conference or symposium that happens once in a while, but a regular place for these conversations. In the beginning, it was mostly about providing a space for those interested in the works of Ray Brassier and Reza Negarestani and their other colleagues, who were insisting on a reconsideration of analytic philosophy, making a new bridge between that and its continental sister. These are people around the publishing house named Urbanomic/Sequence Press, Goldsmith University, and people interested in the legacy of the Warwick University's Cybernetic Culture Research Unit. We created a venue where some of these discussions could be extended, challenged, verified, and discussed.

Another mandate came out of discussions that were forwarded by people that came from art education and the art world, like Suhail Malik, about the need to reform contemporary art, particularly when he gave a multipart lecture at Artists Space in New York in summer 2013 titled *On The Necessity of Art's Exit from Contemporary Art*[2] regarding both the philosophical and political problems of being involved in the production and circulation of contemporary art. It was inspiring. A modified version

2 See Suhail Malik, *Exit not escape — On the Necessity of Art's Exit from Contemporary Art*, YouTube video, 38:54 min., uploaded by Artists Space, June 21, 2013, https://youtu.be/fimEhntbRZ4 (accessed Feb 1, 2020).

of Malik's lectures, albeit with a different focus than contemporary art, have appeared in the form of a book published by Urbanomic called *ContraContemporary*.[3]

And we thought, if we were successful, we would provide job opportunities for younger scholars and people who were not necessarily making big incomes or holding tenured university positions. I hate to say it, but yes, it was also job creation, even for those of us who started it. We were people who had just finished our graduate studies and saw no immediate job prospects. So we said, let's just start something and hopefully this can help us with our own income. So this is what also brought us the idea of starting The New Centre.

And where are you now? How did it develop since then, in the past five years?

We just got better and grew. When we started, we almost exclusively offered online seminars. Our students were people dissatisfied with the existing art and humanities academia and professors were mostly drawn from the people belonging to the philosophical scene known as Speculative Realism. Now we're working in many different settings, both online and offline, in educational institutions, galleries, or magazines—to host events, to bring conversations between our researchers and students to the outside world, to promote not just what we are interested in, but ideas and concepts that are emerging on the margins of global intellectual activities. We're of course a lot better known. We are a place to go if you're interested in certain scholars and want to study with them, or are interested in certain ideas. In the beginning, we knew almost every student and

3 Suhail Malik, *ContraContemporary: Modernity's Unknown Future* (Falmouth, 2020).

member already, but today many are not part of our immediate network. And they hear about us, or they've been following us for a year or two online and they have decided to join. It's quite nice to know that there's growing and ongoing interest in what we're doing. Another reason we thought The New Centre would succeed is that we perceived it as a place where people who didn't enter a graduate program in arts or humanities would get a chance to re-examine their thoughts, make new connections, and we will help place them into a good program.

Not only students, but also your instructors get new job possibilities.

Yes, absolutely! I have a keen interest in young scholars, people who just come out of PhD programs. I follow their work like curators follow an artist's work, right? As an example, look at the program of a place like the Strelka Institute in Moscow. Some of the names that are now teaching there previously taught with us. And one thing you can definitely mention is that we're also a place of rigorous searching for new ideas and their articulation. *The Xenofeminist Manifesto*[4] was developed in one of our early seminars from our first semester. It was an idea that was around in terms of a feminist manifesto for the time of technological acceleration. It was the extension of previous works of people like Donna Haraway's *A Cyborg Manifesto*[5]—as a sort of an update for the twenty-first century. The conversation was presented in a seminar called "Towards Xenofeminism." And then, by the following summer, the manifesto came. It's been one of the most talked

4 Laboria Cuboniks, *The Xenofeminist Manifesto: A Politics for Alienation* (London, 2018).
5 Donna Haraway, *A Cyborg Manifesto*, first published in *Socialist Review*, 1985

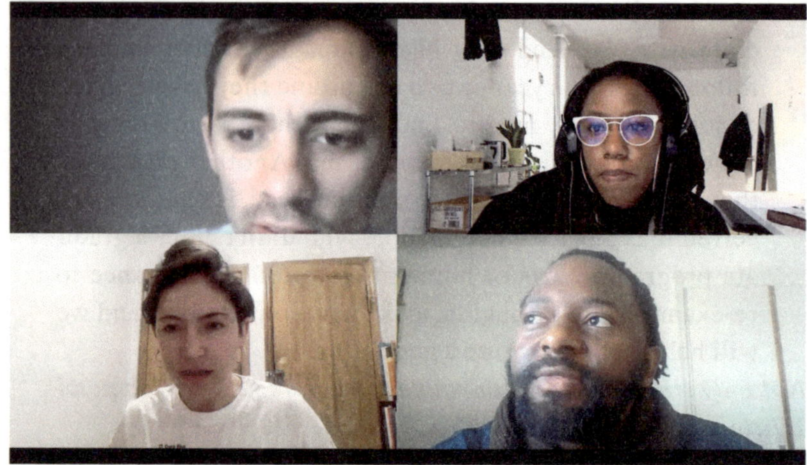

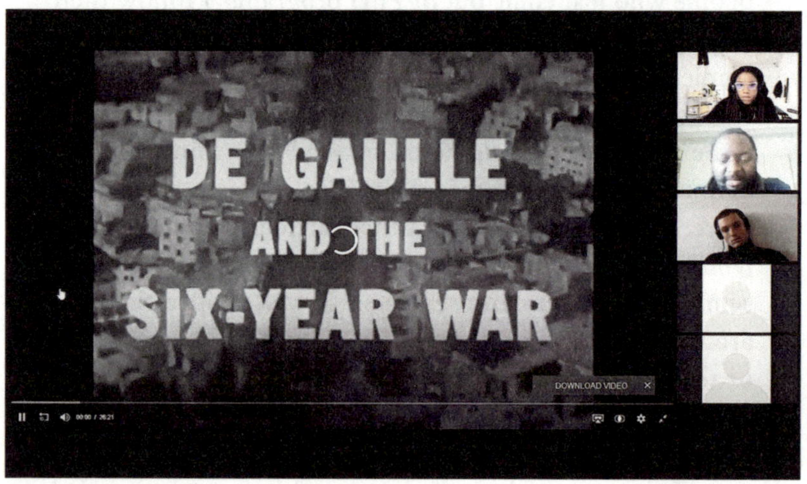

Screen shots from The New Centre course *Postcolonial Theory as Cinematic*, below: session discussion, accessed April 4, 2020

about feminist documents of the past ten years and I'm proud to say we took some part in its development.

What role does social media play in your school? Is it only a PR medium?

Social media is our physical building, our bricks and mortar. Institutions have architects who build them buildings and classrooms that hold the physical identity of a school; social media is where we build our institution. We use it daily to promote upcoming seminars, and interesting things that our researchers, students, and instructors do. But besides that, my own personal social media is also an important part of The New Centre, because, rather than shying away from having an opinion, I try to start or enter conversations online as a real person known as part of the institution. I maintain a very loud voice on social media to indirectly bring attention to The New Centre without constantly referring to what we do there. It makes people realize that real humans with alternative political, philosophical opinion are out there and involved in building an educational alternative.

Is social media helping you to create something like a new collective?

Absolutely. It works two ways. Social media attracts new blood to the institution. When we mention social media, I think it's important to also mention the Slack platform. Slack is important because a lot of dialogues that are not as performative as Facebook and Instagram happen on Slack, which is much more like insider conversation. Most of it is philosophical: it's gossip or outrage politics, a conversation you want to have rehearsed internally before you propose it on Facebook. Then the second layer will be Facebook. And the third layer will be Instagram, which is very surface- and image-oriented.

I also want to add the significance of having the Iranian philosopher Reza Negarestani[6] as the director of our Critical Philosophy Program. In addition, we also consider him our academic advisor because everyone who attends The New Centre as a Certificate Student is supposed to have several meetings with Reza. He's the philosophical core of The New Centre because he not only provides our students with one-on-one feedback but also because in the last year, he's been directing the philosophy program. He's got his own interest in the young and upcoming philosophers that are working either on the continental or analytic side, whether in Europe or in America. Reza has been a major engine of success and growth of The New Centre.

As your school has no (analogue) building in a specific place, is it planetary by definition? Is being a planetary center a conditio sine qua non *for you?*

For the homeless, the whole city feels like home. We nailed this from the get-go with my co-programmers Jaden Adams and Tony Yanick: we thought precisely about how this lack or perhaps disadvantage can immediately be turned into an advantage. This condition has its own complications, for instance, choosing time slots for our seminars which would allow people from different time zones to attend the seminars without inconveniencing people in different places. Imagine producing live programming in this format, for people living as far away from each other as Shanghai and Los Angeles. At some point we seriously thought about writing a manifesto demanding a universal time measurement system which would run against the natural temporality of the sun, moon, and earth. What might be better than conducting a

6 Reza Negarestani, born in 1977, is an Iranian philosopher and writer whose work connects to Speculative Realism.

seminar with people from Kinshasa, Beijing, Tehran, New York, Berlin, London, and Rio?

Last question about The New Centre: How do you finance it? How do you pay people?

The majority of the payments come from the students because ours is a paid program. In addition, we have a membership-level participation, which helps immensely. Because members pay to access the recorded seminars, they help sustain the program. Before we started, we weren't even thinking of membership. But it was something that we articulated very shortly after opening. And we revised our financial plan to consider membership, without which we probably wouldn't have lasted. Today, we have five years' worth of seminars. It's funny, but we are almost becoming a Netflix for philosophy: hours and hours of seminars by different people to watch or listen to. And starting from next semester, we're moving into turning our seminars into podcasts, to diversify the revenue stream.

How many members do you have now?

More than 500.

Let's jump into the future of art education. Think about twenty years from now, 2040. Do you think that The New Centre still exists? Is there anything you want to have changed?

We will have a much more integrated digital platform. A lot of the work we do will be more automated. And if the direction that myself and people involved wanted to go succeeds, we will become more self-organized. Perhaps twenty years from now, we might not even be using the term social media. But whatever social media evolves to be, The New Centre will be an international social media of art, artists, thinkers, and scholars who use it for multiple purposes, including giving or taking seminars and workshops. What we have failed to do so far is switch from

English to other languages, or offer seminars in Spanish, Arabic, or even Farsi, for instance. The dominance of English in the world of art and ideas is a mixed blessing; while its use allows for a form of universality, it allows English with its particular operating logic to dictate the terms of discourse and set the emotional ambiance of our entire catalogue of videos.

And will you grow?

Yes, absolutely. There is a growing interest among young people in the kind of ideas that we have been part of developing since 2014 and the kind of approaches and the proliferation of programs. We are part of this more avantgarde approach to art education, which is combining an understanding of science, technology, architecture, and design that's being taken up by places like Goldsmiths, Stelka, and other institutions. We'll grow because more people are giving up the normal diet of Frankfurt School Marxism and different strands of poststructuralism and instead are being drawn into these newer ideas. However, we will try to remain the sort of the underground institution that we have been thus far.

Will there still be "traditional" art academies as we see them now, or will they disappear?

Of course there will still be art academies. Our role will be to supplement and complement what the studio does and the studio complements what we do, because we don't have a physical space. Art is a phenomenological experience. Let's face it; both making art and experiencing art needs physical space.

The exhibition world is unable to absorb all the people that are going to art academies into proper channels of income, display, and promotion. Meanwhile, its sustainability has been this pyramid scheme of selling art.

Any change that upsets the sales and marketing of contemporary art will have earthquake-like effects. So the news we hear right now is that the sales of contemporary art are low; most galleries that were doing great are now suffering. Many people are educated in art, but only a few could actually find a place to show or sell their work. This narrowing of the bottleneck will have an impact on art education. Young people will reject borrowing thousands of dollars for their MFA degrees, but they are still interested in discussions, and they will go for choices like us. We think it's important to integrate art back into life: This whole model that "an artist's job is to just be critical, sit in the studio and make critical work and this critical work will somehow find its way into exhibitions and then hopefully some collector will be interested down the line and buy it" cannot be sustained. This crisis is a great opportunity to rethink what art will mean in the mid-twenty-first century. Where is the place of artists? We think that blurring the line between art and design and architecture opens up a new space of social life for artists as well.

But also to blur the line between philosophy and art and political activism and social activism and ...

Totally. You took the words out of my mouth: blur the line between the place of the artist and the thinker, but also artist and social change-maker, whether it's true social practice, or activism, or institution building. So our artists would need The New Centre's set of skills to integrate what they do into actual life rather than this narrow way of existence that is increasingly only available to few people who graduate from art institutions.

I imagine that your institution is also a good model for the future of financing education. There is a difference between America and Europe; in Europe many educational institutions are financed by state governments. But the support is decreasing; you never know if our academies will be financed in the future.

There's nothing wrong with governments giving money to art programs. But we need to be prepared to show that there are different ways in which the result of art education can be beneficial to society rather than this idea that the artist will make work that will then end up in exhibitions and state collections, because that's not sustainable.

The New Centre is starting to attract people with good careers. Lawyers, programmers, and doctors are people who feel the need for general knowledge in relation to their profession. They already have money, right? But they feel a certain level of universal ignorance when it comes to certain subjects like art or philosophy, and they feel that their practice will benefit from this knowledge. I like the idea that we attract people from other fields to philosophy and art. The New Centre is another way for us to rethink art education's true place in society. Why do we want to only educate artists? We should try to attract people who are not necessarily artists, and never will be, to art education. This knowledge will be useful for what they do, but it also enriches their consciousness; it enriches their inner and social lives.

That's interesting: it's the same as art production, in a way. I also think it is important for our society that people have a broader knowledge of art and philosophy.

This crisis of art education also applies to humanities, because they went through exponential growth in graduate programs. These questions go beyond art education, but I see humanities as kind of the siblings of art education, so it's interesting to talk about both at the same time.

Yes, I agree with you. You spoke in Salzburg[7] about the future of art education. And you said that there will be new, more collectively-built ideas. Do you think there is a hope that democracy is developing and increasing in these institutions?

We're starting to experiment a bit with that this semester. One of our long-time supporters and students is proposing a course without an instructor. It's not even like every week one person takes a turn as an instructor; it's that every week one person provides a reading list that everybody has to read, and there will be no other formal structure imposed on the seminar. These are ideas that we're developing to look for this collective learning experience that is truly non-hierarchical. It becomes more like collective thinking, talking, and writing.

How do you develop your program now and how will have changed in twenty years?

I am applying what I learned in curatorial school to developing The New Centre programs. But I think the move should be toward self-organization, where you don't need me, or any curator. There will be an automated, algorithmic way in which people who want to teach and people who have something to say will develop a system where the existing data and patterns can predict that they have something to say and it can wave this back into some kind of programming. I mean, these ideas are being experimented with in the art world, take for instance the Art Democracy Project initiated by Berlin-based Stefan Heidenreich,[8] which combines critical approaches

7 Mohammad Salemy, *Back to the Future School: Anticipating Tomorrow's Education in Arts and Humanities,* YouTube video, 1:09:31 min., uploaded by Salzburg International Summer Academy of Fine Arts, July 29, 2019, https://youtu.be/lREaV5FK8og (accessed February 1, 2020).
8 See https://www.stefanheidenreich.de/for-democracy-in-art (accessed March 2, 2020).

to democratic judgment of art using algorithms and programming. I have written a new piece called "Algorithmic Curating,"[9] and one called "A Portrait of the Artist as a Living Algorithm"[10] for a monograph on the work of Polish artist Janek Simon[11] These models of nonhuman organization or a more rational way of putting things together will be the future.

But isn't that frightening?

Sure, it's frightening, but any kind of a rapid evolution is very frightening because you never know where it ends up going. But these things are happening.

Where will you be in twenty years?

I'm always looking at younger people. I think it's good advice for people who are entering their forties and fifties to remember that we all can benefit from involving young people in decision-making; or even if you don't involve them in decision-making just listen to what they think and what they like. Taking the pulse of the young generation is needed to create a dynamic future.

9 The New Centre (website), https://thenewcentre.org/archive/curatorial-expediency-algorithmic-oraganization-exhibitions (accessed December 23, 2019).

10 U—jazdowski (website), https://u-jazdowski.pl/en/programme/wystawy/janek-simon/artysta-jako-zywy-algorytm (accessed December 23, 2019).

11 Joanna Warsza, ed., *Janek Simon: Synthetic Folklore* (Berlin, 2020).

Plastics in the United Arab Emirates: Art in the Time of Climate Change

Rahel Aima

An unusual building has taken shape in Dubai. Designed by architect Shaun Killa and an algorithm, the stretched doughnut structure is shiny and covered in Arabic text, like a punched-in graffitied egg that an alien spacecraft casually dropped by the side of the highway. This is the Museum of the Future, slated to open in late 2020, but its tagline could well be an unofficial city motto: *See the Future, Create the Future*.

What will the museum involve? Most likely, a symphony of VR and edutainment-heavy displays on the threats and opportunities of the future—brought to you by government, in close partnership with technology. Of course, the United Arab Emirates has been in the business of seeing and creating the future—and rewriting the past—since long before the nation's 1971 birth. In recent decades, this has been characterized by a move away from the solidity of land toward the sky and sea. The country's development strategies reflect an orientation toward the aerial: building skylines that look best when photographed by a drone, and dredging up first megaports, then palm and world-shaped islands meant to be seen from the Earth's exosphere. Most explicit is an ambitious space program that emphasizes water scarcity and climatic research, with a side of patriotic jingoism. It aims to land on Mars in time for the UAE's fiftieth birthday in 2021.

As for the past, I think of J. G. Ballard, writing in 1970 that "Deserts possess a particular magic, since they have exhausted their own futures, and are thus free of time. Anything erected there, a city, a pyramid, a motel, stands outside time."[1] The back story of the country is similarly rendered as a squiggle on a bar graph. History here is not fixed, but remarkably malleable to the needs and brand strategies of the present (forty-nine artists competed to design the country's new logo and unified tagline, announced in January 2020). For a long time, the narrative was something like this: first there was nothing and then there was oil, and Dubai exploding out of the desert, in quick succession.

More recently, the image of Dubai has shifted in concert with the broader academic and art-world focus on Indian Ocean discourse: the city's history as a trading entrepot and links with East Africa, Islam's maritime networks and links with South and Southeast Asia, and the still-suppressed history of the Arab slave trade,[2] which was only formally abolished in the UAE's predecessor, the Trucial States, in 1963. The result is a curiously absent center, like the void in the middle of that new museum building: inhabiting the present feels like a kind of time travel.

The nascent field of Emirati art history is equally contingent. A number of recent institutional exhibitions—at the New York University Abu Dhabi Art Gallery, the Sharjah Art Foundation, the UAE pavilion in Venice—have

1 J. G. Ballard, *The Atrocity Exhibition* (New York, 2009 [1970]), p. 82.

2 Qatar is a notable exception here. Doha's Bin Jelmood House, or slavery museum, is a worthy example of how to merge primary sources, oral testimony, and the Khaleeji predilection for interactive museological interfaces to sensitively grapple with a phenomenon that is still very much living memory.

been devoted to the earliest practitioners of the region's contemporary art, cementing an art historical canon and a national hagiography in equal measure. (Of course these now-lionized artists enjoyed little state patronage or broad renown for much of their lifetimes.) These efforts have focused on "The Five," a term referring to a group of Emirati conceptualists associated with the Emirati Fine Arts Society, founded in 1980, and later, the Flying House Collective. They were by no means the first Emirati artists, but are notable for their break with Arab Modernism and the nice pan-Gulf painting exhibitions featuring landscape works and other pastoral representations, otherwise on view at the time.

The work of these early Emirati conceptualists responded to the accelerated pace of development in two ways. One was to take all of this mass-produced plasticky flotsam that flooded the city and use it as the material for their works, the beginning stages of what I've taken to calling a uniquely Gulfi petromateriality. Consider Hassan Sharif, who is best known for the assemblage-style sculptures he began producing in the nineteen-nineties, comprised of junky consumerist detritus like cheap household goods, snack packaging, and assorted industrial bric-a-brac. Viewed today, these works read as kind of material archaeology of the country, as well as a forewarning of the plastic pollution now choking the world's seas.

Yet another tendency is exemplified by Abdullah Al Saadi, whose practice emphasizes the Bedouin traditions—nomadic life, animal husbandry—that were so quickly erased, invented languages, as well as his relationship with nature. Encoded, glyphic semiotics abound: an alphabet of rocks engraved with desert animals, or a collection of the twigs and wrappers that his illiterate mother left outside his door when she visited; a kind of shared secret language.

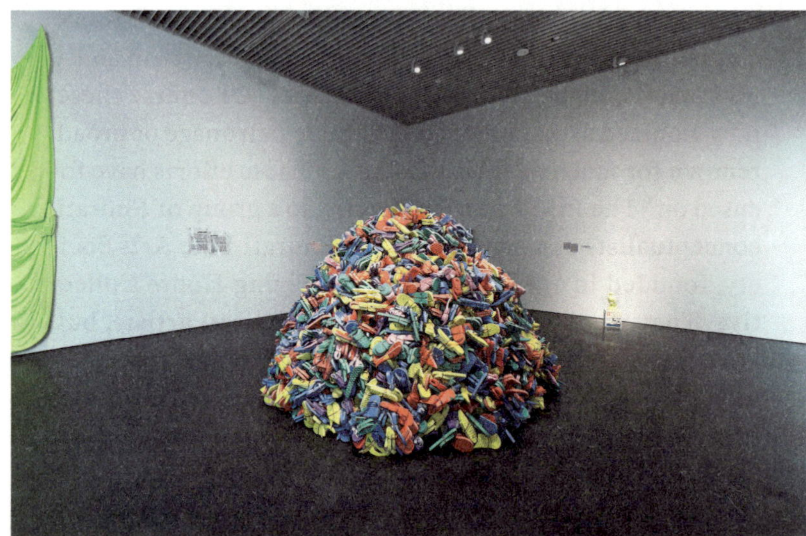

Hassan Sharif, *Slippers and Wire*, 2009, installation view, *Crude*, 2018–19, Jameel Arts Centre, Dubai

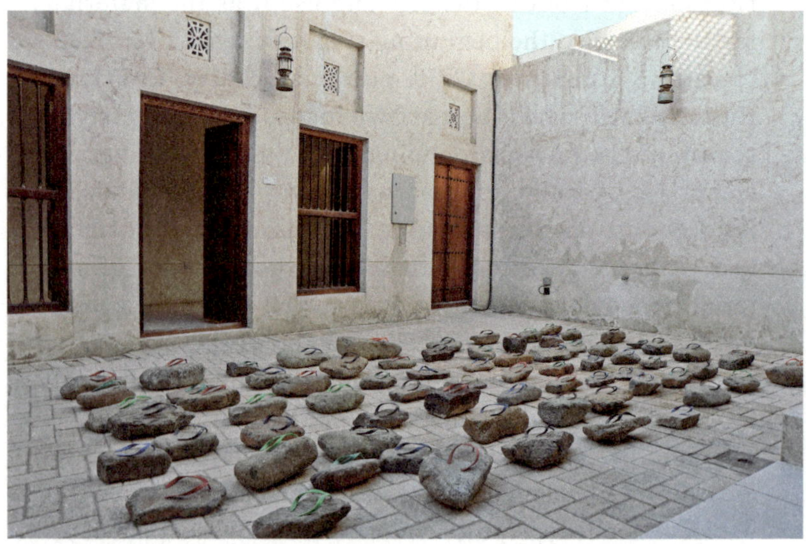

Installation view from the exhibition *Abdullah Al Saadi: Al-Toubay*, 2014, SAF Art Spaces, Al Mureijah, Sharjah Heritage Area

Many works emphasize being on the move, such as an installation of flip-flops that marry cheap rubber thongs with a stone base in reference to arduous journeys in punishing conditions, or a suite of rather lovely watercolors documenting the artist's habit of long, solitary treks, in which landscapes are as much a character as the animals, rocks, and plants he met along the way. Mohamed Ahmed Ibrahim's work is also intimately connected with his home, the small enclave of Khor Fakkan on the UAE's other coast. The town is squeezed between the Arabian Sea and a mountain range that runs almost directly North-South and blocks all sunlight after mid-afternoon in a play of light and shade that is reflected in his work. Similarly, his works on paper feature an inventive mark making reminiscent of the petroglyphs found in the caves near his home while his sculptural practice makes use of found natural materials like palm leaves, mud, clay, sand, shells, and rocks, incorporating them into remarkable, colorful papier-mâché works.

It's worth contrasting both their practices with a younger generation of artists from the Gulf whose engagement with the same Bedouin past stems not from lived experience so much as an abstracted mediated Lawrence of Arabia-type romanticization of "Arabia." The result, as with Ahaad Alamoudi's falcons or Hejazi-Sufi folk dances shot as contemporary music videos, is a fascinating feedback loop and also exemplifies the temporal, cultural, and historical disconnect that characterizes a lot of artists working today. We can also understand this current, heavily present in the artists around Edge of Arabia,[3] as symptomatic of Saudi money's increasing influence—today

3 Founded in 2003 and active through the early 2010s, Edge of Arabia was an independent platform dedicated to promoting primarily Saudi, and later Bahraini artists. One of its co-founders, artist Ahmed Mater, would go on to head the Misk Institute.

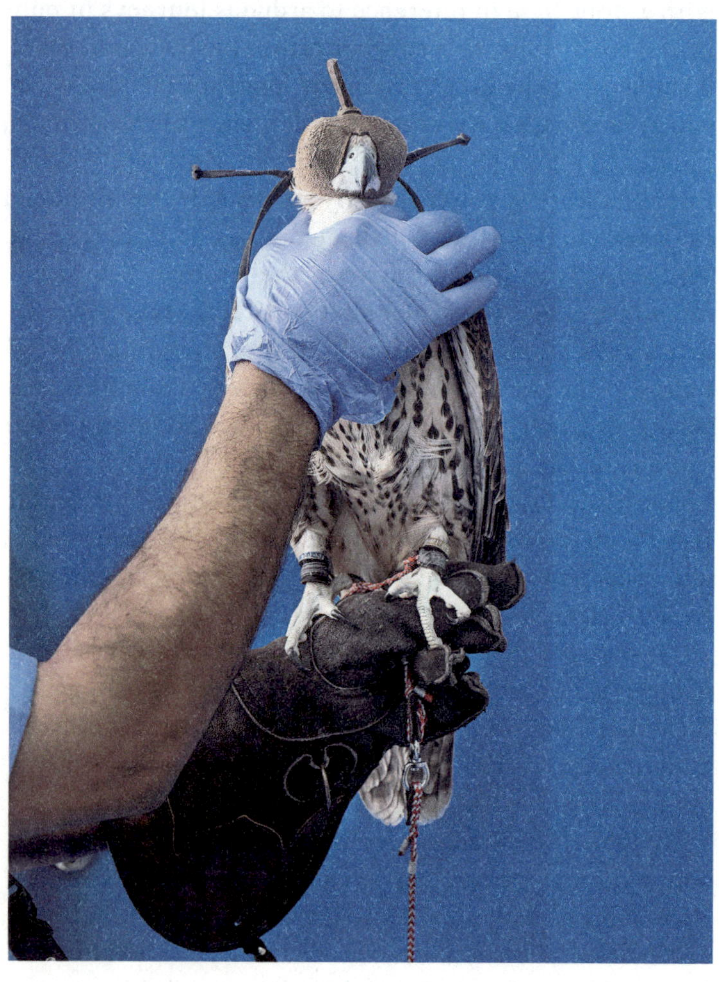

Farah Al Qasimi, *Falcon Hospital 2 (Blue Glove)*, 2016

we have the government funded and sanctioned Misk Art Institute (founded by Saudi Crown Prince Mohammed bin Salman bin Abdulaziz Al Saud to promote "grassroots" art production) and the independent Jameel Foundation, which recently inaugurated Dubai's first contemporary art museum, the Jameel Arts Centre, on its old creek. While Misk promotes primarily Saudi artists, Jameel's remit extends to primarily Arab contemporary art, with an emphasis on discursive and film programming. A unique quality of the latter is that one of its exhibition spaces is a plot of land—dubbed the "Artist's Garden," which features a different cultivation or botany-focused project each year; past commissions have included Asunción Molinos Gordo and Shaikha Al Mazrou.

These same emphases can be found in artists working today, even as they respond to very different conditions: desert journeys are transposed to cars and planes, while nature gives way to hermetically sealed, constructed environments. The constant transience of nomadic life and frustrated placemaking desire is recast into explorations of expat wellness culture, oud-heavy olfactory environments,[4] and all the affective haberdashery of airline travel in Raja'a Khalid's work, and takes on a nostalgic air in Lantian Xie's fast-food delivery motorcycles, Emirati power SUVs, and culture-contingent props for parties. Sharif's maximalist sculptures and lifelong fascination with systems of power meanwhile finds resonance in Farah Al Qasimi's kaleidoscopic, richly textured photographs and in Vikram Divecha's considerations of land, time, and labor, as well as networks of South Asian solidarity in the UAE, where Indians, Pakistanis, and Bangladeshis alone make up some sixty percent of the population.

---

4 Oud oil is a woody, balsamic fragrance component, one of the most expensive in the world.

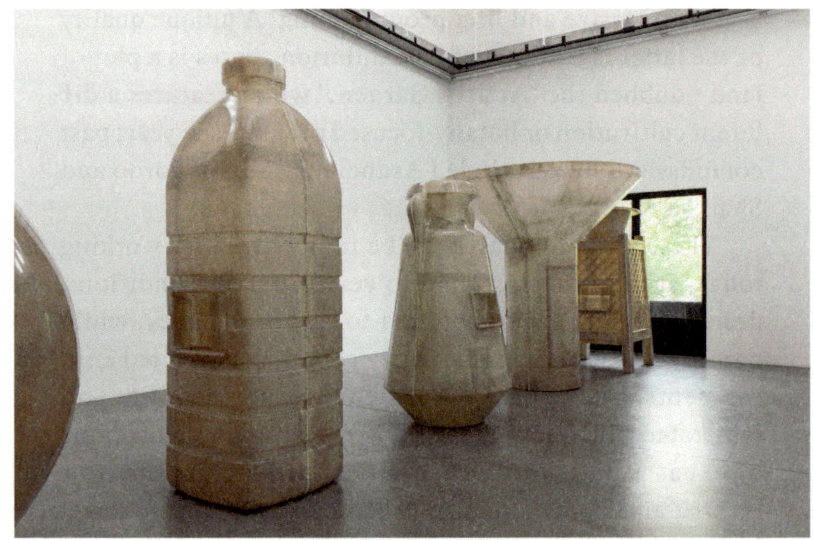

Alia Farid, *In Lieu of What Was*, 2019, installation view, Portikus, Frankfurt

Petromateriality characterizes these practices—sometimes explicitly, as in Alia Farid's jerrycans and monumental fiberglass vessels that chart how the advent of oil changed attitudes to water in Kuwait. Their work features the products of oil culture, and incorporates synthetic oil-derived petroproducts, but above all plastic: viscous, gloopy, in flux. These artists capture the increasingly prevalent sensation of never quite belonging to any territory, having no protection from the state, and never feeling welcome in any place. The historical underpinnings of this kind of work was made manifest in Jameel Art Center's first exhibition *Crude*, organized by Murtaza Vali and running from late 2018 until early 2019, which charted seventeen artists and collectives' engagement with the early decades of the broader region's oil industry—early twentieth century in countries like Iraq, and midcentury in the Gulf. Even as each of these artists evince an interest in Brand Dubai and constructed environments, their work is undergirded by a clashy, hotpot-style multiculturalism (there's some leaching into the broth, but everyone must eventually leave[5]) and attendant regime of racial superiority that places Emiratis and other Gulf citizens on top.

Dubai's cultural fabric can be understood as a kind of urban *kintsugi*,[6] pieced together from the 200 or so nationalities that inhabit it, with the fissures of stratification along class, gender, and national lines lacquered and gilded,

5 All noncitizens are allowed to stay in the country only as long as they have a valid visa. Visas are overwhelmingly provided by employers, which means people must return to their passport countries when they reach the end of their working lives, even if they were born and/or spent several decades in the UAE.

6 This Japanese technique of mending broken pottery uses lacquer mixed with powdered gold, silver, or other precious metals: instead of disguising the repair, it is respected and celebrated. Dubai similarly doesn't look to minimize its seams but instead highlights them.

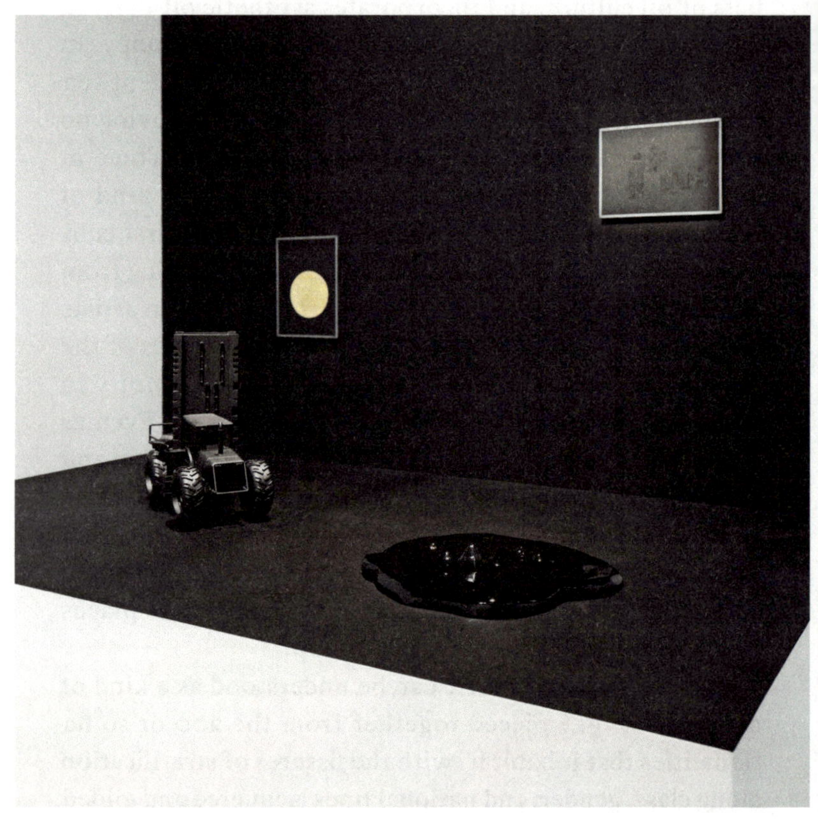

Ala Jounis, *Al Bahithun [The re-searchers]*, 2018, exhibition view from *Crude*,
Jameel Art Centre Dubai

because Dubai. Of course, as with the original ceramic technique there's some cultural territorial pissing at play: suturing Korean, Vietnamese, or Chinese fragments in this way marked them as firmly Japanese. Dubai does the same, fusing together its denizen cultures while painstakingly keeping these cultures' boundaries intact—this is no fondue. And local artists build their visual languages in the same way, even when this regrettably means treating migrant workers as raw material, as in Divecha's practice.

Most interesting is how the aforementioned UAE-based artists (only Al Qasimi is a citizen) have largely bypassed the 2010s flirtation with Gulf Futurism, even as the country deepens its future obsession and the city begins to increasingly resemble an architectural rendering or a fully solar sintered metropolis. It is worth remembering, however, that the phenomenon was a response not only to this heavily mediated experience of the Gulf War, but to the related ecological catastrophe too, namely the unforgettable 1991 burning of Kuwaiti oil fields, those acrid black plumes of smoke that haunt the psyches and practices of a generation now in their mid- to late thirties, like Divecha and Khalid, but is notably absent in the work of younger artists like Al Qasimi.

At the 1991 anti-globalization protests in Seattle, a favorite slogan was *another world is possible*. It's almost certainly too late for this world, but perhaps another *planetary* is possible, one that exists in opposition to the global and the free flow of capital, privileged people, and information. This planetary, to my mind, has the texture of oil, almost as an elegy for this soon-to-be-exhausted resource. It's slow, it's stubborn, it's viscous, it's volatile, and it leaves indelible traces. It has a smell; it hangs in the air like Khalid's oud works. This, of course is aspirational—and to extricate the Gulf region from the oil money that has underwritten its development is nothing short of a pipe dream.

To be clear—Dubai's version of the planetary is not about going to Mars in order to consider the planet as a whole so much as being able to identify Dubai from space. And the most futuristic thing about the city isn't its buildings or technophilia or breathy hyperconsumerism. Rather, it's the aforementioned demographics—only eleven percent of the population are citizens—resulting in a post-nationality, post-rights framework that doesn't need to undo older protections because they never existed in the first place.[7] While it's perhaps overly reductive to claim that the UAE was entirely bypassed by colonialism, it existed largely on the far fringes of other empires, never quite important or lucrative enough to be properly occupied. As such, the defining characteristic of the country is its post-Westernness (while still paradoxically being part of the Global North), which is more a quirk of market and of simply coming into itself at a time when the West had already slid into its long decline.

I think of the rest of that J. G. Ballard quote. He continues: "It's no coincidence that religious leaders emerge from the desert. Modern shopping malls have much the same function. A future Rimbaud, Van Gogh, or Adolf

7 Officially, the UAE is a constitutional monarchy, which has, since 2006, been gradually enfranchising its citizens with the vote, a process that accelerated following the regional upheavals that became known in the West as the Arab Spring. Voters elect twenty members, or half, of the forty-seat parliament known as the Federal National Council and the rulers of each emirate appoint the other twenty seats. In 2018, UAE President Khalifa bin Zayed al Nahyan issued a decree stating that half of the FNC members should be women. As of the last elections in 2019, 337,738 citizens had the vote: approximately a third of all Emiratis, and 3.5 percent of the total population.

Hitler will emerge from their timeless wastes."[8] What kind of artists might emerge from such a place? And what happens when all those diasporic artists, who might have been born in Dubai and lived most of their lives there before moving to other art centers to further their practice, come home, and realize their city is under threat from rising seas, and shift their practices to address this fact?

Perhaps there could be a kind of planetary that pays attention to the planet itself—to its environmental degradation and climate justice. Perhaps it considers the planet as an interconnected entity, plants, animals, and humans all linked and working together in the vein of Gaia theory. For artists, this means paying attention not just to art's modes of production but its environmental impact, too, to say nothing of the practice of shipping or airfreighting artworks thousands of miles between studio and show. We understand that art kills, whether satirized as a cursed painting in the 2018 Netflix film *Velvet Buzzsaw*, or the widespread belief that Vincent Van Gogh suffered the consequences of lead poisoning and Eva Hesse's tragic early death because of a brain tumor was caused by the resins, plasters, and Fiberglass she worked with—and that's to say nothing of the damage caused by the mining and production of art supplies.

Crucially, this applies to the places that artists show, too. It's worth remembering just how closely entwined art and oil money patronage is, beyond the Gulf: J. Paul Getty, and John Rockefeller (whose daughter-in-law would leverage his fortune to cofound MoMA) were both oil tycoons. More recently, many U.K. institutions have come under fire for their links to the planetwide devastation wrought by energy companies like BP, or in the case of the Whitney

8 J. G. Ballard, 1970 (see note 1).

Museum,[9] tear gas, a chemical whose use in warfare was outlawed by the Geneva Convention yet still continues to be casually deployed by police and military forces against their own populations as a means of political suppression or mere crowd control. Other funding sources, including private prisons currently being sued for violating United States anti-slavery laws, and the immigration death camps on the border, might be more likened to environmental racism. Equally if not more culpable here are critics, curators, and other arts professionals who jet about the world with little thought to the carbon miles they rack up. Perhaps this requires a fundamental restructuring in the current international circuit of fairs and biennials.

I think again of the new museum in Dubai and its slogan *See the Future, Create the Future*, an activity that should be viewed as a responsibility, not an opportunity. And I also think of a passing comment critic Louisa Elderton made in September 2019 in Vienna. We were dashing through a climate march to get to the art fair, where I was due to talk on a panel about the future of art. As she so succinctly put it—"How can we talk about the future of art when the planet itself doesn't have a future?" We need to start understanding art, like oil, as an extractive industry. Art doesn't trade solely in immaterial notions of research or beauty or speculative financial capital, but also has a real measurable impact on the environment. After peak oil comes peak plastic, a time not too far off in which another planetary will be not be just possible, but necessary.

9 Former board member Warren Kanders resigned following protests against his company Safariland—a truly planetary company that supplied the tear gas used in conflicts ranging from Ferguson, Oakland, Puerto Rico, and the US-Mexican border to Cairo, Bahrain, Palestine, and beyond—that included several artists withdrawing from the 2019 Whitney Biennial.

Museums, Repair, and Discourse: On Contemporary Art's Planetary Future

Kader Attia
interviewed by Sabine Breitwieser

Artist Kader Attia spent his childhood moving between France and Algeria, an experience that had a profound impact on his work. While cultivating an intercultural and interdisciplinary approach, he researched the notion of repair, a concept he has worked on in his writings and his art. His work *Open Your Eyes* (2010), which started as a double slide projection and later expanded to sculptures, is based on the artist's comprehensive research on modern Western aesthetics, focusing on the repair of the human body, which he compares to the evolution of repair in the non-occidental world. Attia is also the Founder of ~~La Colonie~~, a space in Paris in which to share and debate ideas and knowledge focusing on decolonialization.

"Planetary" and "global" are terms that deal with geopolitics and its limitations, but also with the idea and expansion of space. I recall one of our first projects, a public work I commissioned in 2010 for Utopia and Monument *in Graz. After exploring the city center and a neighborhood across the river, you created a line of couscous on the main public square and filmed pigeons eating it. During the exhibition, this film was broadcast on a large public screen and tram monitors. In a related statement, you explained that you "imagined a poetic and political gesture that will evoke reality, desire, ubiquity, dream, fear, exile, and the failure of contemporary political projects to handle the 'Transnational Spaces,' from Graz to*

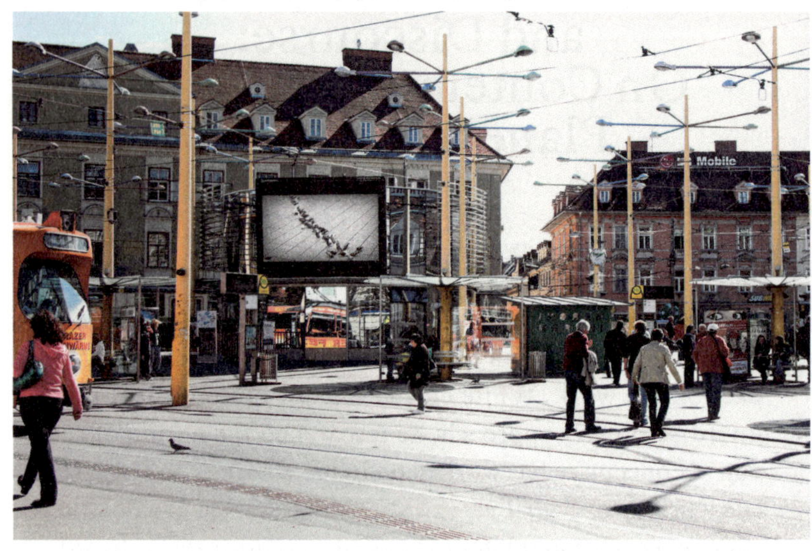

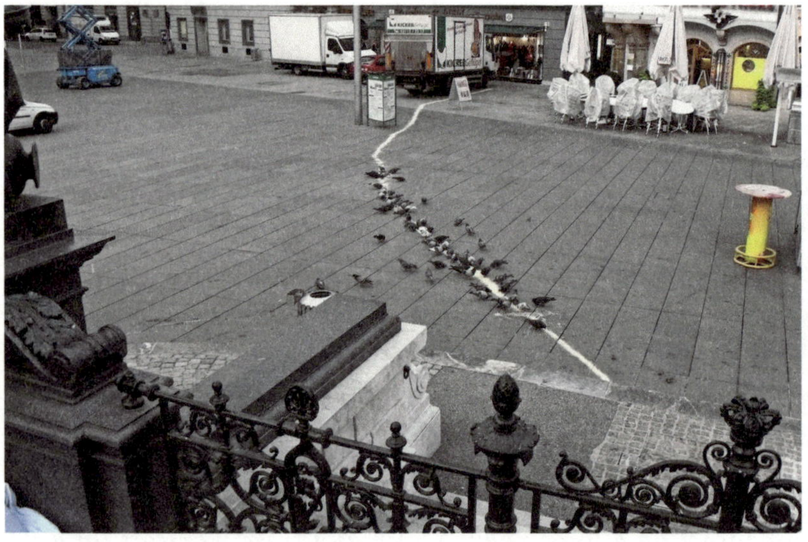

Kader Attia, *Myth of Order*, 2010, Graz, Austria

Istanbul, from Frankfurt to Kolkata, from Qatar to Vienna, because the reality of a boundary is that it both separates and connects two spaces." Over the years you've made several gestures like this. Let's talk about space, transnational spaces, and how you started to work with notions of repair and reappropriation within visual art and its institutions.

I was indeed interested in the invisible border that exists in Austrian society, like in many other European and Western societies, between migrant communities and locals. In this bourgeois city of Graz is a Turkish neighborhood. There was no visible border around it, but people seemed to pay attention to a kind of border, which was basically a road. Beyond it were kebab and sex shops and it was definitely like crossing an invisible wall. The idea of spreading a line of couscous through the city's downtown area in the early morning was a metaphor for a disappearing border eaten by these animals. On the planetary scale, the question of borders has to do with this paradox that borders do not really exist. Especially in Africa, a border can be in the middle of nowhere; between Morocco and Algeria or Cameroon and Congo, there's not even a sign that shows you're crossing into another country.

The question of borders correlates to the time we live in; an era of speed, to refer to Paul Virilio.[1] We are entering a new era of mobility and speed, and the borders that were once fixed are also moving. In Europe—at the border between Germany and France at Mulhouse, for instance— signs of what used to be the border are still there but nobody is there anymore; no customs, no lines. People go back and forth every day and sometimes even live on both sides of the border. But it does not mean there are no "mobile" borders, like police lines. Who has the right to

1 Paul Virilio, *Speed and Politics* (New York, 1977).

arrest anyone at any time on the pretext of boundary in-
fractions? So today, the border rhetoric in the West is a
kind of illusion. It's a delusional process in the sense that
it has disappeared. The only thing that has changed is its
process of controlling the population. Inside Schengen,
the border is mobile. I'm interested in this mobility for
two reasons. For instance, borders between African countries did not exist before colonialism. There used to be
huge areas where two different groups would fight during
a war, but at the same time there were areas of exchange
and trade, and even the language was mixed. So the notion of a border is a line, like Yves Lacoste used to say *La
géographie, ça sert d'abord, à faire la guerre,*[2] which
means we invented geography to make war. The invention
of the colonial border has been enhancing this idea of colonial, imperial hegemony to prepare for war.

We are living in a new era of extreme mobility, but only
for a certain population, because traveling from a non-
European country to Europe has become much more difficult. We have Emmanuel Macron's old discourse about restitution, that we need to repair what colonialism did and
so forth, but the number of visas that France grants people
from everywhere in Africa has completely collapsed. That's
why the notion of the planetary is, politically, a scary paradox. An amazing book about this delusional world we live
in, in terms of ease of mobility, is *Digital Civil War* by
Peter Daou.[3] It's not only an ambivalent or contradictory
world toward those who cannot travel and move like us;
it's much more related to this paradox that the digitization
of society and the relations between humans today do not
suffer from arbitrary borders. A young person in Congo,

2 Yves Lacoste, *La géographie, ça sert d'abord, à faire la guerre*
(Paris, 2014 [1976]).
3 Peter Doau, *Digital Civil War* (New York, 2019).

Senegal, Algeria, or Afghanistan has this incredible proposal of an open world as presented by the internet, but at the same time cannot enjoy it. You cannot move. If I only used my Algerian passport, I couldn't move.

In past years we have experienced how museums aspired to become global organizations in terms of locations, temporary exhibitions, events, and collections. This requires mobility of artists, curators, and scholars. I remember while working in New York it was very difficult to get visas for artists, particularly for people from Africa. How do you envision the future of contemporary art within this setting; in this, as you said, rather scary planetary future?

I see it both ways. One is depressing, and the other hopeful. The depressing way is that many museums are facing a growth crisis. They get so many visitors that they cannot sustain their own administration, but also they cannot afford the time to work more precisely, quietly, and wisely on exhibitions. They—Pompidou, MoMA, Tate—become like malls. I don't think that these institutions see research as the priority anymore. This crisis will automatically generate an evolution toward digitizing the museum, which will become a place you can only visit through Google. This scares me a lot.

But here comes the hope: that curators, artists, directors, and other players in art understand the crucial task of maintaining and actually building museums; or reinventing the museum not as a single place but as a place that appears in multiple locations. I don't believe anymore in these sorts of temples that major museums have been incarnating in the twentieth century. I'm hoping that developing museums outside their original countries is a good idea and can work. It will bring museums to the people. To experience works of art and history, you have to see the objects. The physical experience is necessary. However, we cannot ignore the neoliberal agenda of the contemporary museum. It's dangerous that museums also become brands that do not offer knowledge but only a form of entertainment of this knowledge. A museum is not a mall and if you have a Louvre in Abu Dhabi or a MoMA in Kolkata, you need to work with both local and foreign academia. You need to provide not only a stage for artworks but also a corpus of knowledge, a form of education and infrastructure to explain and maintain this complex activity. Branding the museum is also the end of the museum as we know it.

Why are museums opening branches in other countries? We know it's a new way to generate income; they earn money for sharing their collections and branding new museums under their names in foreign countries, buildings usually paid for by the local governments. Often, these projects don't seem to push an educational agenda. Are you saying that if education were the agenda, such projects would be a great idea?

I think so. Needless to say, we also have to avoid the colonial continuation. Another thing that has to do with my work on restitution is that by developing museums everywhere, we also clearly signify that artworks—classical or contemporary—do not belong to a country, are not nationally owned objects. I don't like the word "universal," but a sort of "planetary" heritage has to be activated. It's one thing to say or write this, another to make it real. I'm afraid that these museums will provide culture only to the most educated people. That's why I want these museums to also produce educational centers.

The other side of this planetary enterprise of museums is that acquisition policies often go hand in hand with a certain buyout of artworks from economically less powerful countries. Consider the many national acquisition committees most of the major Western museums are cultivating now; the national collectors funding the acquisition of works from their countries, in particular Latin American, Asian, or Eastern European art while at the same time these regions' own museums have a hard time acquiring art. It's important to look at art beyond the Western White male lineage on a global scale. But at the same time this has a lot of effects that connect to colonial times.

Yes, and this connects to restitution. I've been working on a film about restitution for a year and a half. I interviewed different people who are both pro-restitution and anti-restitution. What became clear during my research is that restitution somehow reenacts a colonial relation between those who give and those who are supposed to receive. You remember Marcel Mauss and the politics of the gift? It's not for free. There is an expectation.[4] And the question of restitution is a narrative produced by the so-called winners, who are the Western states, rewriting the story of an object. When Macron returns a sword to Dakar or a throne in Benin, the label in the museum of Benin states "This throne was returned by France on April 18, 2019." The object's identity is no longer what it was. It's an object that will always be seen as gift. I found that at the same time when the French Prime Minister came to restitute the sword of El Hadj Omar Saidou Tall, a Senegalese resistance fighter against France, fifty-three CEOs of the French weapon industry were negotiating a weapons contract with Senegal on the basis that radical Islamism was the region's new threat. A Greek archaeologist I interviewed last summer said about the Elgin Marbles that the Greeks have been asking the British to return for two centuries, "What we want is that the British tell us, 'okay, here are your marbles.' Just to answer them, 'We don't want them anymore.'"

4 Marcel Mauss, *The Gift,* trans. W. D. Halls (New York, 1954).

How can power relations be transformed so that "losers" can become "winners"? What conditions would allow them to make such a gesture and tell them, now it's your job to preserve our archaeological treasures and make them accessible? I believe power relationships based on exploitation and repression are ongoing, and it's difficult to stop or reverse them.

Restitution is related to so many fields of research, economy, psychoanalysis, and psychology. It's emotional. France pretends they cannot return the objects because the constitution protects the heritage of France. I think that restitution should enter academia to change the epistemology of the Western world. So much needs to be decolonized. Western epistemology has to include restitution as a field of research because no one, Western or non-Western, is prepared to handle this question that needs decades of discussion and research to find solutions. An anthropologist from Abidjan told me that Africans are not interested in restitution. Why? He says Africans have to map their heritage with objects and artifacts, but it's another thing to bring them to Africa because the Whites have written a story on top of them and the objects have become White as well. We all need to rethink how we understand them. We need to reinvent a language. The question of restitution is also more complex because it has one foot in the darkest past, and one in the future. Restitution should become a field of research like feminism, decolonization, or ecology. It has to become one way to help decolonize Western epistemology. Imagining fields of research like postcolonial studies, feminism, or the Anthropocene at the university would help us to reimagine the museum of the future.

If this museum is a place emphasizing research and education, how would it serve its public? How can the museum become more discursive but also more accessible? How can you include, in particular, people who are involved in this history?

Running my space ~~La Colonie~~[5] the past four years, I got this question in each debate. There are always activists who say that we are not accessible. I'm not saying that they are wrong; some of the minds here are very sophisticated, and you cannot play the Trojan horse without knowing the language of Babel. We need to get into academia. Who decides who writes history? Academia.

But it's also a question of language and format. How can you create accessible formats?

Yesterday, we were in a symposium against fascism[6]—a sort of emergency. The museum question is a long-term one. I would not suffer from the inaccessibility of museum language as much as I'm suffering from the lack of connection with people in light of the question of fascism, which is a massive problem. Fascism is a mass phenomenon, but it is actually theorized by the elite. Accessibility works on a small scale, with intimate workshops and dialogues, even if you do not speak the same language. What I'm trying to do at ~~La Colonie~~ and what I always try to do in the symposia I organize, even *The White West,* is to invite both activists and theorists to the conference. I'm not trying to protect the theorists from the activists and vice versa.

5 ~~La Colonie~~ is a discursive art space in Paris's tenth arrondisement, founded by Attia in 2016. It is a space to share ideas and to provide an agora for vivid discussion. Focusing on decolonialization not only of peoples but also of knowledge, attitudes, and practices, it aspires to decompartmentalize knowledge by a transcultural, transdisciplinary, and transgenerational approach. Driven by the urgency of social and cultural reparations, it aims to reunite what has been shattered or separated.

6 *The White West III, Automating Apartheid,* a conference conceptualized by Kader Attia and Ana Teixeira Pinto, organized by Kunsthalle Wien in cooperation with Burgtheater, where this conversation took place in February 2020.

We have to be aware of the formats we create. The format of the museum in the future may not be only about being for everyone, because we might not overcome social class stratifications. Besides ~~La Colonie~~, what do you think? How should the museum change for a planetary future? Let's address the polarization of our society with wealthy people who have unlimited mobility in every way with those with little or even no mobility who are controlled by our security systems and all kinds of institutions. What has to change? ~~La Colonie~~ is a great project, but it might not be enough, and we would need a lot of ~~La Colonies~~.

I created ~~La Colonie~~ because I felt frustrated by staying encapsulated in the frame of representation that is the museum. I think fewer artists today really engage with the societies they live in. I'm also talking about museum trustees dictating what art can be shown, and using the museum as a money laundering machine. The imperialization of the world is also happening slowly through different processes that are highly problematic; if we think about the future of the museum, we need to understand whether we still trust the project of what the museum was supposed to be. After the aristocracy, France created a *Republique* consciousness; I used to go to the Louvre when it was free on Tuesday. This capitalization of the museum did not exist in France then; it's quite new. This correlation between art and the market is a problem for me; I also feel that the artist has lost power in this conversation. We are losing the notion of ethics: museum directors and curators who operated on ethics and devoted themselves to what they believed was important. It's as if we're returning to the court of Versailles.

Or Wall Street—it's not an aristocratic system but an economic one.

You're right. It's capitalism. This bothers me as well. It has abstracted our concept of art.

Let's go back to your work. You focus on the notion of repair because society obviously needs to be repaired—and the museum requires a certain type of repair. I am thinking about Open Your Eyes *(2010), which I acquired for the MoMA collection. You opened our eyes to the dialectic of injuries and repair. This work was initially neglected because some male trustees were shocked at the portraits of injured soldiers from World War I. Maybe the work mirrored a past they did not want to face; the juxtaposed foreign objects also revealed signs of repair using a challenging, unorthodox visual language.*

Our concept of repair is a modern, postmodern one in which we deny the injury. The importance of this work is that for the first time it shows how much the repair is also the injury. And the difficulty for us to consider is that we've been brainwashed by rationalism to deny the injury. Denying the injury is denying time and history. It's the way that rationally we can control injury and then erase it. The Latin roots of the word repair, *reparare,* means to returning to the original state. Here it's returning to the idea, but never to the original state.

If all museums become globally engaged and show art by marginalized groups—should they just ignore their imperial, colonial pasts in their displays? Or would it make sense if they still showed what they were and why they have changed? Can you simply erase how the museum was generated and informed over the years and what kind of scholarship and collection history it has created? Can artists offer guidance here?

Yes, not only in works or art but also in conversation. What's interesting in your question is whether we display a form of genealogy of art in museums. I have always thought that it's a mistake to separate contemporary art

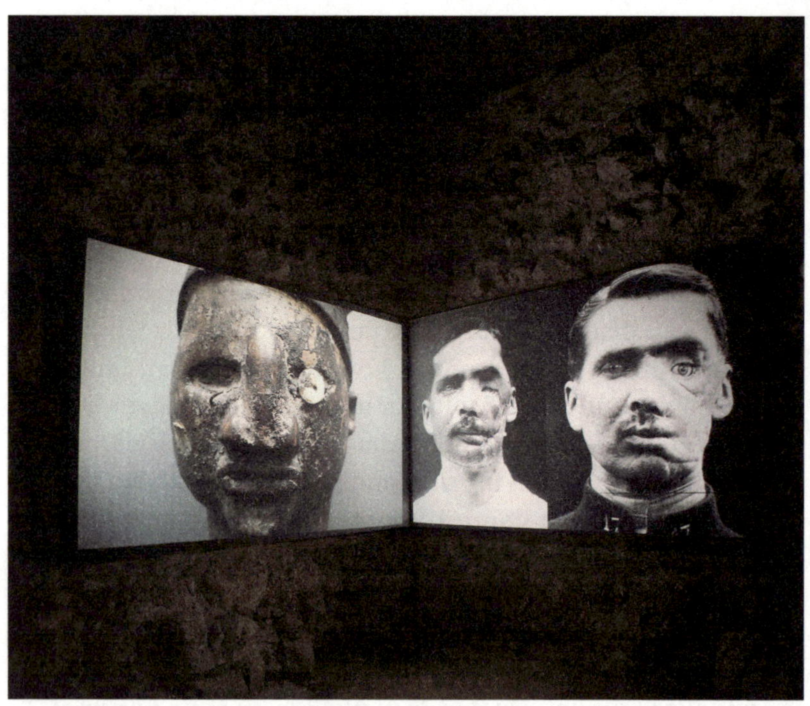

Kader Attia, *Open Your Eyes*, 2010

from other art. Even in my own art I was always interested in conversation. Showing a large evolution and chronology of art is crucial in terms of education. It sounds didactic, but it's crucial. We cannot arrive in Shanghai with a Pompidou and only contemporary art, because then it becomes a discourse that is not properly addressing the histories of the countries in which the museums appear. So the future of the museum will definitely be conversations between times. And this neoliberal society we're living in is totally amnesiac. The reason we look at artworks is to perceive emotional mystery, but also innovation. What do you think about that?

Museums are complex organizations with their own rules; it's about how and with whom the change occurs. And as an artist, once you enter and want to participate, it becomes complicated. So, tell me more about your film.

With the film, I'm trying to build conversations between different positions. My interest in restitution is how to give it enough space and time within Western epistemology to be elaborated. The trap of this discourse on restitution is that it has been addressed by the former winners and colonizers to the colonized as a reparation gift. In the political but also the aesthetic, psychoanalytical, religious discourses, the question of restitution is much more complex, and does not of course repair anything. We cannot bring back the millions of people who died from slavery and colonialism. But what I think and I hope, like Felwine Sarr who wrote a report with Bénédicte Savoy,[7] is that we need to create a new mobility for these objects. The fact is that these objects belong to neither the land where they

---

7 In their report *The Restitution of African Cultural Heritage. Toward a New Relational Ethics* (November 2018), Felwine Sarr and Bénédicte Savoy called for French museums to return to their countries of origin artifacts that had been taken without consent.

come from nor the ones in which they were displayed, they
need to be included in the speed of the twenty-first century.
It's back to the discussion of borders.

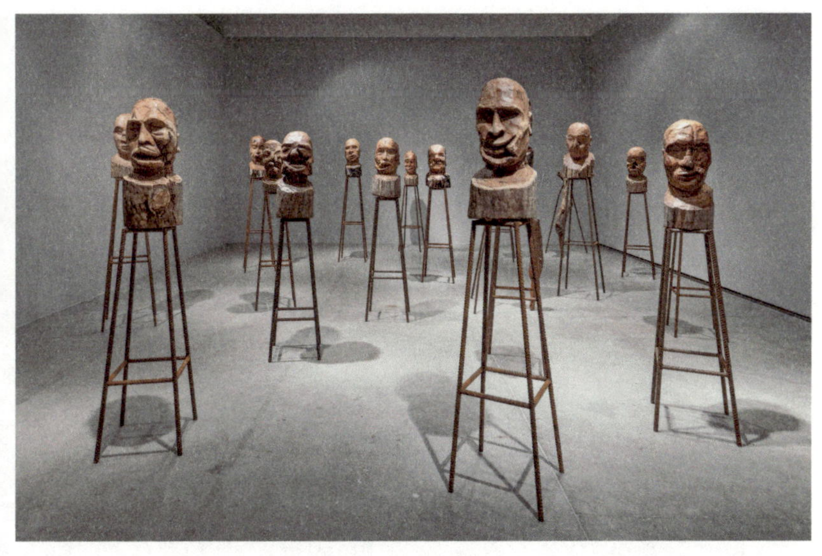

Kader Attia, *J'accuse*, 2016, exhibition view from *The Field of Emotion*, The Power Plant, Toronto, 2018

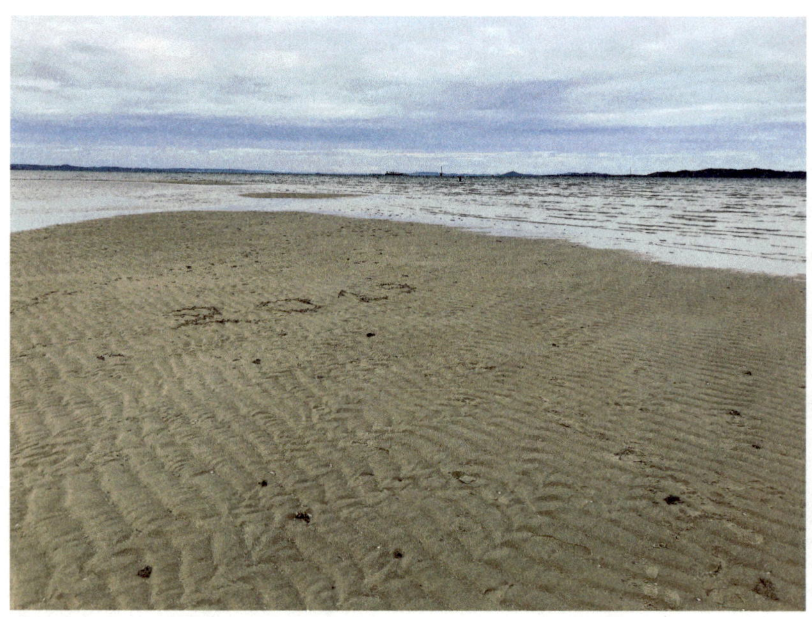

Itaparica, Brazil

Digging into the Future:
An Account of Notions
of Time and Place

Marina Fokidis

Itaparica, Sacatar, Brazil
December 31, 2019, 5:40 a.m.

The first sunlight that breaks through a gray sky at dawn is always the strongest. A few minutes after it appears, reds, greens, and many more colors start manifesting, one after the other, within the black-and-white background. Morning twilight, an ode to obscurity and ambiguity, seems like a numb body in which blood starts to flow the second the sun rises. To inhabit a moment like this, unfolding metaphorically between the Aristotelian notions of *actuality* and *potentiality*, needs patience and care, as well as a sense of bittersweet tenderness; a set of qualities that are lost within the busy courses of our lives, where—bombarded with unfiltered information, in full discontinuity with the natural environment—we run headlong into fulfilling the "obligations" of naked capitalism.

Today, I was awakened by a disobedient sunbeam that found its way into my left eye through the wooden blinds as early (or late) as 5 a.m. Here, on the island of Itaparica, in the middle of nowhere for some, or the center of the world for others, just a thirty-minute boat ride from metropolis of Salvador, everything rushes to enjoy the day. The sun does, too. Again, what are place and time?

***

Rather than articulating a series of presupposed fixations on cultural and historical traits, a further questioning on the issues of time and place as they are being constantly shaped anew seemed to be a more appropriate contribution to a book that seeks paths toward new/old commonalities. Time is relative; a mere matter of perspective. It always was, even before Einstein scribbled the Theory of Relativity on his blackboard. There are thousands of "times" on earth, depending on who is keeping them. Western culture is fascinated with the idea of time progressing as a storyline from past to future. The desire to impose clock time as a common metric agency is in itself colonial. "Time is everywhere in nature," writes Jay Griffiths in her meditative book *A Sideways Look At Time*. "In urbanized life, clocks are needed precisely because there is no other way of telling the time. But while nature knows a million varieties of time, the clock of modernity knows only one. The same one. Everywhere."[1]

In the meantime, we should not forget that in most Latin languages, the word time (*temps/tempo*) means both weather and time. This is how related time is to the seasonal cycle. As to place, what truly informs a place today? Is it exclusively its coordinates on a map? Its history and local culture? Or is it its interactive and interpenetrable relationship to the rest of the hyperlinked transworld? If a geographical place is some locus that can be defined by a common-sense consciousness, what factors shape this consciousness today? How can the *polis*—in the word's Platonic sense, meaning the meeting of citizens to create a place in the form of a city-state guided by philosophical and humanitarian values—be reconsidered? In a 2013 lecture in Athens, Giorgio Agamben argued:

The new identity is an identity without the person, as it were, in which the space of politics and ethics

1 Jay Griffiths, *A Sideways Look at Time* (New York, 1998) pp. 12—15.

loses its sense and must be thought again from the ground up. While the Greek citizen was defined through the opposition between the private and the public, the *oikos*, which is the place of reproductive life, and the *polis*, the place of political action, the modern citizen seems rather to move in a zone of indifference between the private and the public, or to quote Hobbes, the physical and the political bodies.[2]

How can we reinhabit this most recent version of *polis*, of place, which is not only emerging from the ruined boundaries between the notions of "public" and "private," but is also informed by many localities at the same time? The *polis* has indeed become a space of political and spatial contestation. Yet, it is in this contestation that it should legitimate its social body by reimagining itself. In the fifty-second newsletter of the *Tricontinental: Institute for Social Research,* which popped as an email onto my screen just now, Vijay Prashad writes:

> Millions of people are on the streets, from India to Chile. Democracy is both their promise and it is what has betrayed them. They aspire to the democratic spirit, but find that democratic institutions—saturated by money and power—are inadequate. They are on the streets for more democracy, deeper democracy, a different kind of democracy.

A polis should possess the potential to transform itself. And this is what is happening these past months through a series of interconnected street struggles that take place

2 Giorgio Agamben, "For a Theory of Distituent Power," speech from November 16, 2013, https://criticallegalthinking.com/2014/02/05/theory-destituent-power/ (accessed on April 10, 2020).

around the world. Different constituencies protest at the same time, in different places, because of the same need: To reclaim the commons.

***

Fortunate enough at the moment to be on a writing residency, I have the temporary and hard-earned luxury of getting lost in thought. Spare words, fragmented sentences, and brief texts cover every inch of the notebooks around my studio. My laptop is a silent discussant, waiting patiently to hear what must be written every day. Sometimes

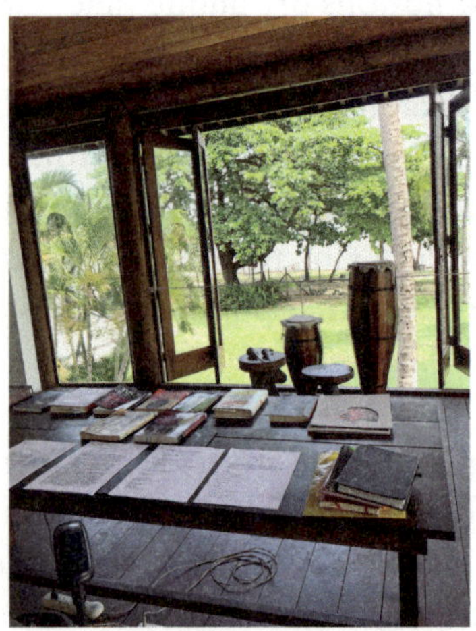

Itaparica, Brazil

it is not so silent. Interruptions for world news as well as personal updates from other lives change the rhythmic continuum. Simultaneous realities penetrate the routine of the natural elements that measure the passage of time here. Different birds sing their own songs at particular moments of the day; the tide rises and falls; the local fisherman comes every morning—for the past fifty-four years—at the same exact time and place to fish; the echo of the Yoruba drums sounds every night together with the faraway sound of Brazilian samba. These things mix occasionally with updates on current events such as the fires in Australia, the protests in India, Chile, Lebanon, Haiti, and Hong Kong; the news of escalating police brutality in Greece, or the killing of Indigenous leaders and environmental activists in Brazil. Yet, as far apart as these actualities seem to be from each other and from nature, they are connected. For various Indigenous communities, the personal, social, and ecological are closely interconnected: "health" is the state in which they are all in balance, a Quechua friend from Bolivia once told me.

In his much-discussed essay "Of Other Spaces," Michel Foucault suggests that the present era is above all the "epoch of simultaneity: the epoch of juxtaposition, the epoch of the near and the far, of the side-by-side, the epoch of the dispersed." He asserts that we are in a moment when "our experience of the world is less that of a long life developing through time than that of a network that connects points and intersects its own skein."[3] How has the over-abundant reception of real-time information—unstoppable wherever we are—affected our sense of "the world"? How has it manipulated our awareness? Are we still able to see outcomes as dependent on human acts? Or has the dissociation between visual impressions and facts been so effective that we've completely lost touch with the "humane," which is meanwhile submerged in cybernetic stimulation? Can we identify a set of new queer capacities that might be emerging, and go beyond the "hip-steria" of hyperconnectivity and navigate the turbulence within the demanding superterritorial terrain in which we all live?

3 Michel Foucault, "Of Other Spaces," in *Politics, Poetics, Documenta X* (Berlin, 1997), p. 274.

Cities have morphed into unfamiliar landscapes. Politics are not the politics we recognize; our belongings are not ours anymore. Public space does not belong to us either; and even private space, if it still exists, is negotiable. We are entities in transit, in which nothing is familiar and everything is banal at the same time. But for how long? We are living through a rupture. As we experience this inevitable change, in which everything is in flux, space loses its shape and transforms into nothingness, an immaterial place: the space for the impossible. Can we transform this uncontrollable oscillation from here to there and elsewhere within a space where "everything" might—again, or at once—be "possible"? How can we bring the past into the present and how can "the future" again become plausible within our lives?

As long as we can be enlightened witnesses of this transitory process and make good use of the realities unfolding simultaneously on multiple levels, there might be a hope for better presents to come. It is, perhaps, time to accept the nature of transition per se—the "and" instead of the "or"—and to find the paths to a series of inclusive spaces where the keys to the entrances are not precut, but are discovered endlessly in the process, through mere interaction. The maze shouldn't be the problem. Closed doors, absolute points of view, and rigid "solutions" are the problem.

Varied observations, dialogues, and desires weave new narratives along the way; they are fluid and open to constructive complexification. These narratives have as much to do with the information we access, people, and places we encounter and relate to, as with our awareness of ourselves. History is tied to geography, but what does history mean before it defines a locality? "History is certainty produced at the point where the imperfections of memory meet the inadequacies of documentation," writes Julian Barnes in *The Sense of an Ending,* one of his most popular novels.[4] Then, what about in times as ours in which the digital networks give us the opportunity to access past documents and doctrines around the world we never could imagine existed? The "complexification" of the process and the notion of modernity seems more needed than ever today. The universal version of Modernity (with a capital M), which was (intellectually) imposed on the biggest part of the world as a single path to progress, is hugely informed by many other knowledges beyond the West/North conglomerate, as is evident by now. Yet, in a world that has been organized by colonial processes for so long, it takes effort and time, courage and introspection to fully admit this.

So how can we fight asymmetries and unjustified hierarchies within so-called meta-colonial times? How can we respond to the popularity of the ultra-right, authoritarian, nationalist governmental morphologies? How can we redefine how our differences bring us together and celebrate them, as Audre Lord suggests?[5] By questioning the notions of place, perspective, and time, we could arrive at the formation of vocabularies that encompass risk and precarity but also promise new forms of solidarity and interconnectedness, beyond the hegemonic relation of the "middle" and the "margin." What about, then, a third space—or a series of third spaces lying between centers and peripheries—where people meet to imagine the possibility of other ways of being in the world? A place "between places," a correlation of space, form, and politics consisting of various

---

4　Julian Barnes, *The Sense of an Ending* (London, 2011), p. 17.
5　See Audre Lord, "Age, Race, Class and Sex: Women Redefining Difference," in *Sister Outsider* (London, 2019 [1984]), no page number (ebook).

interrelated sovereignties? A place that remains constantly open to unexpected dialogues among neighborhoods, cities, regions, associations, and approaches. It is perhaps in this narrow space, between the two or more surfaces—the "heres" and "theres" that have been partially separated—where inconsistencies, flaws, and scarifications can be reconfigured and harnessed with sensitivity and affection.

Or what about the formation of one strong collective (consisting of the so-called weaker marginalized groups) that bypasses national borders and clock times as we have known them so far, and which responds to new commons based on empathy and resonance shared between specific localities? What if a set of new connectivities based on

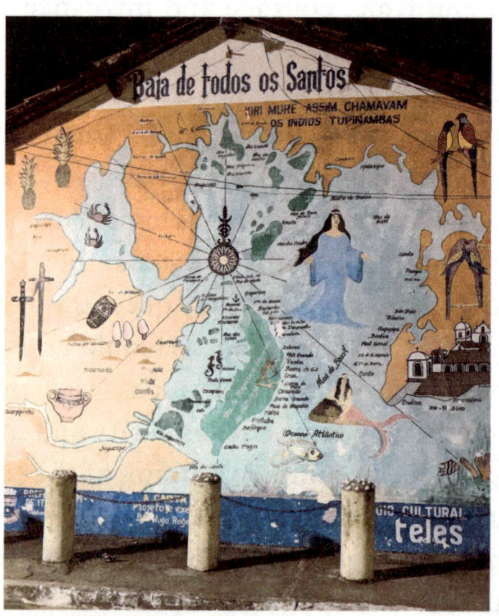

Map of the Bay of All Saints, Brazil

common "worries," as well as a fresh unity under the notion of "lack" and not "power," could be more appropriate and more inclusive?

***

For now, I am at my desk—situated momentarily "here" in northern Brazil—writing for the "future" section of this book. My view is of a place where saltwater meets fresh water. This is an auspicious point for traditional communities and it is often used as a metaphor for different people coming together to share knowledge and reach mutual understanding. In Itaparica, tradition manifests in loops the same way ancestral waters do. Polyvocality, polytheism, syncretism; all seem *ad rem*. If lucky, you can meet the ancestral spirits walking the dirt roads in their elaborate costumes, greeting you warmly and sharing their useful advice for contemporary living; (metaphorically speaking, of course.) Yoruba, coming from West Africa, is the second language after Portuguese, even if it is not taught in school. The reason why is obvious: histories of slavery are still apparent in Bahia. Stories are told and retold; memories blended within today's society and healed through the processes of an alchemical historiography. Or this is how it seems to my unprofessional eyes.

Among the primary obligations of people here is to maintain the sacred connection with everything that exists on Earth and beyond, unfortunately unlike us in the broader Western empire. The authority of traditional knowledge bears on the present, as it is performed in different rituals that take place, far and wide, in this small town. Yet, as customary rituals are tirelessly repeated over time, their reception and interpretation are altered and reinvigorated. Present encompasses past the same way the freshwater embraces the salt and is enveloped by it in the natural microenvironment in front of my modern wooden shack. Synesthesia is the norm here, even if Brazil is currently governed by an enemy of nature and his destructive political party. Candomblé, the Afro-Brazilian religion, among other traditional communities, is still one of the main spaces of resistance. What about the future?

***

The brief for this essay encouraged me to speculate on how a post-global art world and art discourse could look through the lens of art-theory publishing and curating as an activity. Will the precariat revolt? What might become the new normal, curatorially and discursively? These are some of the questions upon which I reflected. Thus I find myself asking: *Which way is South? And what is the time there (here)?*

I was born on the other side of the equator, so when I change sides it takes some time to get a grip on the new orientation and the new clock. From "here" (Itaparica, Brazil) things look different—as different as they would look from any other part in the world. After all, positioning depends on the vanishing point of the subject in question, and this is something we should always keep in mind—especially when we talk about any "global," "post-global," or "planetary" environment.

To attempt an answer, I do not know what will become the curatorial and discursive new normal. I find it difficult to think in terms of normality, as I think that cultural identity and art should be in constant negotiation with the margins. Yet I know that as I write, new art centers and events are being initiated by local professionals in locations that would be considered out of the art world's range in the past, among them Lubumbashi, Accra, Dakar, Jakarta, and Dhaka. As these locations and events gain international agency, they productively shift the cultural dynamics of the contemporary art world. At the same time the so-called proletariat is revolting in many places around the world.

The reasons for protest are almost the same for everyone: access to equal rights and privileges. A day after a duct-taped banana selling for $ 120,000, an "artwork" by Italian artist Maurizio Catellan was exhibited in Art Basel Miami Beach, underpaid janitors marched through downtown Miami with bananas stuck on their purple union T-shirts to protest low wages and poor working conditions. "How much are we worth?" was their question.

* * *

The future might be most about navigating the complexi ties of time and space in a nonlinear way. The fact that the past is no longer and the future has not yet come establishes a general pressure toward constant change—"progress." Yet if we look into different traditions, we do not see the same vectors of progress. In Bahia, daily life is shaped by ancestral spirits. The Aymara people, who live in the highlands of the Andes, think of the past in front and the future behind them. In contrast to predominant Western belief, the Aymara believe that what is known is what we see in front of us with our own eyes and what is unknown lies behind us, where we cannot see. The Maoris hold similar views of time. Even if this perception of "historical time" reads as an oxymoron, it feels logical, sensitive, and sophisticated to approach life by prioritizing the notion of continuity as a vital force. Above all it is urgent to understand that the easier access the West gains into such knowledges enlarges the "universal" meaning (and direction) of evolution and its entanglements.

Art is not separate from culture, but how necessary is it to think exclusively in terms of concrete geography and distinctions, especially if we want to define a destiny that claims real freedom, or at least an attempt at it? Where do we start if we want to open a possibility for discursive change? Whose experiences are narrated here, by whom, and why? Who defines what we, whether artists, audiences, professionals, or people in general, are and where we are at this moment? "Current history might be about false communities and calculated absences," argues the Invisible Committee in their 2009 book *The Coming Insurrection*,[6] "however, 'art,' as a kind of magic operation always offers an exodus from the rigid reality to a more 'invented' one. Often it not only captures an actual time and place, but also predicts and even influences the future."

How is the notion of a "common postcolonial heritage" upheld in times of thriving neocolonialism, triggered not only by the global economy but also by the new ultra-right-wing nationalist and authoritative forces that have gained popularity around the globe? What if we recomprehend the South as polysemic symbol that stands for direction and movement and questioning "South" as a set of idiosyncrasies to be rediscovered?

Like many others, we found ourselves in a similar discussion when we initiated the journal *South as a State of Mind* in 2012.[7] Soft, slippery foundations seem to create a need for territorial quests. In our case, the magazine was the imaginary territory in which we found and still find refuge during the devastating, everlasting crisis in Greece and beyond. The idea was, and still is, to give space to polyphony and cross-contamination—even if the voices that we present sometimes conflict with each other. Yet, how can coexistence be manifested in the form of a journal? How can networks emerge from a concentrated, sometimes even brief, exchange of ideas and shared intensities

6 The Invisible Committee, *The Coming Insurrection* (Cambridge, Mass., 2009), p. 109.

7 With a small group of collaborators, we founded this journal in Athens in 2012, which for four issues over the course of two years served as the official magazine for Documenta 14.

that takes place in the seemingly limited space of a bundle of printed pages?

It seems like yesterday when we began in Athens, possessed by a spirit of absurd authority guided by ideas that derive from Southern mythologies, which proved powerful for facing down an image of our future—an image presented to us as bleak and closed, after much rational calculation. We never thought of the South in purely geographical terms. For us, it stands as a parable upon which we built our endless quest for imaginary territories where intellectual freedom, as well as new/old methodologies, ways, pasts and presents, even new/old words, can flourish beyond any sense of compromise and tactics of crypto-colonization.

Within history (and the realms of theory, political sciences, and contemporary art practice), the notion of the "Global South" has provided a strong defensive mobilization against the hegemony the North. At times, however, efforts to forge a counterdiscourse to hegemony can become hegemonic themselves. Models of inclusion and exclusion, even if profoundly necessary when formed and adopted, can eventually defeat their own purpose. How can the very ideas of liberation and self-determination escape the subjective viewpoint of the "author" that brings them together? How can we go beyond the division of the "civilized" North from the "primitive" South without falling into the trap of self-imposed cosmopolitanism or self-imposed ethnicity?

We must overcome centrism in respect to the myriad of other truths in the world. We must also be careful with our approach to multiculturalism, as there are still structures of power that lie within it. In the past years, the focal point of the so-called art world has shifted from a few major centers to a multiplicity of artistic communities around the planet. Cultural power is still perhaps concentrated in some cities and regions more than others (hopefully not for long), but the affinities between the "peripheral locations" have started to shape a different geography of contemporary art. How can we go even further, besides the cultural dependence between the center and the peripheries? Is it possible to decentralize the canon completely? A spherical understanding of time and geography is urgently needed to fight the renewed demand for exoticism. The historical colonial narratives of "discovery" continue unstoppably within art's geography. Despite all art-market pressure, we need to defend the spaces—museums, art institutions, exhibitions, universities, or journals—that make serious critical thought possible.

The constant redefinition of South can also be a deliberate act of rapprochement, a path that both "swerves away from the influence of predecessors," and heads toward a "third space." In the words of cultural theorist Nikos Papastergiadis, "This relational energy that connects personal and historical claims not only curves away from the compulsive trajectories that head North, but also draws force from the swirling gestures of rapport with other like-minded southerners."[8] Above all, South is a living entity.

The journey South is not predetermined. For us at *South as a State of Mind*, driven by the feeling of *abjoy*—a term from provincial Friulian poetry redefined by Pier Paolo Pasolini as the nostalgia for living toward the possibility of development through simultaneous euphoria and melancholy—this journey has been a sort of return: a dig into the future. Not necessarily a literal return to a fixed

8 Nikos Papastergiadis, "What is the South?," *South as a State of Mind*, available online at http://southasastateofmind.com/south-remembers-south-nikos-papastergiadis (accessed March 12, 2020).

time or topography, but to the rediscovery of the subjectivities that have been and keep formulating the condition of South. Our journal's present became a renegotiation with the past. And our future became many pasts and presents to be. Across his writings, Antonio Gramsci believed that creating a new culture not only means one's individual original discoveries, but also the diffusion in a critical form of truths already discovered and their socialization into the present. The point is to make these past truths the basis of vital action again, and together an element of coordination and intellectual and "moral" order. How can "ruins" transmit knowledge through a series of presences and absences?

"The years between 1492 and 2012 are special years in our current era. In general, for most Indigenous peoples, this period represents 520 years of oppression and dispossession. In contrast, for European colonists and missionaries it represents a period in which the modern industrialized and technological society was born. It was their Golden Age," writes Jorge Garcia in his text on timekeeping, published in the tenth issue of *South as a State of Mind*.[9] For Mesoamericans, however, the "dark" was less about despair[10] than being part of a transitory time. Anticipating a long period of oppression, Indigenous peoples evolved strategies to survive and safeguard their ancestral ways and knowledge. But they knew that this

9 Jorge Garcia, "Timekeepers: The European Golden Age, the Mesoamerican Time of Darkness, and the New Dawn of Indigineous People," in *South as a State of Mind*, Issue 10 (2018), p. 132.
10 This is not to say that the conquest of the Mesoamerican continent was not devastating for millions of Indigenous people, but rather that for Mesoamericans the conquest was far more than simply an earthly encounter. Venus's movement indicated a cosmic time in which their knowledge would be safeguarded until the New Dawn—when it would resurface and people would continue with a way of life Europeans had interrupted.

period would ultimately end, and its conclusion would be announced by the passing of Venus in front of the Sun as it did in June 2012, a moment marking the beginning of a cycle known as the New Dawn of Indigenous Peoples. The post-2012 era is about the future. If we could all understand "facts" the way they did, that changes on Earth are the result of passing time, as marked solstices and equinoxes, and learn to live in harmony with cosmic events, today's planetary concerns would have been solved long ago. There are no entities without irregularities. If we master our fear and find ways to face the darkness within an unwelcome void without being swallowed by it, this emptiness might become a space to fill with brilliance and beauty.

Today is the last day of the decade. As I write, I read on my screen that a "Santa Claus" traveled from Chile to Athens, Greece, to visit an "illegal" squat hosting Syrian and African refugees. He gave presents to the children and encouragement to the adults. Symbols are objectified and made available to users distant in time and space. This is how they stop being parochial. No one can be totally self-reliant. On this island, one of the still-celebrated *orishas* (gods) is called Exu. His function is to bring to each of us the truth that we are all interconnected. This is the bare essence.

United we go South.[11]

11 In the positive sense, contrary to the popular racist definition of the idiom "to go South," which means to take a turn for the worse.

CONTRIBUTORS

Rahel Aima

is a writer, editor, and critic currently based in Brooklyn, New York. She was the founding editor of *THE STATE* and is currently working on a book about color and futurity, and a collection of exhibition fiction set in Dubai. Her writings have appeared in or at *4 Columns, Art Asia Pacific, Artforum, Art in America, Artnet, ArtReview, Bidoun, e-flux architecture, Elephant, Frieze, Harper's Bazaar, Ibraaz, Mousse, New Inquiry*, among others.

RECOMMENDED LITERATURE

- Aima, Rahel and Ahmad Makia, eds. "Vol. IV: Dubai." *The State* (March 2013).
- *But We Cannot See Them: Tracing a UAE Art Community, 1988–2008*. Edited by Maya Allison, Alaa Edris, and Bana Kattan. Exh. cat. The Art Gallery at NYAD. Abu Dhabi, 2017.
- Mishra, Pankaj. *From the Ruins of Empire: The Intellectuals Who Remade Asia*. New York, 2012.
- Unnikrishnan, Deepak. *Temporary People*. New York, 2017.
- Vora, Neha. *Impossible Citizens: Dubai's Indian Diaspora*. Durham, 2013.

Hildegund Amanshauser

is an art historian, curator, educator, writer, and currently director of the Salzburg International Academy of Fine Arts, where she initiated and is the director of the Global/Planetary Academy, a project tackling the question of how art can be learned and taught in a globalized world. In the framework of this project, she organized several conferences, including *Global Academy II, examples of transcultural exchange* with Kimberly Bradley in 2018.

Kader Attia

is an artist who lives and works in Berlin, Paris, and Algiers. His sociocultural research has led him to the notion of repair, a concept he has been developing philosophically in his writings and symbolically in his œuvre as a visual artist. In 2016, Attia founded ~~La Colonie~~, a space in Paris that provides an agora for vivid discussion. His work has been on view in solo exhibitions, group shows, and biennials throughout the world. These include the 12th Shanghai Biennial (2018/2019); the 12th Gwangju Biennale (2018); the 12th Manifesta, Palermo (2018); the 57th Venice Biennial (2017); and Documenta 13, Kassel (2012).

Stephanie Bailey

divides her time between Hong Kong, where she was born and raised, and London, while exploring the global art world as a site for intercultural exchange. Formerly senior editor of *Ibraaz*, a platform for visual culture in and around North Africa and the

Middle East, she is currently editor-in-chief of *Ocula Magazine*, managing editor of *Podium*, the online journal for M+ in Hong Kong, a contributing editor to *Art Papers* and LEAP, a *Naked Punch* editorial committee member, and regular contributor to *Yishu Journal of Contemporary Chinese Art*, *D'ivan: A Journal of Accounts*, and *Artforum International*. Since 2015, she has curated the conversations program for Art Basel in Hong Kong.

RECOMMENDED LITERATURE
- Dick, Philip K. *A Maze of Death.* Boston, 2013 (re-issue, first New York, 1973).
- Dirlik, Arif. *Global Modernity: Modernity in the Age of Global Capitalism.* Boulder, 2007.
- Kohn, Margaret. *Radical Space: Building the House of the People.* Ithaca, 2003.
- Massey, Doreen. *For Space.* London, 2005.
- Wallerstein, Immanuel. *Historical Capitalism.* New York, 2011.

Sammy Baloji

currently living in Rome and Brussels, was raised in Lubumbashi, Congo, a center of colonial, postcolonial, and contemporary entanglements related to resources. Colliding reality and representation, his photography and multimedia installations expose tensions between past and present. He mines the archive, traces social history in architecture and landscape, and probes the body as a site of memory and witness to operations of power. He is cofounder of the Picha Encounters, the Biennale in Lubumbashi. Recent exhibitions include *Senses of Time: Video and film-based work of Africa* at the Smithsonian National Museum of African Art, Washington, D.C. (2020); *Other Tales* at Lunds konsthall, Lund (2020); Belgian Art Prize 2020, BOZAR, Brussels (2020); *Extractive Landscapes* at Stadtgalerie Museumspavillon, Salzburg (2019); and *Sammy Baloji & Filip De Boeck—Urban Now: City Life in Congo* at WIELS, Contemporary Art Center, Brussels (2016).

Kimberly Bradley

is a writer, editor, and educator based in Berlin. Her journalistic, essayistic, and critical writing is often, but not always, about art and the art world, and appears in publications including *ArtReview*, *Frieze*, *Monocle*, and *The New York Times*. She teaches contemporary art practices at New York University Berlin and art writing at the Salzburg Summer Academy of Fine Arts.

RECOMMENDED LITERATURE:
- Deliss, Clémentine. *The Metabolic Museum.* Ostfildern, 2020.
- Enwezor, Okwui. "The Postcolonial Constellation: Contemporary Art in a State of Permanent Transition." *Research in African Literatures*, Vol. 34, No. 4 (Winter 2003).

- Filipovic, Elena, et al., eds. *The Biennial Reader*. Ostfildern, 2010.
- Kauffmann, Stuart. *At Home in the Universe: The Search for the Laws of Self-Organization and Complexity*. Oxford, 1996.
- Reggio, Godfrey. *Koyaanisqatsi* (film), 1982.

Sabine Breitwieser

is a curator and author currently based in Vienna. From 2013 until 2018 she was the director of the Museum der Moderne Salzburg. From 2010 until 2013 she served as chief curator of Media and Performance Art at the Museum of Modern Art in New York. From 1988 until 2007 she was the founding director and chief curator of the Generali Foundation in Vienna. She has organized more than 150 exhibitions throughout Europe and the United States and has also edited about one hundred catalogues and books as well as numerous essays. In 2012, Breitwieser received the Yoko Ono Lennon Courage Award for the Arts in New York.

Tania Bruguera

is an artist and activist whose performances and installations examine political power structures and their effect on society's most vulnerable people. Her long-term projects have been intensive interventions on the institutional structure of collective memory, education, and politics. Bruguera has received many honors such as the Robert Rauschenberg Award, a Guggenheim Fellowship, and a Prince Claus Fund Laureate. Her work has been extensively exhibited around the world, including the Tate Turbine Hall Commission and Documenta 11. Her work is in the collections of the Guggenheim Musuem and MoMA in New York; Van Abbemuseum in Eindhoven, Tate Modern in London, and the Museo Nacional de Bellas Artes de La Habana. She holds an MFA in Performance from The School of the Art Institute of Chicago (SAIC), as well as degrees from the Instituto Superior de Arte and the Escuela de Artes Plásticas San Alejandro in Havana, Cuba. She has been awarded Doctor Honoris Causa at the Maryland Institute College of Art (MICA) and from her alma mater (SAIC).

RECOMMENDED LITERATURE
- Aikens, Nick, et al., eds. *What's the Use? Constellations of Art, History and Knowledge: A Critical Reader*. Amsterdam, 2016.
- Bishop, Claire. *Artificial Hells: Participatory Art and the Politics of Spectatorship*. London, 2012.
- Boal, Augusto. "Invisible Theatre." *Art and Social Change: A Critical Reader*. Edited by William Bradley and Charles Esche. London, 2007.
- Dewey, John. *Art as Experience*. New York, 1980 (originally published 1934).

- Esche, Charles, and William Bradley, eds. *Art and Social Change: A Critical Reader*. London, 2007.
- Freire, Paulo. *Pedagogy of the Oppressed*. New York and London, 2005 (originally published 1970).
- Groys, Boris. "On Art Activism." *e-flux journal* (June 2014).
- Khomami, Nadia. "Abortion Drone to Fly Pills across Border into Poland." *Guardian*, June 24, 2015.
- Ruskin, John. *The Relation of Art to Use*. In *Lectures on Art—Delivered before the University of Oxford in Hilary Term, 1870*. New York, 1875 (first Oxford, 1870).
- Scott, Emily Eliza, and Kirsten Swenson. "Contemporary Art and the Politics of Land Use." *Critical Landscapes: Art, Space, Politics*. Edited by Emilia Eliza Scott and Kirsten Swenson. Berkeley, 2015.
- Sherk, Bonnie Ora. "Position Paper: Crossroads Community (The Farm)." *Art and Social Change: A Critical Reader*. Edited by Charles Esche and William Bradley. London, 2007.
- Wright, Stephen. *Toward a Lexicon of Usership*. Eindhoven, 2013.
- Yank, Sue Bell. "From Freehouse to Neighborhood Co-op: The Birth of a New Organizational Form." *FIELD: A Journal for Socially Engaged Art Criticism 1* (Spring 2015).

Roger M. Buergel

is the founding director of the Johann Jacobs Museum in Zurich, a private museum that looks at art through the prism of global trade and political history. Buergel has curated numerous exhibitions, such as *Mobile Worlds* (2018) at the Museum of Arts and Crafts Hamburg (with Sophia Prinz) and *Suzhou Documents* (2016) at the Suzhou Museum of Art (with Zhang Qing). He was the artistic director of Documenta 12 (2007).

RECOMMENDED LITERATURE

- Ngũgĩ wa Thiong'o. *Globalectics: Theory and the Politics of Knowing*. New York, 2012.
- Zupančič, Alenka. *What is Sex?* Cambridge MA, 2017.
- *Interwoven Globe: The Worldwide Textile Trade 1500–1800*. Edited by Amelia Peck. Exh. cat. The Metropolitan Museum of Art, New York, 2013.

Clémentine Deliss

works across the borders of contemporary art, curatorial practice, and critical anthropology. From 2002 to 2009, she ran the transdisciplinary collective Future Academy with research cells in London, Edinburgh, Dakar, Mumbai, Bangalore, Melbourne, and Tokyo. She also published the itinerant and independent artists' and writers' organ, *Metronome* and *Metronome Press* (1996–2007) that were twice part of Documenta X (1997) and Documenta 12 (2007). Between 2010 and 2015, she directed the Weltkulturen Museum in Frankfurt instituting a new research lab and curating *Object Atlas—Fieldwork in the Museum* (2011); *Foreign Exchange (or the stories you wouldn't tell a stranger)* (2014); and *El Hadji Sy—Painting, Performance, Politics* (2015). In 2016, she was a fellow of the Wissenschaftskolleg zu Berlin (Institute of Advanced Study Berlin). More recently she has taught at ENSAPC Paris, Karlsruhe University of Arts and Design, and she is currently a guest professor of History and Theory at Hamburg University of Fine Art. She is mentor of the Berlin Program for Artists and faculty at large in Curatorial Practice at the School of Visual Arts in New York. Her forthcoming book *The Metabolic Museum* will be published by Hatje Cantz in coproduction with KW Institute of Contemporary Art, Berlin.

RECOMMENDED LITERATURE:
- Benjamin, Walter. *The Arcades Project*. Translated by Howard Eiland and Kevin McLaughlin. New York, 2002.
- Crébillon, Claude Prosper Jolyot de (Crébillon fils). *The Sofa*. Translated by Bonamy Dobreé. Cambridge, Ontario, 2000.
- Hui, Yuk. *Recursivity and Contingency*. Lanham, 2019.
- Kosuth, Joseph. "The Artist as Anthropologist." *Art after Philosophy and After. Collected Writings 1966–1990*. Edited by Gabriele Guercio. Cambridge, MA, 1991.
- Rancière, Jacques. *The Ignorant Schoolmaster. Five Lessons in Intellectual Emancipation*. Translated by Kristin Ross. Stanford, 1991.
- Valéry, Paul. *Eupalinos or the Architect*. Translated by William McCausland Stewart. London, 1932.

Rosalyn D'Mello

is an author, columnist, editor, researcher, and a widely published freelance art writer and critic. She is the author of *A Handbook for My Lover* (2015) and her writing has appeared in numerous anthologies published in India and internationally. Since January 2016, she has been writing a weekly feminist column for *mid-day*, and, since mid-2016, a regular column for *OPEN* based on her visits to South Asian artists' studios, which she has been evolving into a forthcoming book for Oxford University Press, India, thanks to a research grant from the India Foundation for the Arts. She was previously the editor of BLOUIN ARTINFO India and was nominated for the Forbes' Best Emerging Art Writer Award in 2014, and was also shortlisted for the Prudential Eye Art Award for Best Writing on Asian Contemporary Art in 2014. She was associate editor of *The Art Critic*, a 600-plus page selection of the art writings of Richard Bartholomew from the nineteen-fifties to the early nineteen-eighties, and was a member of the jury of the Prudential Eye Art Award 2015.

RECOMMENDED LITERATURE:

- Ahmed, Sara. *Living a Feminist Life.* Durham, 2017 (reissued New Delhi, 2019).
- Cataldo, Antonio, and Katya Garcia-Anton, eds. *Critical Writing Ensembles: Dhaka Art Summit 2016.* Milan, 2016.
- Guha-Thakurta, Tapati. *The Making of New 'Indian' Art: Artists, Aesthetics and Nationalism in Bengal, c. 1850–1920.* Cambridge, 1992.
- Mitter, Partha. *Much Maligned Monsters: A History of European Reactions to Indian Art.* Chicago, 1992.
- Selim, Lala Rukh. "Art of Bangladesh: The Changing Role of Tradition, Search for Identity and Globalization." *South Asia Multidisciplinary Academic Journal* (July 2014).

Charles Esche

is director of Van Abbemuseum, Eindhoven, professor of contemporary art and curating at University of the Arts London and teaches at Jan van Eyck Academie, Maastricht. His focus is on art and how it reflects, provokes, and influences changes in society. His main work has involved the theory and practice of art museums, but also the qualities of the art center or biennial. His writings on institutional possibility and policy are useful aids to rethinking the relation between art and social change.

RECOMMENDED LITERATURE:

- Aikens, Nick, et al., eds. *What's the use? Constellations of Art, History, and Knowledge. A Critical Reader.* Amsterdam, 2016.
- Azoulay, Ariella Aïsha. *Potential History. Unlearning Imperialism.* London and New York, 2019.
- Byrne, John, et al., eds. *The Constituent Museum. Constellations of Knowledge, Politics and Mediation. A Generator of Social Change.* Amsterdam, 2018.
- Mignolo, Walter D. *The Darker Side of Western Modernity. Global Futures. Decolonial Options.* Durham, 2011.
- Vazquez, Rolando. "Decolonial AestheSis." *Periscope Social Text Online* (2013).

Olamiju Fajemisin

is a writer and deputy editor of Zurich-based contemporary art publication, PROVENCE. She is based in London and studies at The Courtauld Institute of Art. Her work is concerned with ideas that lie at the convergence of art, literature, and decolonization.

RECOMMENDED LITERATURE:

- Adair, Cassius, and Lisa Nakamura. "The Digital Afterlives of *This Bridge Called My Back:* Woman of Color Feminism, Digital Labour, and Networked Pedagogy." *American Literature* (June 2017).
- Bhambra, Gurminder K., et al., eds. *Decolonising the University.* London, 2018.

- Chow-White, Peter, and Lisa Nakamura, eds. *Race After the Internet*. London and New York, 2011.
- Hartman, Saidiya. *Lose Your Mother. A Journey Along the Atlantic Slave Route*. New York, 2008.
- Soyinka, Wole. *Aké: The Years of Childhood*. London, 1981.

Marina Fokidis

is a curator and writer based in Athens. She is the founding director and editor-in-chief of *South as a State of Mind* journal. She was part of the curatorial team and head of the artistic office in Athens of Documenta 14, a curator of the 3rd Thessaloniki Biennale of Contemporary Art (2011), and a commissioner and curator of the Greek Pavilion at the 50th Venice Biennale (2003). Fokidis also founded Kunsthalle Athena, one of the first independent art institutions in Athens, and directed it for five years.

RECOMMENDED LITERATURE:

- Achebe, Chinua. *Things Fall Apart*. London, 1958.
- Boal, Augusto. *Theater of the Oppressed*. New York, 1985.
- Borges, Jorge Luis. *Fictiones*, New York, 1962.
- Fisher, Jean, ed. *Global Visions. Towards a New Internationalism in the Visual Arts*. London, 1994.
- hooks, bell. *All About Love: New Visions*. New York, 2001.
- Johnson, Paul Christopher. *Secrets, Gossip, and Gods. The Transformation of Brazilian Candomblé*. Oxford, 2004.

Alexander Koch

is gallery owner, curator, and author who lives in Berlin. In 2008 he co-founded Galerie KOW and is director of New Patrons in Germany, developing initiatives in Nigeria, Cameroon, South Africa, India, and other countries. His exhibitions, publications, and lectures reflect the institutional and economic transformation and their consequences for contemporary art.

Christian Kravagna

is an art historian, curator, and critic. His focus lies on postcolonialism, migration, and globalization. He is professor of Postcolonial Studies at the Academy of Fine Arts in Vienna. His latest books include *Transmoderne—Eine Kunstgeschichte des Kontakts*, Berlin (2017) and with Cornelia Kogoj *Das amerikanische Museum: Sklaverei, Schwarze Geschichte und der Kampf um Gerechtigkeit in Museen der Südstaaten*, Vienna (2019). He is the editor of the books *Privileg Blick. Kritik der visuellen Kultur*, Berlin (1997); *Agenda. Perspektiven kritischer Kunst*, Vienna/Bolzano (2000); *The Museum as Arena. Artists on Institutional Critique*, Cologne (2001); and *Routes. Imaging Travel and Migration*, Frankfurt (2007). He was also joint editor of *Transcultural Modernisms*, Berlin (2013).

RECOMMENDED LITERATURE:
* Appadurai, Arjun. *Modernity at Large: Cultural Dimensions of Globalization*. London and Minneapolis, 1996.
* Clifford, James. *Routes: Travel and Translation in the Late Twentieth Century*. Cambridge, MA and London, 1997.
* Gandhi, Leela. *Affective Communities: Anticolonial Thought, Fin-De-Siècle Radicalism, and the Politics of Friendship*. Durham and London, 2006.
* Juneja, Monica. "Global Art History and the 'Burden of Representation.'" *Global Studies: Mapping Contemporary Art and Culture*. Edited by Hans Belting et al. Ostfildern, 2011.
* Mercer, Kobena, ed. *Cosmopolitan Modernisms*. Cambridge, MA, 2005.
* Mitter, Partha. "Decentering Modernism: Art History and Avant-Garde Art from the Periphery." *The Art Bulletin* (December 2008).
* Okeke-Agulu, Chika. *Postcolonial Modernism: Art and Decolonization in Twentieth-Century Nigeria*. Durham and London, 2015.
* Thompson, Robert Farris. *Flash of the Spirit: African and Afro-American Art and Philosophy*. New York, 1983.

Bonaventure Soh Bejeng Ndikung

is an independent art curator, author, and biotechnologist. He is founder and artistic director of the art space SAVVY Contemporary in Berlin. He was curator at large for Adam Szymczyk's Documenta 14 in Kassel and Athens, the artistic director of Bamako Encounters Photography Biennale in Bamako, Mali (2019–20), and is artistic director of Sonsbeek 2020–2024 in Arnhem, the Netherlands.

Peter Osborne

is a writer, editor, and professor of philosophy at Kingston University London. His focus lies on the historical ontology of the artwork, philosophical criticism, postconceptual art, and global comparativism. He writes critical essays and is currently working on a monograph that rereads Marx's *Capital* from the standpoint of post-Kantian European philosophy, focusing on its articulation of categories of time and the subject. Recent books include *The Postconceptual Condition*, London and Brooklyn (2018) and *Anywhere or Not at All: Philosophy of Contemporary Art*, London and Brooklyn (2013).

RECOMMENDED LITERATURE:
* Adorno, Theodor W. "Progress." *Critical Models: Interventions and Catchwords*. New York, 1998.
* Benjamin, Walter. "Convolute N." *The Arcades Project*. Cambridge, MA, 2002. Translation of *Das Passagen-Werk*. Edited by Rolf Tiedemann. Berlin, 1982.

- Marramao, Giacomo. *The Passage West: Philosophy and Globalization*. London, 2012.
- Nietzsche, Friedrich. *On the Advantage and Disadvantage of History for Life*. Hackett, 1980.
- Spivak, Gayatri Chakravorty. *An Aesthetic Education in an Era of Globalization*. Cambridge, 2012.

Fernando Resende

is a scholar and writer primarily interested in the study of narratives of conflicts and diasporic movements, both in physical and symbolic zones. His research focuses on theory and philosophy of communication, journalism, culture, comparative media, and documentary studies. He currently holds a chair for Brazilian Cultural and Communication Studies at the University of Tübingen.

RECOMMENDED LITERATURE:
- Martins, Leda Maria. *Afrografías da Memória*. São Paulo, 1995.
- Mbembe, Achille. *Necropolitics*. Durham, 2019.
- Sodré, Muniz. *Pensar Nagô*. Petrópolis, 2017.

Mohammad Salemy

is an independent Berlin-based artist, critic, and curator from Canada. His writings have been published in *e-flux, Flash Art, Third Rail, Brooklyn Rail, Ocula, Arts of the Working Class,* and *Spike*. Salemy is the organizer at The New Centre for Research & Practice in Seattle, Washington.

RECOMMENDED LITERATURE:
- Avanessian, Armen, and Robin Mackay, eds. *#Accelerate: The Accelerationist Reader*. Falmouth, 2014.
- CCRU. *Writings 1997–2003*. Falmouth, 2017.
- Cox, Christoph, et al. *Realism Materialism Art*. Annandale-On-Hudson and Berlin, 2015.
- Daston, Lorraine, and Peter Galison. *Objectivity*. Cambridge, MA and New York, 2007.
- Hayles, N. Katherine. *How We Became Posthuman: Virtual Bodies in Cybernetics, Literature, and Informatics*. Chicago, 1999.
- Riegel, Alois. *Historical Grammar of Visual Arts*. Translated by Jacqueline E. Jung. New York, 2004.
- Schutz, Alfred. *The Phenomenology of the Social World*. Evanston, 1967.
- Sellars, Wilfrid. *Philosophy and The Scientific Image of Man*. In *Frontiers of Science and Philosophy*. Edited by Robert Colodny. Pittsburgh, 1962.
- Thornton, Sarah. *Seven Days in the Art World*. New York, 2008.
- Žižek, Slavoj. *The Parallax View*. Cambridge, MA and New York, 2006.

Shuddhabrata Sengupta

is an artist and curator with the Raqs Media Collective, Delhi. Raqs Media Collective plays a plurality of roles, often appearing as artists, occasionally as curators, and sometimes as philosophical agents provocateurs. They have been invited to teach in many institutions and self-organized initiatives. Raqs Media Collective is artistic director of the Yokohama Triennale, Japan, in 2020.

Nina Siegal

has been a journalist for twenty-five years and a regular freelance contributor for *The New York Times* from Europe since 2012. Her articles have appeared in dozens of international newspapers and magazines. Based in Amsterdam, she currently covers art and cultural topics in a sociopolitical context. An occasional general-news reporter, she has also written about migration issues, emerging political parties, and legal cases in the Netherlands. She has published two novels, with the support of numerous grants and fellowships.

Chloe Stead

is a writer, critic, and editor currently based in Berlin. Her writing has been published by *AnOther Magazine*, *art-agenda*, *Art + Australia*, *Artnet*, *Frieze*, *Frieze d/e*, *Mousse*, *Monocle*, *Sleek*, and *Spike*, among others. She also regularly contributes to artist monographs and exhibition catalogues.

Sanjukta Sunderason

is a historian of twentieth-century aesthetics and intellectual histories of decolonization. Her monograph *Partisan Aesthetics: Modern Art and India's Long Decolonization*, Redwood City, CA (forthcoming 2020) studies left-wing aesthetics in India between the nineteen-thirties and seventies. She is currently working on a second monograph on connected histories of post-partition visual art across India, and West and East Pakistan during the nineteen-fifties and nineteen-sixties. This is part of her larger project on transnational formations of Third World cultural solidarities. She is based in The Netherlands, where she is assistant professor in Modern South Asian Studies at Leiden University.

RECOMMENDED LITERATURE:

- Chakrabarty, Dipesh. *Provincializing Europe; Postcolonial Thought and Historical Difference*. Princeton, 2000.
- Cooper, Frederick. *Colonialism in Question. Theory, Knowledge, History*. Berkeley, 2005.
- Harvey, David. *Cosmopolitanism and the Geographies of Freedom*. Berkeley, 2009.

- Ross, Kristin. *Fast Cars, Clean Bodies: Decolonization and the Reordering of French Culture*. Cambridge, MA, 1995.
- Wilder, Gary. *Freedom Time: Negritude, Decolonization, and the Future of the World*. Durham, 2015.

Kate Sutton

is an art historian, writer, and curator currently based in Zagreb after nearly a decade in Russia, where she helped found the nonprofit art space Baibakov Art Projects. A regular contributor to art and culture magazines, she is currently the commissioning editor of international reviews at *Artforum,* as well as a resident professor at the WHW Akademija in Zagreb.

Simone Wille

is an art historian. She currently directs the research project *Patterns of Trans-regional Trails. The materiality of art works and their place in the modern era. Bombay, Paris, Prague, Lahore, ca. 1920s to early 1950s,* funded by the Austrian Science Fund FWF (Project Nr P 29536-G26). She has spent many years of research between Pakistan, India, Bangladesh, Iran, Italy, France, Czech Republic, and Great Britain. Wille has published extensively on artistic routes and transnational relationships between these places. She is affiliated with the University of Innsbruck.

RECOMMENDED LITERATURE:
- Abu-Er-Rub, Laila et al., eds. *Engaging Transculturality. Concepts, Key Terms, Case Studies*. New York and Oxon, 2019.
- DaCosta Kaufmann, Thomas et al., eds. *Circulations in the Global History of Art*. London and New York, 2015.
- Dogramaci, Burcu, and Birgit Mersmann, eds. *Handbook of Art and Global Migration. Theories, Practices, and Challenges*. Berlin and Boston, 2019.
- Flood, Finbarr B. *Objects of Translation, Material Culture and Medieval "Hindu-Muslim" Encounter*. Oxford and Princeton, 2009.
- Mitter, Partha. *The Triumph of Modernism. India's artists and the avant-garde 1922–1947*. London, 2007.

GLOSSARY

GLOSSARY

Planetary Glossary

Crowdsourced from contributors

Hildegund Amanshauser (HA)
Stephanie Bailey (SB)
Rosalyn D'Mello (RDM)
Charles Esche (CE)
Olamiju Fajemisin (OF)
Marina Fokidis (MF)
Christian Kravagna (CK)
Peter Osborne (PO)
Fernando Resende (FR)
Mohammad Salemy (MS)
Chloe Stead (CS)
Sanjukta Sunderason (SS)
Simone Wille (SW)

A

Académie (Academy)

This term generally refers to an institution for the study of higher, usually tertiary education at a college or university. In the context of the RAW Material Company, the *académie* is an experimental residential program for the research and study of artistic and curatorial practice and thought. Its *académie* is held in French-speaking Dakar, Senegal, over a period of seven weeks each year. (OF)

Aesthetics of Decolonization

Decolonization—the undoing of European colonial empires in the twentieth century—was not only a political movement, but also one that generated modes of cultural imagination, social thought, and ideological dynamics. By introducing new visions and visualizations, decolonization generated an aesthetic field where questions of freedom, rights, sovereignty, and struggles could be staged, debated, and negotiated. Aesthetics of decolonization captures this dynamic field of visions. (SS)

Anthropocene

Name for a proposed geological epoch characterized by the decisive effect of human action on the earth's geology via its ecosystems. Has the political function of drawing attention to the catastrophic effects of human-produced changes to climate and other ecosystems. (Sometimes mistakenly associated with the self-contradictory standpoint of the organic planetary naturalism of the "Gaia hypothesis" of the earth as a maternal self-regulating system violated by human intervention.) (PO)

Arte de Conducta

A term that Tania Bruguera uses to describe her specific approach to performance. Bruguera: "Many things have made me feel uncomfortable over the time with Performance Art: the expectations people have of it, its transformation into visual iconography, and its apparent fatalism to become entertainment. But the biggest discomfort for me is with the place art has is society, and this is the most important aspect of my work: trying to find a way in which art can situate itself in society as a useful resource, not in the psychological sense, but in an active sense, as an agent of social change; as an element that interacts with life not as its mirroring moment but as one that can build an alternative structure to live; and how could it be transformed from a contemplative form (even when the work is interactive there is an expected passivity) into an active sphere." (https://www.taniabruguera.com/cms/866-0-Arte+de+Conducta.htm, accessed April 7, 2020.) (HA)

Arte Útil

A term that artist Tania Bruguera often uses for her art production. "Arte Útil is not neo-liberal art, it's not relational aesthetics. Arte Útil is the form of practical utopia; it is also civil disobedience art. Arte Útil is trying to close the gap between contemporary art and our contemporary non-art trained audience. I always say that the world is divided into two kinds of people: those who think who are going to change the world by making fun of it, and those who have fun trying to change the world." (https://vanabbemuseum.nl/onderzoek/bronnen-en-publicaties/artikelen/arte-util-and-the-attempt-to-change-the-world, accessed April 7, 2020.) (HA)

Arte Popular

An umbrella term used to describe traditional handcrafts and folk art from Latin America. Including textile, glass, pottery, furniture, and other

methods of art-making, Arte Popular (engl. "popular art") draws on the practices of indigenous peoples and French, Spanish, and Portuguese colonialists. In Brazil, enslaved Africans brought by the Europeans also contributed their own traditions and rituals. (CS)

Colonialism

Colonialism can be understood as a common sense as well as historical terminology used to understand European expansionism and subjugation of colonies across Asia, Africa, and Latin America for economic and political gains. Colonialism has resulted in the creation and maintenance of colonial empires—by Spain, Portugal, Netherlands, France, Great Britain, and Germany—since the fifteenth century, and consolidated most strongly over the eighteenth to twentieth centuries. Apart from its economic and political subjugation of colonies, colonialism has also produced deeply exploitative regimes of social segregation (racialism) and cultural and epistemic dominance (Eurocentrism) of Europe over histories and thoughts of its colonies. The undoing of colonialism—or "decolonization"—in the twentieth century forms one of the most important political, cultural, and social movements in global history. Colonialism, despite the fall of European colonial empires, continues to remain active via economic subjugation of under-developed or developing nations across the world, particularly in formerly colonized nations. The drive for decolonization, likewise, continues to persist in the twenty-first century in calls for decolonizing thought, cultural imagination, and social structures. (SS)

Computational Paradigm

The physical manifestation of networks ushering a paradigm fa beyond the media. It is marked by the substitution, mass production, and automation of human functions, including thinking, by machines. It marks our era, in which not only computers are used to solve problems or speed up work processes in all aspects of life, but also when their operational logic is employed to explain both natural and social processes. (MS)

Crypto-colonialism

Coined by anthropologist Michael Herzfeld, the term signifies that radical capitalism, as per extraction, orchestrated contamination, or germification, the instrumental division and conflict between people and communities, dispossession, the unstoppable destruction, the instrumentalization of refugees, the administration of terror, and other negativ systems are forms of colonialism. If the demand in the past was the conquest of the land of Others, today it is the accumulation of wealth to the few at the cost human lives, the environment, and the planet at large. Thus, the colonization process never stopped and has always been driven by excessive greed. Crypto-colonialism could be a more astute term than postcolonialism for the description of present times. (MF)

Decoloniality

A term that has largely been developed in South America by thinkers such as Aníbale Quijano and Walter Mignolo. It addresses the need to delink from colonial narratives that control much postcolonial discourse and to understand coloniality as an ongoing matrix of power that is exercised across the world. To decolonize mind, body, and spirit is to open up to a pluriversal understanding in which parallel tracks become possible and living and breathing on and between the borders becomes

a common condition for all planetary life forms. (CE)

Demodernization

The question of the "modern" as an ideology is Europe's creation, but has become the world's problem. While decolonial thinking serves most of the world as a way to work on delinking from the toxic ways of the past and propose different routes to understanding the present, in Europe such action needs to be qualified by the term "demodernizing." To undermine and question the "modern" is to test the core European bellef system in universal values and singular notions of the future, progress, growth, and society. It has achieved much through its power and persuasion and has led us to our current planetary crisis at all levels. Whereas to decolonize can easily be seen as exclusively the task of those originating outside Europe, demodernizing strikes at the core of European exceptionalism. Planetary demodernization is therefore a process that can only occur once Europe has come to terms with its past in a way most related to the incomplete social processes of post-1945 Germany. At that point, it may be possible for those originating outwith Europe to repurpose or link back to certain modern values that can still be useful for our collective present, but this is a task the world must embark on together and from different starting points and locations. It is also a process in which Europe must see itself as one place amongst others—neither center nor periphery, neither civilized nor primitive, neither traditional nor modern. (CE)

Diaspora

A form of exegesis that reveals an inherent normalizing of the trauma of migration. (RDM)

Global/Globalizing

An adjectival qualification denoting a state or process of extension of something over the whole of the planet Earth, in which the wholeness of the planet is imagined, in a geometrically ideal manner, on the model of a "globe" [Latin: *globus*], a sphere with a continuous smooth surface. Mainly used since the nineteen-eighties to refer to the worldwide spread of the capitalist mode of production and digital communications technologies. As Gayatri Spivak puts it: "Globalization takes place only in capital and data. Everything else is damage control." The smooth surface of a globe lends itself to the (false) imagination of this process as quasi-natural yet ideal, non-contradictory and uninterrupted. This act, by which "globalization" is revealed to be an imaginative process of "worlding" [*welten; mondialisation*]—the projection of a world [Latin: *mundus*] as the space of experience for a particular social subject —points to the ideologically contested nature of both the concept and the process it purports to grasp. "World" is associated with finitude and mortality (as opposed to otherworldy divine); "globe" carries the geometrical associations of infinity and perfection; "globalization" combines these associations. See *Planet/ Planetarizing*. (PO)

Global South

Avoiding a binary North/South shape, a space—one can also think of a territory—that is constitutive of cultural and political disputes. The idea of the Global South, in this sense, seeks to draw links across nations and societies that share a history o exclusion and oppression, though highlighting ways in which those histories are not necessarily confined to specific geographical limits. As part of structured and structuring

processes of constant disputes, entangled temporalities, and conflicting regimes of subjectivities, Global South is nevertheless a "concept" that would work, more precisely, if thought from specific contexts of cultural and political disputes. (FR)

Global South

A forged reality premised on notions of similarities in the experience of oppression on the basis of geography. Catchphrase. A means of dislocating and equalizing the specificities of imperialist trauma and its residual remains. (RDM)

Indigenous Communities

Culturally distinct groups affected by colonization. The people belonging to these communities are the following generations of the earliest known inhabitants of an area as opposed to groups that have settled. Any community may be described (or self-named) as Indigenous in reference to some particular location that they see as their traditional Indigenous land. In that sense, Indigenous Communities seems to be an open-ended term that can be constantly redefined and renegotiated specifically by their own members. (MF)

Modernism

A generic term customarily used to describe late nineteenth and twentieth centuries' advanced art of Europe and North America. Usually based on Eurocentric notions of progress, originality, universalism, as well as center and periphery. (CK)

Museum (and its redefinition)

Museums are storytelling machines using objects and narratives gathered out of the past. The stories they tell speak about the present and what a society or a subset of society finds valuable and worthy of remembering in the moment of creation. Because the kinds of stories change, museums cycle through phases of remembering and forgetting constantly, although they are often overconfident and discard unwanted stories that tomorrow might become essential. Museums work on these narratives collectively and are subject to the influence and control of their owners, political stakeholders, and users, usually in that order. Nevertheless, curators do have a certain agency and museums can compete for narrative hegemony, especially when the owners and stakeholders are not united in their own political vision. Redefining the museum today means taking a position in relation to modernity/coloniality and collectively rethinking which narratives are most able to help different global societies come to terms with the modern/colonial past. (CE)

Narrative Territoriality

If we understand territoriality as a result of the fight that occurs within a territory, we can extend such an approach to the comprehension that territorialities are also built by and within narratives. Identification of subjective processes cross distinct space and time dimensions (in art, media, and so on). In this sense narrative territoriality is a fundamental concept for us to track lines of thoughts and/or actions, helping us to comprehend, for instance, ways of being South. Furthermore, the term suggests it is from and within these narratives—aesthetically built territorialities—that we also interpret and build our understandings of the space and time we all inhabit. (FR)

Nation-state

The nation is not a state nor is a state a nation. The former relates to a group of people bound by a sense of shared

identity; the latter describes a designated territory presided over by a government. A nation-state is when the two come together. "The idea of a homogenous nation governed by its own sovereign state—where each state contains one nation … is almost never achieved." (Melissa Y. Rock, *State, Nation and Nation-State: Clarifying Misused Terminology*, Penn State College of Earth and Minerals Sciences, https://www.e-education. psu.edu/geog128/node/534, accessed February 13, 2020.) (SB)

Networks

Networks are relativizing engines, undermining absolutes and replacing them with permanent uncertainties. They are the sum of connected particles. On the human level they are the connections between individuals with some consequences for the older concepts of representation and metaphor. (MS)

New Materialism(s)

A loosely related set of revivals of the philosophical materialism of the French Enlightenment. Opposes itself to the anthropomorphic tendencies of other (rhetorically older, but often actually newer) materialisms in the name of a dynamic ("vital" or "agential") naturalism, based now on recent developments in the life sciences. United, ideologically, by a rejection of Marx's "historical materialism" and the "materialism of practice" as "sensuous human activity" on which it is based. Rides the posthumanist wave in the wake of antihumanism (despite the idealism of its structuralist ground); opportunistically exploits the political revaluation of Indigenous knowledges for spurious philosophical effect. (PO)

Optic/Haptic

Described by art historian Alois Riegl in his book on late Roman art (*Late Roman Art Industry*, Rome, 1901/1985) as two different modes of experiencing the world privileging either visual perception or physical (tactile) sensations. The two modalities correspond with different types of representation regarding the relations of objects, bodies, and space that have been illustrated by other writers, such as Viktor Lowenfeld, with Impressionism and Expressionism. (CK)

Order/Disorder

By using these terms, Comaroff & Comaroff ("Theory from the South: Or, how Euro-America is Evolving Toward Africa," in *Anthropological Forum 22* July 2012, p. 113–31) emphasize how one cannot be isolated from the other; they are imbricated ideas. In other words, whenever we think of a certain order, we must always be aware of the fact that there is an imagined disorder from where legitimacy is invented. Such an approach is fundamental for us to think of Global South as part of a dispute, rather than a physical and homogeneous space/time dimension. (FR)

Planetary

Not necessarily relating to cosmic. Still singular, still deriving facets of identity and selfhood from orbiting around an entity that is separate from its own physical and intellectual mass. Still denoting aspects of agency-lessness. Still bound to aspirational knowledge of what exists outside of one's immediate ecosystem. Not "inter" enough. Not "trans" enough. (RDM)

Planetary/Planetarizing

An adjectival qualification denoting a state or process of extension of something over the whole of the earth,

in which the planet is imagined in its literal astronomical sense as part of a solar system—iconically, as photographed from outer space—and hence as an essentially natural, geological entity or system. Preferred by some to the terms "global" and "globalizing," as purportedly less ideological and more "scientific"; considered by others, in some uses, to be equally ideological, in its naturalization of social processes. See *Global/Globalizing*. (PO)

Polis

Platonic sense: a body of citizens; the citizens meeting to create a place in the form of a city-state guided by philosophical and humanitarian values. For Plato, the best form of the *polis* is the one that leads to the common good. (MF)

Postcolonial

The time of independence and thereafter that usually coincides with great hope, expectation, movement, possibility, uncertainty, and promises met and not met. (SW)

Postcolonial narratives

Just as postcolonial literature addresses the consequences of and problems arising from the process of decolonization, postcolonial narratives too exist in multiple, literary, and nonliterary mediums. These narratives are the manifestation of social, academic, and professional discourses surrounding and reacting to the action and effect of decolonization. (OF)

Postmodern

A term that has become more or less meaningless. Originally it denoted a kind of architecture but now it has become a punching bag for the political right while being of no interest to decolonial discourses. It would be better being retired and left to gather dust for a couple of generations. (CE)

Postwar modernism

The worldwide historical condition after 1945 is generally referred to as postwar. Postwar modernism is therefore used as a term to describe the situation under which modernist art practices around the world were able to develop under disparate conditions. Postwar modernism comprises of essentially different aesthetic and ideological arrangements and is not restricted to geographies considered either central or peripheral. It is therefore seen as an inclusive term. (SW)

Precarity

Often also referred to as precariousness, signifying a condition of vulnerability, unpredictability, displacement, and dispossession within which the individual lacks material and physiological security. Much of the world population—namely in the broader South and, increasingly, beyond it—lacks stable work and income. This new/old social class is referred to as the new "precariat." Words like precarity/precariousness/precariat are used largely within the academic research in the wake of the twenty-first century. This is not surprising as neoliberal politics and climate crises make apparent the irregularities and asymmetries between the precariat and a very small percentage of people on the planet that have accumulated all the capital. (MF)

Residency

"Artist residencies can be a part of museums, universities, galleries, studio spaces, theaters, artist-run spaces, municipalities, governmental offices, and even festivals. They can be seasonal, ongoing, or tied to a

particular one-time event. They exist in urban spaces, rural villages, and deep in nature. Hundreds of such opportunities and organizations exist throughout the world." (https://resartis.org.) (CS)

South

A living entity as per the tradition of many animistic religious present in the Global South; a polysemic symbol that stands for direction and movement; a parable upon which we can build an endless quest for imaginary territories where intellectual freedom, as well as new/old methodologies, ways, pasts and presents can flourish beyond any sense of compromise and tactics of crypto-colonization. (Within history, and the realms of theory, political sciences, and contemporary art practice, the notion of the Global South has provided a strong defensive mobilization against the hegemony the North. The constant redefinition of South can also be a deliberate act of rapprochement, a path that both "swerves away from the influence of predecessors," and heads toward a "third space," in the words of cultural theorist Nikos Papastergiadis). (MF)

Speculative Realism

A strand of contemporary philosophy posited on the idea that the world, or "reality," might be independent of human thinking about it. It is the realism of the wanderer, also a wandering of the philosophy of science between and over existing forms of realisms. Speculative Realism, given the very different work of affiliated philosophers, should be considered a spectrum at one end occupied by Graham Harman, whose rejection of phenomenology and placing truth in the human experience erects a new phenomenology in negative or reverse, to Reza Negarestani on the other, whose rejection of human experience as the basis of truth leads him to embrace scientific rationalism. The realism in Speculative Realism has little in common with European traditional philosophy and is in dialogue with the Anglo tradition of analytical philosophy. (MS)

Talanoa

"*Tala* means to inform, tell, relate, and command, as well as to ask or apply. *Noa* means of any kind, ordinary, nothing in particular, purely imaginary or void," writes Tongan scholar Timote M. Vaioleti ("Talanoa Research Methodology: A Developing Position on Pacific Research," in *Waikato Journal of Education*, January, 2006, pp. 23–24). "In Talanoa, it is the sum of *noa* and *tala* that adds to the total concept. It requires researchers to partake deeply in the research experience rather than stand back and analyse. Talanoa, then, is subjective, mostly oral and collaborative, and is resistant to rigid, institutional, hegemonic control." (Ibid.) (SB)

Territoriality

Deriving from the idea that a territory is not only a physical space, but also part of a symbolic structure that involves constant and conflicting construction, the term "territoriality" serves as a form to comprehend how such construction takes place. It gives us room to understand that any territory is made of multiple forms of being/acting, opening perspectives for us to think of the disputes which occur within any inhabited space. For Carlos Zambrano, this would mean thinking of the plurality that exists within any territory, for Rogério Haesbaert, it means thinking of the multiplicity of forms by which a territory is constituted. (FR)

Thirdspace

Building on the work of Henri Lefebvre, Edward Soja's theory of

thirdspace describes "a limitless composition of lifeworlds that are radically open and openly radicalized; that are all-inclusive and transdisciplinary in scope yet politically focused and susceptible to strategic choice; that are never completely knowable but whose knowledge nonetheless guides our search for emancipatory change and freedom from domination."*(Thirdspace: Journeys to Los Angeles and Other Real-and-Imagined Places*, Hoboken, 1996, p. 70). Crucial to this conception is trialectical thinking, which Soja has described as "difficult" since it "is disorderly, unruly, constantly evolving, unfixed, [and] never presentable in permanent constructions." (Ibid.) (SB)

Third World

The Third World is part of a vocabulary of post-World War II politics of the Cold War in the twentieth century. It refers to the formerly colonized nations of Asia, Africa, and Latin America that were characterized as "developing nations," and which presented a "third front" vis-à-vis the "First World" nations steered by the United States and the NATO allies and the socialist "Second World" steered by the Soviet Union. The Third World, while initiated as a political category, carried strong resonances in generating solidarities among Afro-Asian and Latin American nations, reflected in political alliances, cultural thought, and social movements. (SS)

Transcultural

An approach that engenders learning to grapple with and embrace structures of difference that perforate our preference towards seeking similitude. How to inhibit the tendency to "other" through the still unrefined project of empathy lies at the heart of this mode that requires a rewiring of forms of conditioning that have encouraged "passing" as survival strategy or have impelled disempowered cultures towards "catering" to privileged ones for semantic validation. (RDM)

Transculturation
One of the early postcolonial concepts of culture based on notions of colonialism, migration, and global capitalism, "transculturation" was coined in 1940 by Cuban writer Fernando Ortiz Fernández in his book *Cuban Counterpoint: Tobacco and Sugar* (New York, 1947; reissued Durham, 1995). "The word *transculturation* better expresses the different phases of the process of transition from one culture to another because this does not consist merely in acquiring another culture, which is what the English word *acculturation* really implies, but the process also necessarily involves the loss or uprooting of a previous culture, which could be defined as a deculturation. In addition it carries the idea of the consequent creation of new cultural phenomena, which could be called neoculturation." (Ortiz, Durham, 1995, pp. 102–03). (CK)

Transitional vision
A transitional vision (of decolonization) suggests modes of viewing, imagining, and initiatives that emerge from and respond to the critical transitional decades of decolonization in the twentieth century. Covering the decades between the nineteen-forties and the nineteen-seventies, when nations across the formerly colonized worlds in Asia and Africa were gaining political independence, transition into postcolonial nationhood generated unfolding and transformative ideas of freedom, arrivals into political modernity, utopias, and solidarities. Transitional vision captures this dynamic energy that was attuned to shifts and instabilities, and moves beyond static ideas of

postcolonial identity, driven often by narrow nation-statist rationalities. (SS)

Transmodernism
A multifarious worldwide tendency in modern art based on transcultural contacts and exchange of ideas, concepts, and styles. Transmodern attitudes, which usually counter Western modernism's logics of exclusion and purity, often originated in contexts of decolonization and anti-racist movements. (CK)

Transnational
Located outside of the confinement of the nation, a transnational approach opens a space outside the national framing of historical research, pushing boundaries so that questions of origin and originality can be interrogated. (SW)

Vā
In Bernida Webb-Binder's essay "Pacific Identity Through Space and Time in Lily Laita's Va I Ta Taeao Lalata E Aunoa Ma Gagana" (in *The Space Between: Negotiating Culture, Place, and Identity in the Pacific,* Andrea Mārata Tamaira, ed., Mānoa, 2009, p. 27), Webb-Binder elaborates on the concept of vā by quoting acclaimed Samoan writer Albert Wendt: "Vā is the space between, the betweenness, not empty space, not space that separates, but space that relates, that holds separate entities and things together in the Unity-that-is-All, the space that is context, giving meaning to things." Webb-Binder advises that "vā is best understood when it is perceived holistically, since it encompasses multiple times and places. That is, all aspects of temporality are present within a single designated space." (SB)

Xenofeminism

A feminism for the time of structural feminist acceleration and biotechnocultural gender transformation; a feminism that includes the Other. It addresses the challenge of updating existing feminisms by infusing new philosophical insights and realities with what we know of feminism. Xenofeminism is a form of feminist language game whose reality will get us out of the business of language games once and for all. (MS)

INDEX

INDEX

COLOPHON

COLOPHON

Introductory Essays
p. 16 Photo: Krishna S. Joshi, Shutterstock; p. 17 Bridgeman Images; p. 19 Bridgeman Images; p. 25 PM Press; p. 26 © NASA; p. 30 Courtesy Shuddhabrahta Sengupta; p. 33 Film still used by permission © 1977 Eames Office LLC. All rights reserved; p. 35 © NASA; p. 40 © NASA; p. 44 X-ray: NASA/CXC/Villanova University/J. Neilsen; Radio: Event Horizon Telescope Collaboration; p. 53 Courtesy Shivanjani-Lal and Artspace, Sydney.

Past
p. 60 Photo: Timm Rautert, © Salzburg International Summer Academy of Fine Arts; p. 63 (top) Photo: Studio Exclusiv, © Salzburg International Summer Academy of Fine Arts, (bottom) Courtesy Prantl Family; p. 70 Courtesy Green Art Gallery Dubai; p. 72 Fondation Zao Wou Ki/© Bildrecht, Vienna 2020; p. 76 Courtesy Prantl family; p. 84 © Chichico Alkmim/Instituto Moreira Salles Collection; p. 90 © Yasmin Thaniá p. 94 Publicity photograph released in connection with the exhibition *Young Negro Art*. MoMA, NY, October 26, 1943– November 28, 1943. Gelatin silver print, 4 ½ × 6 ½" (11.4 × 16.5 cm). Photographic Archive. The Museum of Modern Art Archives, NY. Object no: 1N243.6B. New York, Museum of Modern Art (MoMA) © 2020. Digital image, The Museum of Modern Art, NY/© Photo SCALA, Florence /© Estate of John Biggers © Bildrecht, Vienna 2020; p. 99 Collection of the Hampton University Museum, Hampton, VA; p. 107 Dallas Museum of Art, Museum League Purchase Fund/© Estate of John Biggers © Bildrecht, Vienna 2020; p. 108 Collection of the Hampton University Museum, Hampton, VA; p. 111 © bpk/ RMN—Grand Palais/Patrice Schmidt p. 112 © Estate of John Biggers; Courtesy Michael Rosenfeld Gallery LLC, New York © Bildrecht Vienna 2020; p. 116 Courtesy Coco Fusco; p. 117 Courtesy Walker Art Center, Minneapolis MN;/© Bildrecht, Vienna 2020; p. 126 Photo: Glenn Halvorsen for Walker Art Center (All Fusco/Peña images: © Bildrecht, Vienna 2020); pp. 139, 141, 144: Every effort has been made to trace the copyright holders and obtain permission to reproduce this material. Please get in touch with any inquiries or any information relating to this image or the rights holder.

Present
p. 154, 156, 161–62, 164 Courtesy Savvy Contemporary, Berlin; pp. 167–68, 176–77 Archives Van Abbemuseum, Eindoven, The Netherlands, Photos: Peter Cox, Eindoven, The Netherlands, p. 178 Archives Van Abbemuseum, Eindhoven, The Netherlands, Photo: Ernie Buts, exhibition curated by Christiane Berndes and Steven ten Thije; pp. 181–82, 186 Photos: Geyson Escuta, Courtesy Belojardim Residency; p. 193: Photo: Tim Kaiser; pp. 194, 196 Photos: Geneviève Frisson, Courtesy Johann Jacobs Museum, Zurich; p. 197 Photo: Tim Kaiser; p. 198 Photo: Geneviève Frisson, Courtesy Johann Jacobs Museum, Zurich; p. 207 Photo: Antoine Tempé; p. 208 Courtesy RAW Material Company; p. 212 Photo: Anna Karima Wane; p. 222 Exhibition: *Tania Bruguera, Neighbors*, TATE MODERN, 2 October 2018–24 February 2019/ Photos © Tate (Andrew Dunkley); p. 227 © Habiba Nowrose/Courtesy the artist and Dhaka Art Summit 2020; p. 228 Photo: Pablo Bartholomew, exhibition curated by Maria Balshaw and Diana Campbell Betancourt; p. 232 Courtesy the artist; p. 236 Courtesy the artist and OAGOMA Collection; p. 238 Courtesy the artist, Labor and Otazu Foundation, Photo: Randhir Singh; pp. 244, 251, 253 Courtesy the artist and Axis Gallery, New York.

Future
pp. 258, 264, 270, 274 © Wolfgang Günzel, Weltkulturenmuseum 2013; p. 286 (top) Photo: Philippe Piron, (bottom) © Les Nouveaux Commanditaires-4; p. 290